T0328528

Township Girls

Township Girls
The Cross-Over Generation

compiled by

Nomsa Mwamuka
Farai Mpisaunga Mpofu
and
Wadzanai Garwe

WEAVER
—PRESS—

Published by
Weaver Press, Box A1922, Avondale, Harare, Zimbabwe
2018

Cover design: Farai Wallace

Photos courtesy of Farai Mpisaunga Mpofu, Nomsa
Mwamuka, Rutendo Hadebe, Wynne Musabayana Joy
Chimombe, Farayi Mangwende, Wadzanai Garwe,
Sophie Chamboko

Printed by Lightning Source.
Distributed by the African Book Collective
www.africanbookscollective.com/publishers/weaver-press

ISBN: 978-1-77922-325-8 (p/b)
ISBN: 978-1-77922-326-5 (epub)

This book is dedicated to

The women of Africa who dare to
tell their story

and in memory of

Emelda Musariri
1963-2014

Contents

Contributors' biographies

Sophie Shingai Chamboko is a journalist by training, Sophie has worked in the field of broadcasting for over 25 years. Educated at Harare Polytechnic and Wits Business School, her experience has been in broadcast operational management as well as in front of the camera and behind the mic. Sophie was born and raised in Zimbabwe, but has also lived in the USA and is currently based in Johannesburg, South Africa where she works for DStv Digital Media. 'Love in Great Abundance' is Sophie's first foray into the world of writing and it has sparked such an interest in her that it will, no doubt, not be her last.

Joy Chimombe studied for a B.Sc. Honours in Economics at the University of Zimbabwe (1984). She then worked briefly as a journalist at the Zimbabwe Broadcasting Corporation but soon decided to follow a career as an economist, and joined the Ministry of Finance, Economic Planning and Development. Joyce moved to the UK in 1990 where she lived for four years during which she studied for an MBA at the University of Hull. Moving back home in 1994, she worked for Zimbabwe Sugar Refineries as a Trade Relations Manager. She married in 1996 and joined her husband in Spain, becoming a stay-at-home mom, and teaching her children to read and write English. She now lives in Pietermaritzburg, South Africa where she is a researcher for Xubera Institute for Research and Development. She is also a qualified personal trainer (fitness), a photographer and an avid golfer, playing off a 9 handicap. She has a 23-year-old daughter, Lourdes, and a 20-year-old son, Mudiwa.

Cathrine Chitiyo attended junior school at St Martins, followed by boarding school at Nagle House, completing her high school education at Arundel School. She studied law at the

University of Zimbabwe and began her legal career with the Ministry of Justice as a public prosecutor before going into private practice as an attorney/legal practitioner. Cathrine is a partner with a law firm in Harare and sits on various boards of mainly commercial institutions. She has one son.

Tsitsi Stella Dangarembizi is a former broadcaster and news reader who is now a development consultant working largely on programmes in the HIV/Aids Sector. She has a Degree and a Diploma in Social work and obtained a Certificate in Non-Profit Management through Walden University in the USA. She is the proud mother of a son in his twenties.

Runyararo Bertha Faranisi was born in Harare. She began her primary education in England and completed her secondary and tertiary education in Zimbabwe, studying languages at the University of Zimbabwe before completing an Honours Degree in Translation Studies. 'My most fulfilling years were when I was actively involved in sport, the engagement with people, the drive and determination that I had to get things done. Sadly, change is the only constant in my life and that chapter has been paused. Now I am trying my hand at other things including confectionery – my journey continues.'

Wadzanai Garwe is a mother of two wonderful adult children. In her professional life, she is a development practitioner specializing in financial and economic analysis and management and assisting governments in designing community based investment projects. She currently works for Food and Agriculture Organisation in Rome. She has and previously worked with the United Nations High Commissioner for Refugees in Zimbabwe, Food for the Hungry International in Mozambique, Macpherson Consulting Group in Zimbabwe, and for 13 years was a free-lance consultant working mostly with the International Fund for Agricultural Development. She holds a Bachelor's degree in Finance from the University of Maryland and an MA in Community Economic Development from Southern New Hampshire University.

Rutendo Pfende Hadebe studied print journalism at Harare Polytechnic and worked at *The Herald, The Gweru Times* and the Bulawayo based *Bulletin.* In 1992 she broke into the NGO sector as Communications Officer of the National Council of Disabled People of Zimbabwe. Subsequent work would see her co-founding a consultancy RUSH to assist small businesses to access World Bank Funds in Zimbabwe, working with Munyati Consultancy, Environment 2000 and Crisis in Zimbabwe Coalition. Following her passion for women's rights she worked for Feminist Political Education Project, the Women in Politics Support Unit and then went into full time consultancy, specialising in documentation of key political and social issues as well as proposal writing and fundraising. In 2010 Rutendo relocated to Cape Town where she works with the University of Cape Town's African Gender Institute. She is married and has two children.

Nyasha Katedza is a fiction writer, poet and playwright whose plays focus on women's issues in the workplace. She lives in Canada.

Constance Machibaya is a Real Estate Agent and Property Development consultant based in Zimbabwe. An alumni of Arundel School, she obtained an Honours Degree in French, with Psychology as a second major at the University of Zimbabwe in Harare. She has four children.

Matilda Madekurozwa (Dr) was born in Zambia. She is a paediatrician with specialist knowledge in autism. She is based in Pietermaritzburg, South Africa.

Nyarai Majuru lives and works as a Clinical Specialist in Mental Health in England. She is also co-founder and Creative Director of a small media company in Zimbabwe. When she uprooted her young daughter years ago to go to the UK, Nyarai could never have foreseen the challenges in raising a child in a foreign country and as a single parent. But with the unrelenting support of family and friends, many of whom were strong, vivacious and independent women, especially her mother, such challenges become more manageable. As her daughter is in her final year at university, she has had more time to explore avenues and goals that had been temporarily shelved.

Farayi Mangwende is a seasoned communications and marketing executive with more than 25 years' experience. A mother of one and a Christian, she is passionate about community transformation and mentorship of young adults in order to ensure that they reach their full potential. Farayi has had exposure in various industries and gained experience in Zimbabwe, the UK and sub-Saharan Africa. Her career successes include rebranding and brand strategy formulation for First Mutual Holdings Ltd and African Sun Ltd. She was selected by the US State Department, Washington D.C. as one of 33 women leaders from emerging economies globally to participate in the FORTUNE / US State Department Global Women's Mentoring Programme in April 2010.

Spiwe Kachidza Mapfumo was born in Mutoko and attended various mission schools before going on to study in for a BA and MA in the USA in 1975. She currently lives in Calgary, Canada working for an NGO called HIV Community Link.

Sithabile Garet Mari is a BCOMPT Accounting graduate with a Post Diploma in Business Administration and an MBA from the University of Pretoria. She works in the Public Sector division of a large international software company as a Sales Excellence Lead Developer. Her motto in life is 'Don't sweat the small stuff' as life always has its trials and tribulations.' A mother of three, she lives in South Africa with her husband whom she met at junior school.

Isabella Matambanadzo is a development, human rights, women's rights and media professional with vast experience working mainly in southern and eastern Africa. She holds a BA (cum laude) from Rhodes University South Africa majoring in English Literature, Journalism & Media Studies and Theatre

Studies (with Distinctions.) A recipient of Sally Mugabe Foundation/Reuters' Foundation Scholarship she studied Mass Communications at Harare Polytechnic and holds a Diploma from Zimbabwe Institute of Public Relations. In 2008, she took the Advanced Management and Leadership Programme at University of Oxford's Said Business School. She has worked for organisations as diverse as ZBC, SADC Press, Inter Press Service, the New Delhi based Women's Feature Service, Africa Information Afrique, Zimbabwe Women's Resource Centre and Network, OSISA, and the Virgin Unite, Nduna Foundation, Humanity United and Enterprise Zimbabwe amongst others.

Manyara Matambanadzo is 21 years old. She went to the UK when she was eight in 2004. In her poem, she speaks of her experience of adjusting to life in the West Midlands. She is in her final year at the University of Sheffield, where she studies Law and Criminology. She recently returned from Sweden where she spent a year abroad as part of her degree programme, an experience she found deeply rewarding. She hopes to pursue a career as a solicitor. In her spare time, as well as being part of a student-led university pro-bono legal programme, Freelaw, she is also part of her university's cheerleading club, the Sheffield Sabrecats.

Geraldine Matchaba has worked with the Standard Bank Group since 1998 starting up in the Marketing Department to Heading up Corporate Affairs in Zimbabwe, South Africa, India and Hong Kong. She has worked as Senior Manager Media and Research and specialises in media strategy of the Group Brand campaign with a focus on Asia, Africa and Middle East and global media. She conducts analysis and insights from brand tracker research on key brand metrics in 13 key markets.

Sara Nyaradzo Moyo is an intellectual property attorney and the senior partner of Honey & Blanckenberg. In addition to her expertise as a lawyer, Sara is one of the founding members of Zimbabwe Women Lawyers Association, a prominent women human rights organisation. She sits on the board of a local listed financial institution and has held various leadership positions on the boards and committees of local and international organisations that deal with the promotion and protection of intellectual property rights as well as access to justice and women's rights.

Farai Mpisaunga Mpofu is co-founder of VIRL Financial Services P/L (est. 2010) and is country director of VIRL Social Foundation (est. 2014). A senior Communications, Marketing and Investor Relations professional, she served in the Insurance and Banking environment for over 20 years. Among her board positions are the Microfinance Association, Women's University in Africa, Culture Fund of Zimbabwe Trust, Junior Achievement Zimbabwe and St Martin's Convent Primary School. Farai holds a Special Honours degree in English from the University of Zimbabwe and is an alumnus of the British Council leadership and Harvard Executive development programmes. Farai serves as patron of the youth blood donors club, Pledge 25.

Wynne Musabayana's formative years were spent on Zimbabwe's copper belt. Born at Alaska Mine, she did her primary education at Shackleton Mine, and attended Chinhoyi High School, before moving on to the University of Zimbabwe. She worked as a producer, anchor and chief PR officer at ZBC, before venturing into the private and international sectors as communication manager at First Mutual, and the International Federation of the Red Cross. Since 2009 she has been a Deputy Head Communication and Information at the African Union Commission. She is married to Dr Joni Musabayana. They have four children and had their first grandchild in December 2015.

Emelda Chiedza Musariri was a Development Consultant who worked on assignments associated with the Global Fund to Fight AIDS, Tuberculosis and Malaria. Prior to that she worked with Price Waterhouse Coopers providing Health Sector consultancy. She ventured into commercial agricultural farming activities and was building a primary and secondary boarding school on her farm with a vision to build a clinic when she passed away in 2014. In contributing to this project she fulfilled her long hidden desire to write and tell her story.

Tambudzai Glenda Muzenda spent most of her life boarding at mission schools before heading off to gain 'living knowledge' in, Vancouver, New York City and The Hague, working for various NGOs internationally. 'The experiences of life grow and develop on a daily basis as I have witnessed in many cities and global "townships" alike'. She says. 'My interests as a sociologist scholar prompted me to write for this project.' Glenda is interested in human rights issues of gender, sexuality and identity with a focus on young girls, adolescents and boys. An avid writer and reader, she has a daughter named Maya, and 'two cats'.

Nomsa Mwamuka is a researcher, writer, producer and project manager with over 20 years' experience working across various media platforms from film, TV and radio to print, focusing, in particular, on arts events and cultural festivals. Nomsa contributes feature articles to various publications and is the award-winning author of *Makeba: the Miriam Makeba Story*. She is currently conducting interviews and research for a series of biographical stories documenting the lives of pioneering and influential African women, cultural and political activists, and icons under the working title, *Acts of Activism*.

Chiyedza Nyahuye is a consultant at Westfield training and World Ventures. She has worked in various capacities empowering women through advancing their education, including leadership training for teachers and parliamentarians, and in peace building and conflict resolution with Envision Zimbabwe Women's Trust as a founding member. She has also had opportunities to explore her artistic talents by performing in various plays at Reps Theatre, and writing and performing her own play, 'Telling HerStory: Warrior Women of Zimbabwe' and singing in multiple cabarets.

Debra Patterson completed her A-Levels in 1987. She then worked in a bank in Harare for one year before travelling to Spain in 1989 to study Business for Tourism, Spanish and Translation. Thereafter she moved to Germany and set up a consultancy business offering communication and coaching services to mainly law firms. She has a Bachelor in Law from the University of London. acquiring a masters in Germany. She is married to Mark and they have two children.

Mona Lisa Pfende has a BA degree, majoring in English and Geography from the University of Zimbabwe. Initially intending to be a High School Teacher her life path led her into Marketing. After obtaining an IMM Diploma in Marketing Management from Speciss College, she worked for Trinidad Industries for several years and has spent almost two decades at Blue Ribbon Foods. A part time Marketing Management tutor, Monalisa sits on the boards of on Bumhudzo Old People's Home Board and together with her husband serves as Deacon for Outreach Ministry in Celebration Church Ruwa. She has three daughters.

Theodora Rondozai is a chemist by training. She studied at the University of Zimbabwe and Hull University. She works as a management systems (ISO 9000 & friends) trainer/consultant and is an avid network marketer in the travel industry. She is a single mother of two.

Jacqueline Kuziwa Rugayo is an Emergency Human Resources Specialist. She has worked in humanitarian emergencies in Zimbabwe with UNHCT in Nyamatikiti Refugee Camp, with UNDP Harare, UNICEF Zimbabwe, World Vision Food Aid Program in Bulawayo, WV Sudan in Nyala and Darfur, for the Asia Tsunami Response in Sri Lanka, East and Southern Africa Regional Offices, and as an International Recruiter, Staffing Team Leader, Americas and as People and Culture Director for the WV Syria Response team in Jordan. She is the co-founder of SurgeAfrica, an online recruitment network that showcases the wealth of talent in Africa.

Xoliswa Sithole is producer/director of films focusing on human rights, Xoliswa is a two-times BAFTA and Peabody winner and a three-times BAFTA nominee. She began her work in cinematography as an actress in films such as 'Cry Freedom', and went on to learn production on feature films. She was the producer of 'Orphans of Inkandla', the South African producer of the Oprah Winfrey Leadership Academy's 'South Africa's Lost Girls' with True Vision, and for the BBC's 'Zimbabwe's Forgotten Children' which was shot entirely undercover (Peabody/BAFTA). Xoliswa produced 'Child of the Revolution', which explored the revolution in Zimbabwe. Some of her documentaries have become impact films: 'Zimbabwe's Forgotten Children' raised money for to educate children and to build a school. 'Orphans' was used to raise money for 'Make Poverty History', and for two years in succession, Elton John used a clip of the film to raise money (about £7m) for ARV research in Kenya. She is currently producing the documentary 'Mandela Man of Peace', exploringMandela's global peace efforts plus a documentary on Chief Albert Luthuli Africa's first Nobel Laureate. Xoliswa Sithole has produced 18 documentaries, is a member of BAFTA, and has been a juror three times.

Maryanne Situma was born in Kenya and moved to Zimbabwe with her family in the early eighties shortly after the independence. She is tourism specialist at Zimbabwe Tourism Authority in Harare

Chiratidzo Zhou is the owner at Zhou Paralegal Services and lives in Arizona, USA.

Foreword

S. N. Moyo

Township Girls: The Cross-Over Generation is a compelling anthology of the deeply personal reminisces of women growing up in Zimbabwe during the transition from colonialism to independence. Written by lawyers, doctors, businesswomen and other professionals, the book is a unique narrative of an oppressive political system as experienced by children and the youth.

Whilst the book has a special focus on harrowing school experiences in a racially segregated Rhodesia, it is also an account of political consciousness during the war years and the challenges of navigating post-independence crises.

Many of the writers were hitherto unpublished authors and their reflections, which are frequently written in dramatic prose, are an interesting account of lives of privilege lived under political oppression. Alternatively sad and funny, 'Madora to lobster, in one quantum leap' [Mpofu], their interpretation of the events of that time evoke feelings in of joy and sadness in the reader.

In many ways, the book is an important historical record of the unheralded lives of the women who lived in 'two worlds' [Mpofu], 'I lived with Africans but went to school with whites' [Garwe] and were 'raised to be confident and proud' [Chitiyo].

At a time when the feminist discourse on gender equality was not as commonplace as it is today in Zimbabwe, the book provides a unique insight into the strong influence the writer's parents, whose academic ambitions for the girl child was no less than that for the boy child, had on the successes of the writers.

'It was assumed that high school ended at A-level and not before, and that this exam was but if stepping stone to University. The only questions were: after a level what subjects would you do for a level? And forward to degree course would a level prepare one? Girls were not exempt from these expectations.' [Chitiyo]

The writer's parents were in many instances teachers and nurses by profession. All were acutely aware of the freedom and opportunities that education gave to those who possessed it and were prepared to work hard.

Whilst the writers' parents strove to give their children the very best education and amenities that their personal resources could buy, which included private schooling in multiracial schools and exposure to white cultural activities and practices such as classical music, ballet and other forms of dance - even if such classes were taken 'generally *anchored {in} the back row'* in the downtown studios of Joan Turner's School of Dance [Mpofu] - the anthology also documents in disturbing detail the trauma and distress suffered by the writers who underwent sudden transition from community township schools in which the they had excelled and had lots of friends to suburban schools which, though better resourced, were populated by white teachers and 'droves of white children' [Hadebe], racially prejudiced and abusive.

In addition to narrating 'the loss of their language and African identity and history' [Hadebe], and the irony of being 'sold on whiteness' [Garwe], authors like Hadebe and Chimombe document in detail the humiliation and ridicule they personally suffered in the quest to fulfil their parents' desire to give them as broad an education as possible.

Hadebe writes:

'I never shared this painful event, or the many more that reflected racial prejudice, with my parents. Instead I chose to live it alone. This I did, because I knew my parents' decision to move me to this white school had and then a favourable status in the community. They were revered, and they saw themselves as pioneers. The whole decision was also a financial drain on them and I was not about to tell them that I hated the school and missed my simple township friends.'

Chimombe describes the embarrassment and demoralisation she suffered at the hands of a high school teacher who constantly harped that 'Africans were not made for swimming as their bones were only designed for running' to such an extent that any hopes she had of becoming a swimming champion were 'immediately dissolved'.

Garwe describes with wry humour the incongruity of being the best student in English literature and language but being discouraged by the Domincan Convent nuns from excelling in English because the 'Rhodesian government's doctrine did not allow that an African child could speak English better than a white child.' As a consequence, and in an effort to pacify the consternation caused by her being the best English student, the nuns decided that a white would receive the English prize and she had the 'dubious honour' of being the best History Student for 1983 - 'thereby depriving a more deserving History buff'.

In addition to the writers' personal interpretations of their schooling experiences, the book is at the same time a record of rising political consciousness of the writers during the war years.

In spite of their privileged existence, the writers had first-hand experiences of the brutality of the war waged by the liberation fighters and the Rhodesian army. Theirs was not just a sheltered existence – they were often sharply aware of the fears and concerns of their parents

Xoliswa Sithole writes an unnerving account of her experiences of the war at a rural primary school at the age of nine:

' ... we got used to seeing the comrades at night and singing songs to early hours of the morning and the Rhodesian soldiers coming to school in the morning to arrest student activists. At times, the soldiers would take the older girls and burn cigarettes under their breasts as part of the interrogation process. A friend of ours – let's call her Maidei – also suffered when her father was buried alive by vakomana/comrades. He was suspected of being an informer, a dzakutsaku.'

Katedza's poem poignantly captures the brutality of the war years and the ways in which the adults' fears and anxieties concerning the war overwhelmed the innocence of youth.

Machibaya, Dangarembizi and Hadebe narrate with great candour of the fears and anxieties they suffered as children concerned for the physical wellbeing of their parents and family members as well as the impact of the war on family finances, the challenges of accommodating in modest township housing extended family members fleeing the war in the rural areas, political activism in urban areas, police brutality and the eventual-euphoria and excitement attendant on Zimbabwe's attainment of independence.

Township Girls is more than just an unnerving narration of the educational, political and economic challenges experienced by the contributors during the seventies and eighties, it is also a humorous and loving tribute to parents who straddled the rural and urban divide with determination, aplomb and finesse – organising lift clubs to ferry children to and fro school and dance classes; ensuring the children spent part of their school holidays with extended family in the rural areas; providing entertainment for their children in the way of ' 'flicks' in town', 'pop festivals at Gwanzura Stadium, the Salisbury show complete with Luna Park and fireworks'; equipping themselves with new culinary and deportment skills to help them navigate the new area of entertaining in a multiracial milieu in an independent Zimbabwe; and with the new dispensation seizing the opportunity to acquire spacious homes in the former white only suburbs.

On the mines, writers like Musabayana experienced a vibrant cosmopolitan life where different languages and dialects were spoken; Christians, Muslims, atheists and traditionalists co-existed; children played outdoors; sporting and cultural activities were common including live shows by popular local musicians and entertainers such as Safirio Madzikatire; beauty contests were held for the women *'some of whose marriages did not survive the wives' newfound celebrity status'* and sewing competitions in which the winners' *'exquisitely embroidered table cloths ... disappeared ... with no compensation, into the homes of the madams who lived 'kumayadhi'* ' and housing cleanliness competitions.

In conclusion, the *Township Girls* is a timely collection of childhood anecdotes by women who look on life as an adventure and regard their skills, experiences and contribution to society as worthy of documenting for posterity.

Introduction

Nomsa Mwamuka

This anthology documents the experiences of women who lived through a time of transition from colonialism to independence. The setting is largely Zimbabwe though the seventies, the years of war; and from the eighties, the years of independence, to date. The stories are expressions of emotional, psychological, spiritual and personal change set against the backdrop of the social, cultural, political milieu of the times.

Written in first-hand narrative, the authors tell different stories. There are reflections, memories, odes to forebears, parents and mentors and acknowledgements of current achievements. Most importantly, though, these stories document elements of Zimbabwean, southern African and African history and will serve as an inspiration to future generations.

Background

The vision for the book was born when former school friends Patience Mbofana Mavhima and Farai Mpisaunga Mpofu were at their Alma Mater seeing off their own teenage daughters, when they began reminiscing about their personal histories and experiences at that same school, several decades before. Bittersweet memories came to the fore. Women of action that they are, they decided that such memories could form the basis for an important book, and put out a call for contributions. This is a collection of the responses they received and the words of the women who dared believe they had a story worthy of sharing reflecting their own individual reasons and concerns.

Farai Mpofu has this to say about her vision of the book:

The contributors to this literary work share something not previously discussed or honed into an anecdotal account of what it meant to grow up in Rhodesia, and to experience the transition to black rule in Zimbabwe. With the benefit of hindsight, this anthology offers a personal glimpse into events, and decisions made by parents and guardians, which moulded this unique cross-over generation. It also offers a tribute to the older generation, without whose wisdom, resilience and foresight, we would not be what we are today.

Rutendo Hadebe focuses on what for her was a holistic transition:

For me, the word 'transition' represents fundamental personal change and circumstances. Thus, I have returned to my childhood and tried to share the many ambivalences, conflicts and understandings that I associate with Zimbabwe's political transition. While for many the signifier was the ecstatic crowd of a hundred thousand people that welcomed Robert Mugabe on his return to Harare from exile in Mozambique, on 26 December, 1979, mine is a little different. My notions of the transition do not begin in 1980 when ZANU-PF and Robert Mugabe came to power but rather when a Methodist Bishop became the Prime Minister of the country with a 'surname', Zimbabwe-Rhodesia in March 1978. It was during this critical period that my life took a drastic turn and I experienced transition of my persona, society and nation.

Wynne Musabayana has more personal reflections:

When I got the invitation to contribute a piece for this anthology, I thought, 'What a great opportunity to reminisce over my youth' while paying tribute to the two people, my parents, who gave everything to provide me with a firm foundation in life.

She paints vibrant picture of growing up on the copper mines: Our friends were a cosmopolitan bunch; Manyika, Karanga, Zezuru, Korekore, Ndebele, Shangani, Ndau, Chewa, Nyanja, Zulu, Sotho, Bemba, coming as they did from Zimbabwe, Zambia, Malawi and South Africa. A world which prepared her to be an 'international citizen' though she didn't know it at the time.

Isabella Matambanadzo's contribution sets her on a path of enquiry:

My contribution is prepared for a series of stories of Zimbabwean women who were born and raised in the country's ghettos. For its preparation, I have reviewed various family historical records and photographs in my custody. In the tradition of oral story telling that is part of my inheritance, I have listened to assorted accounts of our family stories as told by my uncles Edmund and Francis Matambanadzo, my aunt, Ronia Kahari and my mother. I have also re-visited various places in Zimbabwe to establish as accurate a record as possible. I am indebted to my brothers for their collective remembering of certain key events. I have also relied heavily on records housed at the National Archives of Zimbabwe. In addition, I have utilised school reports and records, and raw interview notes that were generously availed to me by Volker Wild from his research in the 1990s on African entrepreneurs in Zimbabwe. To the best of my ability I have relied on the reservoir of my memories to create an authentic record.

Xoliswa Sithole wrote with a sense of ambivalence:

When I was first asked to contribute to this book I was conflicted because I did not think that I could write a decent piece. As an artist who values honesty and openness, how was I going to write about my wayward, wonderful and glorious life and at the same time pay homage to a country that raised me? Grew me and most importantly, to a mother who knew that there had to be something better than apartheid even though it was still Rhodesia when we arrived in Zimbabwe in 1969...

For Tambu Muzenda her reflections provide a personal exposition of a life straddled between the rural areas and townships of Mabvuku and Tafara. She awakens her youthful sense of what sex and sexuality meant and considers the prevailing attitudes around HIV/AIDs. She remembers life with the nuns – *'Missionaries and modernisation yani?'* – in a context of traditional customs and practises around life and ultimately death. It is an initiate story written largely in Shona, with interspersions in English.

Style and Content

Only a handful of the contributors in this anthology have been published before, few dared to think they had a story to tell ... but here it is: words from mothers, daughters, housewives, nurses, bankers, doctors, lawyers, farmers, travellers and business women, all of whom have experiences to share. While the contextual space is Zimbabwe, every voice and experience is unique and this is what makes this anthology special.

Themes

Various themes came to the fore during the compilation of this anthology. Recurrent motifs include the search for identity, the value of education and hard work, cultural displacement, transition from rural life to city living, questions of race and racism, the ambition and aspiration of parents passed down to their children, and the yearning for a sense of legacy.

Conclusion

The stories are as much individual biographies, as they are stories of a country. The question is: how do we harness these experiences, to inspire a desire for change, to make a better future for our country and the continent as a whole?

Traditionally we say, *Paivapo,* to which the response is *Dzefunde.* May you enjoy the stories!

November 2015

With these hands...

I create wonders, work hard
 negotiate terms of trade
I empower, I refuse to be a door mat
With these hands
I survive *Murambatsvinas*[1]
I am ingenious,
finding numerous alternative ways
to make a living, thrive and prosper

With these hands
I gain economic independence
Who would have thought that even
a rural woman from a township
could travel the world
Dubai, China, Singapore, Sweden
selling my products, generating forex
supporting my family,
building businesses,
supplying secondary industries,
with imported raw materials and chemicals

With these hands
I show my daughters and sons
how to be industrious,
never to bow down to tribulations,
that with every failure, every obstacle,
there are opportunities

With these hands

---

1   Operation Murambatsvina (Move the Rubbish), also officially known as Operation Restore Order, was a large-scale Zimbabwean government campaign to forcibly clear slum areas across the country. The campaign started in 2005 and according to UN estimates affected at least 700,000 people directly through loss of their homes or livelihood and thus could have indirectly affected around 2.4 million people.

I renew and nurture my *hukadzi*,[2]
I discover my infinite, amazing gifts
Yes my back hurts,
my hands are raw,
my feet ache,
tears burn down my cheeks
but my heart is light and rejoices
For these hands are my freedom
All of you amazing warrior women, I salute you!

Chiyedza Nyahuye
June, 2012

---

2   womanhood.

Two Worlds and Everything in Between

Farai Mpisaunga Mpofu

This is your life

I was born at the Municipality Clinic in Mufakose and delivered by Sister Holmes to a township primary school-teacher, Ruth Emma Muchawaya, and a manager with a multinational company, Etherton Francis Mpisaunga. My first home was a semi-detached unit, 8 Mutondo Street, Mufakose, the third oldest township in Zimbabwe, after Harari (now Mbare) and Highfield, which was our home from 1968-69 and again 1978 to 1988.

In 1970 we moved to Beatrice Cottages, another exclusive corner, in the rough and tumble of Harari. We had two rooms in the house of a woman we children considered quite mean. For example, if my brother and I broke the branch on one of her frangipani trees, she threatened our mum with an end to her tenancy. (At the time, Dad was at school in the USA.) Jelly powder, generously ladled into the palm of one's hand, and then allowed to dissolve under the drip-drip of the newly hung laundry, was a sure way of keeping us entertained and out of trouble. However, our lifestyle was generally assumed to be inferior to the landlady's, so treats were enjoyed surreptitiously. My first taste of yoghurt caused me to fall off a chair, *negotsi*, backwards, causing the landlady to enquire after the cause of the tumble!

New clothes for Christmas and Boxing Day was non-negotiable and meant a trip to Milton's Store on Gordon Avenue in the city centre. Two complete outfits and footwear for two days of celebrations. Middies, maxis, platforms, hair pieces, revolution trousers and more. The new clothing required family get-togethers accompanied by great food and as many soft drinks as we could drink.

In 1971, we house-sat for family friends in Marimba Park, a mere three kilometres away from Mufakose, and a middle-class enclave for black people in racially segregated Rhodesia. From a semi-detached abode with an outside loo, to a fully contained house with everything under one roof, this home featured a long driveway, a rose garden and a gardener, who was distinct from the maid (in the township, these roles were usually performed by the same person). I clearly remember balmy evenings on the veranda with mum eating *ipwa*, a type of sugar cane, admiring the rose garden and absorbing the scent of the flowers, before attending to my homework and helping to make dinner in the kitchen.

Marimba Park, Westwood, a small section of Highfield, and Beatrice Cottages offered middle-class enclaves for black people and mixed-race families; the 'ghettoes' were the townships established in the western locations to provide labour for industry and bachelor quarters for working men: (some of these hostels were later augmented to include family accommodation). Such enclaves are where disenfranchised black people of means – professionals and businesses people, now called entrepreneurs – deliberately re-created or mirrored the white western lifestyle from which they were excluded on racial grounds. Children of these families led a privileged, exclusive, 'greenhouse' existence in private, multi-racial schools, often boarding schools, which ensured that children were more comprehensively inducted into western culture. They acquired hobbies, bicycles to ride, some danced – usually modern dance or ballet – and they learned to play a musical instrument; they had domestic help, three sit-down meals a day, study time, extra lessons, and they played with their own. Occasional unaccompanied forays into the neighbouring township usually resulted in them being bullied, or having obscenities hurled at them; sometimes they were even thoroughly beaten. Yes, it's also true that quite often they enjoyed a good game of football with their poorer peer group, but the game always ended when the posh boys picked up the ball, at end of play, to take home.

Hair plaiting *kwa*Mai Linda, near Machipisa, was perhaps a once-a-month weekend ritual, *vairuka nemawoko* (corn rows) before it became common, and used *kamu yesimbhi* (metal comb) to create accurate paths in my hair. Then there was Bester Kanyama Photo Studio; there was not a household without a 'Foto Bester Kanyama' on display. In the same way, few escaped a visit to Dr Mazhindu's surgery from which one came away with a sore bum and the all-weather Gees Linctus. Higher up the pecking order, Dr Gordon, was a white liberal medical doctor, operating out of Amato Arcade, on King-sway, Salisbury. Her bedside manner is legendary, and typically included the question, '*Uri kutshaya kazhinji kashoma?*[1]for those suffering from stomach ailments and diarrhoea. She had a calling, her mission was inclusive health for all, delivered with care and sensitivity. We did not drink as minors, but we were reasonably well acquainted with kuFed (Federal Hotel), kwaMushanz (Mushandirapamwe Hotel), kuSeven Miles (Seven Miles Hotel), and other places where typically dads would park under a 'tree', open all the windows, enter the den of iniquity and over a three- or four-hour period send out a waiter with our 'order' of cold drinks and crisps… An age of innocence and trust.

My next move was to a room that our family of four shared

---

1 Your stomach is running a lot, or a little?

in my late paternal grandfather's house. It had sufficient space for two beds, though it also accommodated a wardrobe, lounge suite, stove and fridge – a squeeze as we were in-between homes. Through the cracks in the door, which separated us from the family next door, we were able to follow the latter's lives in both intimate and minute detail.

Through all of this, my parents were clear that they wanted more for their children and that it would be possible to have more, in the future, provided we had a solid education. They chose the Catholic education offered by the Dominicans and Jesuits. These two religious orders pioneered integrated education in Rhodesia and my parents instinctively knew that this was the way forward. Possibly their worldview differed from many because they had been exposed to a wider world early on in their lives and from a reasonably privileged perspective. Dad read for his first degree in Politics and Economics in India, where he lived with his young bride. He went on to undertake postgraduate studies in the USA and Canada. Mum was a qualified teacher, a singer and an actress: (she performed as Lady Macbeth in a 1960s in a production directed by Adrian Stanley staged at Amai Musodzi Hall, in Harari Township.) She spent nine months studying towards a diploma in development, and then some years later, at the age of 70, attained a BA in Theology.

St Martins 1972-77, KGI to Standard 4

St Martin's was the first multi-racial school in Zimbabwe, or so I was told, by one of the 'visionary' mums whose children attended the school before I did. One of her younger daughters, now deceased, was a great friend. Dominican religious belief and values were just what we needed, I suppose, to side-step the difficulty of confronting the demons of traditional culture, racism and colonial separate-existence policies. I have fond memories of sporting excellence – rounders and netball – building grass houses (after the elephant grass bordering the sports' fields had been cut on the extensive grounds), and being awarded the victrix ludorum for two consecutive years. Sister Daniela, whom I was privileged to meet again in 2014, was a young but capable headmistress.

Reflecting back on that time, I ask myself: how did a single, family car manage to ferry two children to school and two adults to work all in the requisite time (at least on most days) over a distance of over 20 kilometres? The situation was exacerbated by a zoning system in which the townships (residential areas for black people) lay in the same area as the factories for which they supplied labour, and far from the city centre. The answer can only be, with tremendous determination and some luck!

At 6 p.m. the school dogs were allowed out to patrol and keep the Dominican Sisters safe, especially given that the boys – which referred to either terrorists or freedom fighters, depending on your politics – were at large, and appeared capable of anything. This meant that the family car had to make sure it met the school pick-up deadline. The Convent parlour was a welcome refuge from the canines.

At times, we spoke 'our own language' at St Martin's derived, I believe, from the coloured community, the B-language, which entailed punctuating each word with a couple of 'Bs'. So, for example, my name 'Farai' would be 'Fabarabai' and 'School', 'Schbool'. Going to full sentences 'Ibai woulbud libike tobo leabeve thebe clabassrooboom befobo thebe teabecheber cobomes' – (I would like to leave the classroom, before the teacher comes). Spoken fluently this lingo was not only intimidating but inscrutable. Its purpose was subversive. Teachers and others not-in-the-know would have no idea what we were talking about. (For this reason, the transition to the Convent, an English-speaking school in town, was somewhat traumatic, as English was spoken with more loyalty to those who introduced it, than was the case at St Martin's.) The annual braaivleis is my biggest single memory from my years at primary school. From what I recall, the music consisted of one track 'Popcorn' playing *ad nauseam*. The braai was probably one of my earliest evening functions: the magic of seeing your school and friends at night under floodlights was great fun, as was the distinct aroma and taste of roasting meat.

Mr Chiweshe was a transport entrepreneur way ahead of his time. He provided a door-to-door school transport service for a monthly fee. It was as safe, efficient and reliable as an ageing over-used people carrier could be. Mr Chiweshe was the driver, conductor, chaperone and mechanic; his wife would occasionally step in to help. A fearless woman, she would often get behind the wheel of the bus or the soft-top family convertible to shuttle smaller numbers of children to and fro, depending on where the bus had broken down. Meanwhile, her husband would be at the engine, trying to coax his vehicle back to life just one more time!

The Dominican Convent, Harare 1978-84, Standard 5 to Form 6

The Dominican Convent, Harare was a happy and fulfilling academic (perhaps not stellar) and sporting period of my life. Sisters Octavia, 'Occy', Kate, Gundula and Pancratius 'Panny' were institutions in our day and will be cited in most bios of Convent old girls. As a piece of history, I was honoured to serve the school in my final year as the first black head girl, from amongst the day-scholars, as there had been one previously selected from the boarders as deputy head girl. Another piece of history was made when I took my little Radio Shack – sent to me from Canada by mum who was studying there – to school to follow the 1980 election results. From the perspective of fourteen-year-old girls, the outcome changed nothing and yet changed everything, especially had one been a fly on the wall in the various households at dinner-time. Still, lifelong friendships were formed then.

Central to their search for something better and extending their horizons, was the shared love my parents had for people from all walks of life. Their love for and enjoyment of such company, and for entertaining and bringing people together meant that as children we too were able to appreciate the freedom and fulfilment that comes from socialising and exchanging ideas unfettered by one's racial or social background.

Holiday entertainment, prior to 24-hour television, Internet, Playstation, etc. was *nhodo, dunhu,* water, *tsoro, chisveru,* and tree climbing. As an early 'greening' initiative, each township house was issued with two fruit trees: a peach, mulberry, mango or guava tree by the local authority. Hide-and-seek, and generally playing truant, were other pastimes. Inevitably, home-time and bath-time would arrive. For the little ones, bathing was either outside the stand-alone bathroom to avoid an accidental fall into the open pit latrine or, for the older children, inside and out of public sight.

Mornings would include an early visit to the *horda,* the mobile bakery, to buy fresh bread. However, our breakfast typically included more than the basic township one of tea *nechingwa,* for we nearly always had eggs, baked beans and a breakfast meat of some kind. But this was not information for public consumption. My parents seemed to instinctively understand that preparation for life included knowing some things which may have been considered non-essentials, by others. Their desire to replicate and introduce their children to what they had seen and experienced was nothing short of visionary.

I recall thinking I was nearly drowning at our next home – a brand new concrete block Glen Norah house. This was 1972. It had rained heavily. The storm-water drainage was not very effective, the floor of our old Anglia was not water-tight, and water poured into the car. Neither of my parents noticed. I was distraught. I imagined disaster. I survived. In Glen Norah, none of the rooms had doors. Occupants innovated with curtains draped across each doorway. *Sisi,* our domestic helper, slept in the kitchen.

I recall our neighbour, not the one with whom we shared a wall, but the one with whom we shared a two-strand fence, causing a stir at least once a quarter, when his rural, home-based, legal wife came to town for a number of essentials. Invariably, a 'town wife' would be ensconced in his city home, and unseating her required unprintable name-calling, blows, screeching, scratching, disrobing, chasing, and, finally, disgrace ... we would dine out on these incidents for days. It was our introduction to 'domestic bliss'.

We were the three F's at Joan Turner's School of Dance, where every Saturday in sky-blue leotards, pink tights, and black shoes we generally anchored the back row at ballet class, and 'Uncle Dzi' and our parents formed a lift club to get us to the down-town studio. Apart from breaking into a white stronghold, we learnt to appreciate ballet and other forms of dance, as well as classical music, and poise. It seems to me that there exist some physiological differences between the races, which may influence whether or not one has a lead role in a performance or becomes a prima ballerina; once in a while, a slight black girl, generally believed to have 'white' body structure would go a little further than others. Just nearby was *muPutukezi*, the Portuguese Sweet Corner, which was strategically located for us to hurry there after classes, as we waited for our transport back to Highfield. Treats available included sweets and pastries, handy for black ballerinas who were desperate for a five-cent sugar fix after the rigours of 'Swan Lake' rehearsals. The storekeeper would tickle our palms as he handed over the goodies and the change. No, not acceptable, but it happened.

The biggest treat was Highfield, Kuma U, a whole house for three years in the second oldest township which was certainly more upmarket and more genteel than Harari. Sis' Martha was the best maid ever. She always had lunch waiting for both of us after a long bus ride home when I was harassed by those who insisted – just to annoy me – on reading aloud, my names written in large easily legible print on my school

8

case. During the war years, in the event of a bomb, identification was necessary. Quite how a naïve Convent girl could turn out to be a terr, or used by terrs, (terrorists) to smuggle bombs into white schools, is beyond me.

Lunch was a medley of leftovers when all the flavours seemed enhanced, and always followed by sweet rich tea and bread and butter. Amazing! And just what I needed after a morning of speaking English and various other forms of cultural immersion. If one stayed at school for the full day, lunch consisted of a tired sandwich, warm juice and a brown-skinned banana while sitting cross-legged in the 'Rec', an enclosed, unexpectedly lush, city centre garden. This day-scholar option was no comparison to a vegetarian lasagne lunch followed by a cool glass of water and a mini debrief with a parent/guardian, before changing into crisp sports clothes and returning to school. The reality is that the black girls who lived too far away to return home for lunch, or whose professional parents could not manage the 'dash' in an hour, became stronger, more focused and resilient faced with an unbroken day at school. Becoming a boarder had a distinct appeal, on some days, when the aroma of freshly cooked meals wafted across the quad.

Cyril Jennings Hall 'CJ' formed part of the community facilities which every township offered and where various aspiring bands assembled for rehearsals, including some big names. There they sang lyrics that were often 'made up' from songs heard on the radio, strummed guitars and banged on drums that often sounded tinny and hollow; but there was no shortage of enthusiasm as the girls, the backing vocals, all sopranos, belted out a chorus and 'wiggled' to the beat. The weekends were busiest at CJ, but I would also see the bands during the week, as I walked past the hall after disembarking from the 'United' bus, which offered a reliable service provided to all residential areas of the city. The CJ's big slide, swings and netball pitch were great. I never went to a film – *firimu* or *filim* – but I knew what was showing from the audience's live commentary: *'Awu ye!'* suggested an action movie in which the indefatigable villain is pummelled to the ground by an invincible hero.

The Convent was different. They appeared to operate on quotas: a third white, a third black and a third coloured and Asian combined. Names were problematic. To this day, I am 'Ferai' to many dear friends. Surnames were even more difficult, 'Empasunga' was the best many could manage for my surname 'Mpisaunga'. Blacks gave more to any relationship, or so it seemed to me. Life was comprised of back-to-back tests: what break or lunch did you bring with you? What hairdo did you sport? Did your uniform have proper name tapes? What stationary did your pencil case contain? What accent did you have (coming from St Martin's many of us were coloured, ekse)? How did you read aloud in class? It took tremendous focus to speak and think in a way which would promote fitting in as quickly as possible and conforming to the expected standards and rules. This would include how one sounded while reading aloud in class, the pronunciation of certain words, decorum and much else. Today, we marvel at how our parents knew that we had the stamina, intellect, flexibility to achieve these daily feats, benefit from the experience, and acquire an advantage by dint of these bitter-sweet years. Did our chameleon-like existence have casualties? Yes, I think so – the permanent mismatches, fish out of water, the misfits ...

At term end, everyone you met was fully authorised to ask you what position you had come in class, so from the bus stop to the gate, seven or more total strangers would call out, *'Waita number ani?'*[2] My response, as I was not enrolled in the black township schools, which ruthlessly ranked pupils, was *'Hatiite zvemanumber'*.[3] If I deigned to ignore an enquirer, they would use and abuse my name, the one emblazoned on my bomb compliant school case, all the way home.

2　What position did you come in class?
3　We are not given class positions at my school.

Eastlea, Mutare Road, was unimaginable luxury. Our initial post-independence, house-hunting forays took us no further afield than five kilometres from Highfield, to modest, white working-class and upwardly mobile coloured areas, near the railways stations, namely: Southerton, Houghton Park, Lochinvar, Waterfalls, and Hatfield. These western and southern suburbs were fringe areas bordering, as they did, the black areas. Somehow, my parents decided there would be no half-way or half-hearted approach to racially integrated living. In Eastlea, our first home in a 'white area' stretched from 1981 to 1988. We had as neighbours, the Gunnings, to the left and a Sikh family behind us. Our new home featured a sunken lounge (how did my parents even know what it was?), a generous veranda, a bar and an entertainment area. The house was conveniently located along a suburban bus route. The bus driver appeared to enjoy his job. He actually stopped dead for passengers to disembark, unlike the township trend, where the bus slowed down enough for the sure-footed to disembark. The property was on a whole acre – what privacy and seclusion. The garden was in good shape most of the time. Thanks to A'Rabson, the gardener.

Newlands, our next home area, was the acme of *rugare*, and the one on which my forward-looking parents decided. Very upmarket. Indeed, today, the best restaurant, Victoria 22, was situated next door, though not a restaurant at the time. Our home boasted character, and rambling, generous proportions. How my parents understood the value of this type of house, I'll never know – a scullery, en suite bathrooms, guest loo, two lounges, and pedestrian gate – small but significant features. To have spotted such a property and mobilised the funds to buy it meant that their children absorbed a distinct reality, one that reflected particular values. Black families had little induction into house hunting and what constitutes a good buy. Township homes were allocated according to need. So, when suddenly Independence made it possible to live where one wanted and attend any school one desired, all this meant having to make decisions about very new issues. The default is what one knows, so many families found themselves in homes which were merely bigger than what they had had before and not necessarily more interesting from an architectural or aesthetic perspective; in other words, a standard house. Against this background, we discovered that our parents had been very shrewd and had used their combined exposure to make an excellent buy.

Who shaped me?

Mushakata Youth inducted me into a God of miracles (though people today seem to believe that He has only just begun performing them). As a member, we travelled to places which seemed far away such as Kadoma or Bazeley Bridge in Manicaland for youth church conferences. On one such outing, which were typically done on very modest budget, mainly donations from the youth themselves, I lived on mangoes as the standard menu consisted of offal and sadza, for which I had not then acquired a taste. During these outings, we prayed with youthful fervour for the growth of our independent African church, our youth group and our faith, singing *'Tiri Hondo Imwe'*[4] and *'Fambai Majoni*[5] with *ana* Mbuya Machingura and Tsododo, and our 'Mother Advisor'. Mbuya Mareya.

My maternal grandmother was a market woman, a woman of God, with deep faith. Her prayer was, *'Mwari makaita mukasandipa mombe, makandipa vana, ndivo vanondichengeta'* – God, I thank you for providing me with wealth in the form of children, who care for me, not cattle.

My paternal grandparents were also an inspiration. *Sekuru* would peel and slice *nzimbe*, sugar cane, from his garden for me and sit with me while I ate it. He also allowed me to catch the grasshoppers which delighted in the floral border along his garden footpath, as long as I let them go. Gogo, who died

---

4   March [God's] soliders.

5   We are one [God's] army,

before I was born, was – as I can see from her photographs – a tall elegant woman, a teacher at a time when few black women had qualified for this respected position. Their family mode of transport was two bicycles. They shared reading glasses!

Tete, dad's sister, taught me cleanliness, to be house-proud and to love my family. She introduced me to pilchards, butter, a rose garden, stainless steel kitchenware and high standards. She was also my nurse on the days when I was ill and could not go to school. Mum would drop me off, and *tete* would scrub and exfoliate (*kukwesha*) my cousin and I in the late afternoon. All mum had to do after she'd picked me up at the end of the day, was feed me and put me to bed.

Maiguru's husband, mum's sister, took us to his employers' children's parties at the showgrounds. From my recollection, Magden was a refrigeration company for which my uncle worked, and they hosted Christmas parties for the children of their black staff. My uncle brought his natural children and all of us to this orgy of food, sweets, crisps, fizzy soft drinks, and entertainment. Maiguru also introduced us to jelly. Maiguru was an avid knitter, my first plain and pearl knitting lessons came from her.

The 'Queen', mum, what can I say...? She was a professional, a homemaker, a chef, a lover of life; she had an amazing wit, a great sense of humour, and was afraid of nothing. Always ambitious for herself and her children, she was also mother hen and friend. She believed that travel was the best form of education. Before she became an accomplished travel co-ordinator, there was Kariba. It must have been September school holidays, in knee-high boots and a winter dress, we flew to the dam for the day. The discomfort I experienced is unimaginable, but all that pales into insignificance when I recall the thrill of first aeroplane ride and first visit outside Harare, and many other firsts. This was the amusing result of the black middle class trying something for the first time, with limited local knowledge or research, and little guidance from the travel agent ... wow! Working with progressive and like-minded travel agencies, in the seventies through to the early noughties, my mother designed packages and interested women in taking the trip. Her travels took her to Canada, America, the UK, Switzerland, Austria, Australia, France, Kenya, Ethiopia, culminating in several groups of women taking advantage of group packages to travel to regional destinations such as Mauritius and South Africa. Mum empowered herself, before it became a fashionable concept, and went further to create opportunities for other women and mobilise for them to assume active roles in organisations including the Young Christian Women's Association (YWCA), where she served as an employee and a non-executive member of the board, so we naturally became YWCA children. People talk about role models now, as if this was a new idea; but in my childhood, amazing women walked this earth and did great things, often on a voluntary basis, while still finding time to be daughters-in-law, wives, mums, women of God, community activists, politicians, etc. Our role models were tangible, approachable, remarkable in the institutions they established, some of which are still amongst us today and the organisations have endured. Zimbabwe African Women's Association, among other noble endeavours, held year-end parties for their families. They were festive occasions which taught us how to entertain when the time came, and brought the members' children together – some of us are still friends today.

Among her achievements which inspire me included writing a book, *Entertaining in the Home*,[6] in the seventies. It was conceived for middle-class black families to help them navigate the new area of entertaining in a multi-cultural milieu in the new multi-racial nation. Zimbabwe would require new skills and social graces, so mum was amongst a group of women who enrolled at Connie Makaya's modelling school

---

6   Longman Publishers, Salisbury, 1980.

for a full course. Husbands were invited to the graduation ceremony. Many arrived already a little tipsy and proceeded to drink a little more. By the time the ceremony started and the graduands walked elegantly along the ramp, their cat-calls and howls were not the most appropriate, but their enthusiasm was appreciated. Professionally, mum was appointed first woman Branch Manager at Old Mutual, Marketing Division ... I could go on.

The 'Barley', dad, was a Princeton graduate after completing his first degree in India. He had a wide network of friends and was nominated Communicator of the Year in 1984, owing to his successful positioning campaign for the country 'Amazing Zimbabwe', when he served in the Ministry of Tourism as Director. He was debonair, a marketing, advertising and PR practitioner who also loved jazz. His sense of style, huge story-telling talent, and marvellous sense of humour made he and mum much sought after guests and wonderful hosts. As a father, he was present, loving, patient, demonstrative, never intrusive and a good companion.

'The Special One'

These are the reasons why I know I was living an extraordinary life, a charmed life, in which one had a certain sense of entitlement:

- It was okay to speak Shona badly and sometimes behave inappropriately, to be politically incorrect.
- I drank tea cooled with milk, not tap water.
- My aunt, Tete Rosie, introduced me to tinned pilchards in tomato sauce, cheese and *real* butter, not margarine, in Mufakose.
- Play was generally within the boundaries of the fence or hedge of the property we lived in, to minimise the potentially corrupting influence of the township.
- If I was able to gain a pass to play 'outside', I had to be home by 5 p.m., washed, and by 6 p.m. sitting in front of the TV in time for the national anthem.

- Watching the *Christmas Cheer Show* was a must each year. It was anchored by Sally Donaldson, to support the 'Boys on the Border' to whom 'little brown bottles' – *dumpies* – were being sent and who, no doubt, consumed them with gusto upon arrival.
- It was expected, acknowledged and accepted that you would do better, and go further than the rest.
- There were much lower household chores expectations of me, even if I was a girl, no sweeping away the top soil, daily at day-break, except at holiday time when rules were relaxed and activities and chores became more 'inclusive'.
- Modelling and advertisement appearances meant semi-celebrity status. In my case, it may have been an advantage that both my parents were linked to the advertising industry, dad as a mainstream 'ad man' and mum more on the market research side, for a while. Membership of a modelling agency, Photogenic, the first agency for non-whites, established by Jubi, a successful model of mixed race who saw an opportunity in the new Zimbabwe to create a stable of alternative models for the jobs that were becoming more interesting and diverse as things opened up in a new multi-racial dispensation. These product promotion advertisements included Tanganda Tea, 'Up, up, it lifts you up', Sun Jam, whose main character was Ms Connie Makaya, a successful black model and entrepreneur, whose main line 'Sun Jam, I love it' came out as 'Sun Jam, I laive it' and Buff Puff scourer and exfoliator, in which I co-presented with the colourful and funny Mary Mushore, a childhood friend, who is no longer with us.
- The ability to live concurrently in two worlds, from township to exclusive multi-racial *school, and everything* in between. *Madora* to lobster in one quantum leap, as it were.

2

'Please send me chocolates!'

Constance Machibaya

In 1967, David Dawanyi, a high school mathematics teacher at Highfields Secondary School married Christina Chopera, a trainee nurse at Harari Hospital, *paGomo,*[1] as it was known then. They had a customary marriage followed by a white wedding. In June of 1967, they welcomed their first son, Tendai Edward Dawanyi, into the world. A few years later, while still at their home in Highfields, Salisbury, they welcomed their daughter Nomusa Constance Dawanyi – me – into the family. In 1977, the family had a last son, Tinashe David Dawanyi.

By the time I was born, my mother, Christina Dawanyi had left her nursing career to become a social worker in Kambuzuma. As a result, once I was ready for pre-school, I attended Kambuzuma Crèche. Having aspirations for their young family, my parents then sent my older brother and me to St Martins Convent School for my KG1– the first year of school – Kindergarten 1. This was 1977.

At the time, my dad received a promotion – from being a secondary school teacher he became an education officer. His assignment was to the Ministry of Education in Umtali (Mutare) to oversee schools in the Manicaland area, which also covered Buhera. I did not know it then, but this was

---

1   Literally, '[the place]on the hill'.

the time of war in Rhodesia, so my parents were not keen to move my brother and me to Mutare,[2] so we lived for a year with my mother's younger sister, her husband and family. They moved into our home while my parents moved to Sakubva, a high density area in Mutare, with our baby brother. Mr Chiweshe, who lived in the neighbourhood, had a minibus. He would pick my brother and I up at the gate every morning and take us and other children to St Martins School, and at the end of the day, he would bring us home. We would carry our school bags, and in them, besides our books would be polony sandwiches and a one litre juice bottle filled with raspberry squash. Friday, after school, was one of my favourite days. We would stop at a small shop in Ardbennie, where I remember having enough pocket-money to buy a huge, brightly coloured dummy – a sweet that I would enjoy for many happy hours. On days when we were not at school, I remember the sweet sound of the Snoman, a blue and orange soft-serve ice-cream van.

One of my earliest childhood friends was Anastasia Rushambwa, a neighbour who went to school at the Convent. Across the road from us lived the Mazaiwana family and around the corner lived the Mutambirwa family. My older brother played with Simba Mutambirwa and I played with his sister Kudzai, who was my age.

In KG2 I moved to St Michaels Prep School in Borrowdale. This was another Catholic school, one where I was taught by nuns. In the boarding house, there were two senior girls, and though they were black, they bullied us and would hit us with coat hangers. To this day, I am not sure why.

My joy was writing weekly letters to my parents, which I always ended with: 'Please send me lots of chocolates!' For our exeat weekends, my cousin, Winnie Mashiri and

2 Umtali (Mutare) is on the border with Mozambique which is where the liberation armies were based. Guerrillas or freedom fighters moved easily over the border, and the fighting in this eastern border area could be intense.

Babamukuru would pick me up and we would go to their home in Mabvuku.

In Grade 3, I moved schools once again. I became a boarder at Bishopslea. From what I remember, either St Michaels closed due to the war, or girls were no longer allowed at the school. This time around we had a lift club from Mutare for the young Bishopslea girls. We shared this lift club with Omega and Lydia Mavengere and Mpho Chizarura. Towards the end of my third grade, my parents had found a place for me at Mutare Junior School in Greenside, not far from our first home on Kingsway Avenue and a bit later at 11 Oriole Drive. Soon after I was to move schools yet again, this time to Chancellor Junior School, this was on the other side of Mutare. Initially, my older brother and I would cycle the long distance to school in the morning and return after school activities. The environment was safe then, even though we had to cross three bushy areas with a footpath, and Main Street all alone, so my parents had no fears of me riding back home alone when my brother had to stay at school for activities in the afternoon.

During this period, I remember stories of my father travelling in a government Land Rover in a convoy to inspect schools. It was a scary time for us. We would hear many war stories of suffering families in the areas to which he travelled. I remember missiles being fired from the hills in the Vumba to Christmas Pass[3] one evening. So, I had to sleep on a mattress in the shower as this was considered 'the safest place' (some of our friends had underground bomb shelters but we didn't have one). The following morning there were reports of a house that had been damaged in Morningside.

When I was in Grade 6, my father was suddenly transferred to Bindura, so then I moved to Bindura Primary School where I became a boarder. This was because around that time, my mum found work as a manager at World Vision, an

---

3   Approximately 27 kilometres.

NGO in Harare and moved there, while my father lived in Bindura. On Fridays, he and I would travel to Harare to visit mum and my brothers, driving back on Monday morning.

I entered Form 1 in 1984 and attended Arundel, a girls-only private school in Harare. The headmistress was stiff and strict but had a very loving husband and a gentle dog. The deputy headmistress was as powerful and scary as a bulldog! There were only three black girls in my class, Form 1 Azure. It was at Arundel that I fell in love with Latin and French. This resulted in me going to the University of Zimbabwe to do an Honours Degree in French, with Psychology as my second major.

In my third year at university, I met a simple, down-to-earth young man at a Christian retreat in Nyanga. He had no car, no cash and no cell phone, and I was happy with that. Six months later, we agreed to have a serious, steady relationship. He graduated during my third year and I graduated the following year, as I was then pursuing a post-graduate certificate in education. On completion of my studies in 1993, I got married under customary law and at the beginning of 1994, we had our white wedding. Today we have four children. We run a real estate and property development company that has felt the flames of the harsh economic environment in Zimbabwe. My childhood was rich and full of so many colourful and heart-warming memories. I often wonder how my children will ever picture where I came from and how that shaped who I am today?

3

The Seventies – A Special Time to Grow Up

Sithabile Garret Mari

We grew up in the seventies. We wore fussy mix-and-match outfits, complete with little handbags, platform shoes and boots. We were glam! Even the helper was glammed up.

To avoid the hustle and bustle of township life, my sister Nancy and I were shipped-off to a mission boarding school in Chishawasha. I was seven years old and Nancy was six. To say the least, Chishawasha was a character-building school where the education standards were extremely high. I learnt Shona in two months. We had no luxuries but lived a life where children were expected to do the right thing and not to step out of line. It was a world ruled by nuns, and civilian teachers.

During the school holidays, we would travel back to the township where our peers regarded us as curiosities. My dad jogged daily and had all the township kids running behind him. My dad's nickname was 'Big Johns'. Nobody dared mess with him. My mom, on the other hand, was a mid-wife. She was called on to assist in almost every medical situation in the area. She was the township angel.

To keep us away from all the 'unsavoury' characters our house was fenced off. The gate was locked at all times. If you wanted to make Big Johns mad, you only had to let him find you walking down the street when he drove home from work!

That would spell big trouble. Big Johns' kids were not meant to be 'loitering' on the streets.

We got our own back on the restrictions on a few occasions. A few of us boarding school children would meet at Mabvuku Primary School during the holidays, ostensibly to study and revise. We were friends with the Matare family whose father was the headmaster of the school. The reality was that while some of the time we would study, we would later have good clean fun turning the classrooms upside-down and causing mayhem before tidying up and going home, to return for the same the following day.

Once, I remember, one of our friends had a 'crush' on a local boy. The boy's mother who was in favour of the playful relationship arranged a 'mock-wedding' complete with us all acting as bridesmaids. She prepared a proper meal of rice and chicken. The non-working adults, both male and female, sat around smart and smiling as if it was a real wedding! We children danced. I was a good dancer. Indeed, some of the adults threw coins at me to urge me to dance some more. When the clock struck five, the bride pulled off all her bridal paraphernalia and we all raced home.

Our house was neat and small, comprising two bedrooms, a lounge and a kitchen. We had a little patch of lawn and grew dahlias in the front garden. We had chickens running about the yard ... and oh, how I hated them pecking around in the vegetable garden. We had two small cars and my mom drove one. We did our shopping for necessities almost daily. Under a timed watch we were sent to the shops constantly to buy meat or vegetables.

One scary memory, though, about that time, was how many kids disappeared to join the war. Many felt it was our duty to do that, but some of us were far 'too protected' to make that move. Perhaps, I would not be writing this story today had things been any different.

When I look back, the seventies were a very special time to grow up.

4

Street Juggling Champion

Monalisa Pfende

Being the eldest and only girl in a family of four, I was a typical 'daddy's girl'.

I grew up in the dusty, red streets of Kambuzuma where we played *dunhu, nhodo, raka-raka,* tag, *chisveru,* and hide and seek. I could juggle a soccer ball on my right foot up to 100 'ups', as they called them. I was the street champion! My brother, now in Dublin, does not demur. He says that I should teach his young son how to play soccer!

Every New Year's Eve, *taitamba ma-records* into the early hours of the morning. These were the only times that my brother and I were allowed to play outside at night.

Then one day we moved to Mabvuku Township. I remember it well. I never really had a chance to say goodbye to my friends. I came straight from playing, was taken into the car and off we went. We moved into a much bigger, nicer, suburban house, which was on a corner just as you drive into Mabvuku. It was one of three houses which had previously belonged to white superintendents and city council officers. These white officials had been forced to move out of the townships for security reasons. The war of liberation was intensifying and slowly creeping into the cities.

We loved our new home. We enjoyed washing in a bathtub rather than in the showers, as had been the case in

Kambuzuma. Sadly, the houses were not for sale. My father wanting more secure tenure for us, soon moved us to an eighteen-acre plot in Mandalay Park in Ruwa.

At the plot, we had to go *kumunda* every day during the holidays. We had pigs and cows that I hated having to look after, though we always had plenty of milk. So, we would eat porridge with milk, and sadza with sour milk after *mugwazo* and a long day *kumunda*.

As much as I disliked being at the plot in the early days, I have now come to love farming and farm animals. Farm life taught me the value of having a work ethic. I appreciate the inheritance that my father left for us and I have since gone back to reclaim it. Two of my brothers are also involved in farming elsewhere, one bought the plot next door to the one we grew up on.

I did my O-levels at St John's High School in Emerald Hill, Harare. I am more *St Johnian* than any other school that I went to and I am grateful for my time and the moulding that I received there. It was there that I learnt how to play tennis, basketball, learnt how to swim and where I enjoyed singing in the choir.

I did my A-levels at Goromonzi High School and then went on to the University of Zimbabwe, where I read for a General degree, majoring in English and Geography. I was looking forward to a career as a high school English teacher. While I was looking for work, I got offered a job as a Marketing Officer at Trinidad Industries, an adhesives company. Since I was not equipped for a marketing career I enrolled for an Institute of Marketing Management Diploma through Speciss College in Harare. I spent five years with Trinidad and later worked with Blue Ribbon Foods, where I have now worked for over 18 years.

I have held positions of Marketing Development Manager, Marketing Executive and General Manager Baking Division; I have taught Marketing Management at colleges, sat on the Board of an Old People's Home, and together with my husband served as Deacon for an Outreach Ministry in the Celebration Church in Ruwa. In addition, my husband and I run a poultry and piggery project at our family home in Ruwa. We have three daughters. Our eldest was born after a long and difficult wait, so we named her Ruvheneko[1] Zoe. Our second child was born during a period of financial difficulty when we were trying to finish building our home so we named her Kushinga[2] Jade. When the third one came along, we were expecting a boy but we realised that God loved us no matter the outcome, so we named her Munotida[3] Olive.

---

1 The light
2 Being brave
3 You [the Lord] loves us.

5

Legacy

Cathrine Chitiyo

I grew up in Marimba Park, Harare. It was the centre of my universe. You could get into town by riding the Mufakose via Kambuzuma bus for 9 to 13 cents. 'Town' began from Market Square Bus Terminus, whence you walked several blocks into what is now called the CBD or Central Business District. You would pass Liberty Cinema en route. During the school holidays, we would go to town or visit friends in Highfield, or relatives in Mbare and elsewhere.

Schoolgirl holiday entertainment were the 'flicks' in town, visiting friends, or pop festivals at Gwanzura Stadium, Highfield. There, live bands would compete for popularity. During the August holidays, we had the Salisbury Show, complete with Luna Park,[1] and fireworks.

Education in the black community was cherished. One was expected to achieve. I attended, as a boarder, first Nagle House school in Marondera, then Arundel School in Harare. Luckily, I was raised to be confident and proud. This was a necessary tool in navigating the multi-racial school turf as a member of an ethnic minority during the immediately pre- and post-independence years.

It was assumed that high school ended at A-level and

---

1 A fairground located in the showgrounds for the duration of the annual agricultural show.

not before and that this exam was but a stepping stone to university. The only questions were: after O-level what subjects would you do for A-level? And for what degree course would A-level prepare one? Girls were not exempt from these expectations. Although, back then, parents were not as hands-on in their children's education as is expected of them today, failure was not an option. A parent did not have to sign a book as proof they had given a child's homework the once-over. Indeed, they may not have done so. But come school-report time: you were answerable to your parents – no excuses allowed – for your classroom performance. You might be good at sport, but this was less significant. Academic accolades far outshone those for athletics.

Nor was one rewarded for academic achievement. You were doing it for yourself. Beaming smiles of approval were the reward, not anything material. From that, it was learned that success is its own reward. Further, because 'it takes a village to raise a child' in our community, you wanted to emulate the classroom pacesetters. You wanted to have a good response to the adults' overt and covert enquiries about how you were doing in school. It was possible from a young age to discern disapproval, just in the facial expressions or vocal tones of our elders. This was true for every aspect of one's life, and growing-up years, though any judgement was tempered with love, affection and concern. As a girl, among other things, you had to learn how to keep house, also, to understand cultural mores, and be respectful.

The standard solution to less than stellar academic results was the dreaded extra lessons at colleges in town. This was a walk of shame to be avoided at all costs; one which motivated us to work harder, self-prompted, in order to achieve the expected results. Today, extra lessons have become a way of life.

One's parents did not need to articulate expectations: they were implicit in one's life and lifestyle. So, it wasn't a question of 'you will or you should' but rather 'why wouldn't or shouldn't you' achieve this or that? Very quickly, it became hard to tell where parental aspirations ended and where one's own began. Sometimes though, tough love guidance was more explicit: '… You want to study what!?' Then you knew you faced a challenge. University, UZ as it was called, was the only local university then, and one's next epicentre. A good time was had by all. Work hard. Play hard. Get the degree – all within the expected time. No gap years. I studied law.

Work followed immediately. In my field, it was standard to work in government, which I did as a public prosecutor for three years. Following that, I started in private practice as an attorney – a legal practitioner, and this has been my career to date.

It's funny how you become your parents … Having recently lost my beloved father, I now increasingly contemplate issues of legacy. What does God say about you? What footprint will you leave behind in your family, community, profession or the world at large? What activities are you putting off, that you should be doing – like writing this brief memoir? I really would encourage everyone not only to write down their memories, but also to record those of your parents and close relatives. It's amazing what you don't know about your own parents and your own family?

6

Path of Feet - Extremes

Emelda Emi Musariri

Prologue: to write or not to write

The bathroom was hot and steamy. I turned the cold water tap on, and stood shivering, not from cold but dread. I thought that if I could just wash myself, I might feel better, cleansed and fresh. I ... realised that it was time.

For years, I had heard that 'Each one of us has a book in them'. I believed this but struggled with the prospect of putting the truism into action. I spent a large part of my adult life prevaricating on the delivery of my story. The main reason being fear of offending in an environment that seemed dangerously treacherous in its defence of age-old habits and beliefs. As one grows older, the strength imparted by life's experience, acquired knowledge and some wisdom, lends courage to the exploration of the secrets of the mind.

But where do I begin this cathartic process? I am certain that many people believe they have brilliant ideas, which they desire to turn into a best-selling work. Perfect in their own estimation, they have clearly made captive a flow of words, emotions, memories, knowledge and fantasy. On the other hand, many have succumbed to the demands of life's final destination without answering the call of the pen or the keyboard. Often *baba* lamented that our generation were good at talking but capable of little or no action echoing Goethe, 'Knowing is not enough, we must apply; willing is not enough, we must do'.

Although uncertainty and fear circle me like vultures, the need to share my life's roller-coaster ride is overpowering. The anger, frustration and helplessness I have felt within an environment where simple things are complicated for the sake of a little drama or for a little bribery and corruption, knows no bounds.

If I am not entirely clear why Salman Rushdie was motivated to write *The Satanic Verses*, I truly appreciate the emotions that must have been churning within him. I was brought up to believe in the inherent goodness of life; to be a confident, kind, responsible, the qualities of a person, who attends church; but instead I encountered my nemesis, maybe we all do? I expected the universe to conspire in my favour. I lost track of the beginning and end, second-guessing much, caught up in a snare of manipulation, control and incomprehensibility. I had believed that people were nice, friends supported one and husbands protected and cared for one. I never imagined myself to be naïve nor did I believe that man is inherently evil. Surely religion, modern thinking – human rights, democracy, freedom of thought and speech and choice – guaranteed a safe passage on life's perilous road, and provided opportunities to leave a footprint, no matter the journey. I concede that in comparison to the starving, poverty-stricken, oppressed, degenerate masses of the world, I should count myself fortunate.

I am now able to write this story, however, as I once was one of those struggling 'unfortunates', but despite the colonial conditions my parents were blessed with a vision, a mission and a conducive environment. It seems Africans in general, at least in my part of the world, seem happy to believe that prevailing conditions are God's wishes, and therefore should be accepted with equanimity. Well, I beg to differ.

I am, however, now in my forties, and beginning to

appreciate the benefits of my unusual childhood. In retrospect, there was nothing lacking. While I might have been imprisoned in my circumstances, I was also undergoing intensive empowerment training. The simplest things are often the most edifying.

Reaching back into this enchanted time has provided me with joy and a sense of goodness, often during very difficult moments when my reason for being became unclear. I finally realised that I was created with the ability to choose and I had to exercise this gift wisely. I have finally made my choice.

The study has become my refuge, my place of peace and expression, the shower a place where new ideas are born and clarity of thought achieved. My bed, a place of the sweetest rest and dreamless sleep. My home, a place where I am.

Inspiration

It was 13 January 1993, ensconced between vaChihera's lace-draped coffin and the warm rough walls of her kitchen rondavel, perched on a made-to-fit cement bench which circled two-thirds of the hut's inner perimeter, that I was struck by the profundity of telling this story for 'prosperity' actually posterity. You see vaChihera was a phenomenal storyteller – witty, informative, wise and correcting. VaChihera allowed one to dream of the future and to leave the irrelevance of the past behind. But now she was gone, with all her untold stories. I should have spent more time with her, taken down notes, made a documentary, something; however, at least she had lived to see me reach womanhood and imparted a measure of her inner strength and fortitude, which is particularly necessary for all women... And men.

The drums plaintively begged me to discover their rhythm. Oh! If I got it, it would be beautiful I knew. As the night wove its magic, I chased the cockroaches with a stick up and down my grandmother's thatched kitchen distracted and miserable. I had cried all the tears for both of us. For her pain and suffering, I prayed that her spirit had soared to a peaceful enclave to 'watch from' that eternal territory. The inherent assumption at that time was that the dead continue to have input into the lives of the living, and, therefore, assume supernatural powers. '*Rangarira, rangarira zuva riye, wakasiya mhuri yako ichingochema here?*' – remember the day you left your family in tears. It is a song of regret, of guilt, a reminder to the deceased for having the temerity to die. In our culture, it was not acceptable that life ended at some point. Someone living was behind the nefarious act that had been permitted indirectly or directly by the ancestors for wrongs committed and unrepented. A vicious circle, perhaps, for once all possible scenarios have been played out – visits to soothsayers, witch doctors, *vapurofita,* and someone had been blamed for the act which had resulted in death, it became acceptable to pass everything over to Nyadenga, Mwari, Almighty God, who knows and sees all. However, sacrifices of goats or cattle, as may be determined by the *gata,* may still need to be made to appease the spirits, who will, in turn, intercede with Mwari for blessings upon the clan. I was not convinced. My beautiful vaChihera, could never be an avenging, restless or interfering spirit. She was resting in peace.

Almost fifteen years later, when every hopeful person on earth was chanting, 'Yes we can' with audacious verve, Barrack Obama was on the verge of becoming the first African American President of the United States of America, with the magnificent Michelle Obama as his First Lady, it was clear the story was mature, and ripe for the picking.

Accident at Chikomo Village

The mango bug was to blame for the very first hiding I received. My mother in true African tradition, used to spend *zhizha* with vaChihera in our Tribal Trust Land (TTL) village of Chikomo in Chikomba and *chirimo* in Salisbury (Harare). Here she not only planted her small plot with maize, sweet potatoes, watermelon, groundnuts, peanuts and millet, but made time to help my grandmother with her chores. At the time, we were too young to do anything other than watch, learn, mimic in our small ways or play. My sisters Ruva and Tina and I helped our mother to clear dirty tin cups and plates by loading them into the metal dish and taking them out of the kitchen to the washing area by the wooden drying rack. Mother cleared the excess ash from the cooking hearth in the centre of the room, by sweeping them with a *mutswairo* onto a piece of corrugated sheeting which took the place of a dustpan. She threw the ash in the usual place, in the empty space besides the herb garden but near the mango, peach and orange trees. We were not allowed to play there, but the mangoes and juicy oranges, red kissed by the sun were too tempting. The moment mother disappeared to the bedroom hut, I coaxed Tina, then two years old, to let me give her a piggyback in exchange for her help in acquiring the enticing fruit. Ruva, two years older than Tina, refused to risk a spanking. I was a little girl in a hurry lest I be discovered. Throwing caution to the wind, I found myself under the mango tree urging little Tina to 'reach out, reach out and pull the branch closer to you'. Then, suddenly, my feet felt as though they were burning, I yelped in pain and jumped, losing my hands from the piggyback grip. Tina slipped from my back onto to the burning ground while I hurried away. When mother eventually returned from the mission hospital, I was mortified by the sight of Tina on mother's back with both feet in dressings and bandages. I wept silently adding more salty tears to my heavily stained cheeks and wet collar. Surely my misery exceeded that of any other living person, I felt so sorry for myself. My uncle Joe, father's younger brother, had delivered some choice cuts with a thin sapling to a part of my calves, soon after the screaming Tina had been discovered.

Village life

Each school holiday, I spent at least two weeks, approximately half the break with vaChihera. We visited vaAmaria once in a while. Life in the village had its moments. The standard demanding routine, according to my parents, was character building. During the early years, there were always many children of many families in the village: life consisted of rising with the sun to collect dry grass and firewood to feed the previous night's glowing embers. The sticks would have been collected by villagers on their way home from their different activities. Only dry or dying trees and branches would be collected for firewood. One could see which households were up and about from the smoke spires drifting from the kitchen huts. Breakfast was large cups of *zambani putugadzike* to warm the innards or sometimes black English tea sweetened with sugar, condensed milk, or with fresh milk from Maduve the Africander heifer. This was accompanied by boiled or roast sweet potato or pumpkin. As the years passed, it was not uncommon to have bread, eggs, liver or other meat savoury made available in limited quantities by visiting city dwellers.

Division of labour worked well in accordance with tradition. Women were basically responsible for the organisation of the home, which included: cooking, washing, cleaning, fetching water, rearing chickens, subsistence farming, and child bearing, rearing and nurturing. The men helped with the heavy duty tasks, such as cutting down trees, and looking after the cattle, goats and sheep which were taken out to barely fertile pastures during the day, and enclosed in the wooden kraals at night. Of course, some of the men helped in the fields, but, as I saw it, the men had an easy time, now that the onerous task of the hunt was more or less extinct. With the progress of time, the able-bodied men, excluding old and infirm, migrated to the towns or 'joined the struggle'. The women had to adjust or perish.

The clan

The entirety of Chikomo hill housed various households of

the clan. *Sekuru* – a direct descendant of the famous chief Mutasa, who is said to have caused the sun to rot on the day he died, such was his legend and greatness – had six wives who bore him sixteen girls and sixteen boys. VaChihera was the last, but the vaHozi, and here is how it happened. *Sekuru* left Binga Guru during the chieftaincy wars of the late 1800s when a Portuguese hunter by the name of Guevara (probably not his real name) passed through the village recruiting trackers or hunters. In accordance with folklore, this was a gift from heaven because Sekuru's family had perished, save for him and two brothers. One Mteme, left with him and the other remained with relatives, the Chifambas.

Tete Femi was an entertainer, alcohol-dependent, loving and hard-working but possessed of a sharp reproving tongue. She lived about five hundred yards down the hill, on the way to the river, the water well, the grinding mill, the hospital, school, stores and bus stop. Thus, she was strategically positioned, given that she considered herself the village administrator of justice and information. Every evening, unless something was very wrong, she paid a visit to the house. While we, the inhabitants, at any given time pottered around preparing to settle down for the evening, a side show was in progress. You must understand that most homes in the village were situated along the road. VaChihera's settlement was bypassed by a road to the big river Mwerahari, to the back of the hill, and most of the village fields, to the south.

The neighbours on the hill to the south; vaChiheras' step children *vekwa*Peta, (children were usually identified by first name followed by their fathers' first name in the possessive. That's right, I belonged to a patriarchal society – all the nieces and nephews *vekwa*Chari. It was rumoured that a member of this family was involved in witchcraft, because they were said to commit unimaginable acts on people at night and, as if that were not enough, eat cats. Indeed, a sizeable number of the village inhabitants had seen one of the boys, skinning a cat in many different ways, salting it and hanging it out to dry. Well! Tete Femi was determined to bring this family to book. She was fearless, she was the African Judge Machete and I admired her gumption. Hands on her hips, swaying slightly from the effects of the *dhoro* which she consumed at any given opportunity, aptly positioned on high flat ground outside vaChihera's kitchen, she launched into a vicious invective at vaChira. 'You should be ashamed of yourself, *voetsek!* Vultures! Feeding off rotting meat!

A posse of children, laughed, asking questions; 'Haaa... what did they do, *zveshuva Tete? Rinhi?* When?' Talking all at once and urging her to continue. This was fun, great entertainment after a hard day's work in the fields and a major distraction from grumbling tummies waiting for the evening meal.

In 1975, the liberation struggle wars began in earnest, and by 1976 we were warned that it was no longer safe for us city dwellers to venture to the TTLs. VaChihera and some of the villagers were safe. By virtue of her old age, she was revered and respected by both antagonists. Additionally, some of the relatives were combatants who, years later, were to tell us stories of how they silently protected our village whenever they were deployed to the area. Stories of heroism abounded, but so too did those of horror, sadism and pain. In some cases, it provided a time of retribution amongst contending neighbours. Yet, I remembered an even better time, when the sun rose and went down, when faraway lands were only in the mist.

The shaping of a young strong mind

The sun was already high in the sky when vaAmaria woke me up to share her meagre but filling mealie porridge, gently simmered with a little salt, sugar and peanut butter. I helped her fold my blankets and roll up the straw sleeping mat that provided me with warmth and comfort at night while also being a place of terror. I was prone to 'watering the garden' even at the age of four, and as much as vaAmaria loved me, it would be irresponsible of her to permit the despoiling of the new second-hand mattress on her high wrought iron vintage bed given to her by *vanavangu*. She talked about *vanavangu* to her friends and neighbours with passion and gratitude. I wondered who they were and found out during the 'school break'.

I discovered to my delight that I was blessed with two aunts who attended the Catholic boarding school at Mt St Mary's Mission and two on 'short leave' from nurse training school at Mpilo Hospital in Bulawayo. They arrived unexpectedly, two by two, over two days amidst much laughter, gifts and supplies from town: a dress and panties for me – a real treat since I mostly wore none or very old ones with many holes; lemons from the mission at St Mary's; a sarong for vaAmaria, shorts and a T-shirt for Stephan, the youngest of the *vanavangu*, and my friend, my brother, my uncle who attended the mission primary school at St Peter's; as well as stories of faraway places and the people who lived there. '*Eeeh!* Things in town are changing...*mabhunu*... the Boers... arresting our leaders... liberation war... *ku*Zambia *neku*Moza.'

Too complicated for me to fathom, I went and dragged a reluctant Stephan away from the sisal that he was plaiting into a *chitorobo* for the cattle, assuring him that he could finish it upon our return, but now was the time to take the 24 cattle out to the pastures. Besides we could strip a young bush or tree of its bark and use the inner fibre or *gavi* to make this tool of discipline. I loved manoeuvring, the cattle around and round with shouts and whistles and occasionally tested the effectiveness of my thin *shamu* by tapping Sekuru Stephan's calves asking: 'Is that sore... heh... is that sore? Tell me and then I shall stop.' Usually he humoured me by pretending to cry, but once it was real, because I had truly exerted too hard. I was already honing my management and organisational skills at this early age. Going to pastures, was an extension of playtime, treasure hunting for delectable forest fruits and edible flying insects, including grasshoppers.

Those anthills rising out of the ground as though they were mighty citadels of an alien life form, were not only a source of food, but also held immense fascination because of the manner in which the inhabitants went about their business – so methodical, determined and sure. If I inserted blades of moist sweet grass down into the aperture, the soldier ants attacked the foreign object by digging in with their sharp pincers. This was indeed a formidable display of their military prowess, but also their downfall. Once embedded, the ants were nutritious protein and fat for the *rwaenga* and my stomach. During the rainy season, they morphed into ants with wings, decorating the humid balmy summer evenings with their translucent wings only to be snared for meals or lose their wings after a short flight and wander aimlessly around, fat and juicy. Their cousins *mhamhatsi*, were on the other hand deadly in meting out punishment on behalf of all docile ants. They covered the smooth hard hot mud road in their thousands, moving about busily, with a purpose, as military men, probably related to the Amazonian army variety, although not quite as destructive. We hopped up and down to avoid the stinging bites, and prayed for the end of the infestation. The verges offered no relief as they were littered with stinging nettles, African variety, and *mafeso* – upside down drawing board pins, with three or more sharp and sturdy piercers, to do damage to bare feet. I hated spring.

The settlement

We lived at the extreme end of this particular settlement which was scattered over a rough circular shape of approximately five hundred metres at the top of a plateau in Wedza to the east of Harare. Our thatched hutments of a kitchen, a *dandrum* (our forefathers must have struggled with the pronunciation of dining room) and a granary – the *hozi*. Much later when I had moved to town, modern additions sprang up as *vanavangu* earned more money and husbands prospered. Among them two small three-bed-roomed brick buildings topped by corrugated iron sheets for the accommodation of the visiting growing families as *vanavangu* married and produced grandchildren for vaAmaria. Of course, her kitchen was upgraded and she was the proud owner of a modern state of the art (by village standards) bedroom complex incorporating an inside toilet, bathroom and a veranda.

A stone's throw away from us, to the south, separated by a shallow levee to prevent mudslides during the rainy season, was vaAmaria's sister-in-law married to her husband's cousin-brother vaEmerenza. Her *vanavangu* would visit regularly also thus contributing to a very festive atmosphere in the village. I truly loved these times. We were swamped by wagonloads of happiness love and gaiety. When the full moon dared to grace us with its presence during these periods, all those of a youthful disposition would answer a call to whistles from the boys and yells of '*Vasikana uyai titambe*'. Akin to the nursery rhyme 'Boys and girls come out to play'. This call would be answered by whoops of spirited singing to drums, *hosho*, ululation, and rhythmic dancing in circular format with the opportunity of moving to the centre for any willing to exhibit their gyrating prowess. We would try the different dance styles: *agogo*, *chips* and *jit*.

Life with vaAmaria was on the whole idyllic, varied and fulfilling for the precocious, curious child that I was. So, I am told, and assisted by grainy memories. Regularly after breakfast, I went to great-grandmothers', vaKuru, a few hundred metres to the south west, and slightly uphill into the escarpment. The entrance to her small hutment area was an archway usually festooned with dark ruby and purple sweet grapes of the cabernet sauvignon type. Yes, you know it, I drink wine. I always sampled the produce before my standard shout of, 'Good morning vaKuru are you awake yet?' A delighted quivery response emanated from within the dimness of the kitchen. VaKuru was very old, and had to walk doubled over, because her back had seen many years of hard cruel work and child bearing, but she was still in perfectly good health and able to look after herself, although I am sure I often smelt whiffs of urine on her rather sparsely washed self. She was keen to preserve water that had to be brought for her, and perhaps washed once a week. It was now impossible for her to climb down the hill to the well at the bottom near the river. As a result, body lice and other bugs happily made a home in the folds of her clothes particularly around the neck area. VaKuru usually sat outside on the straw mat with me and I helped her shell peanuts or groundnuts, and then by squashing the little bugs in her clothes, in an effort to limit population numbers and improve vaKuru's comfort.

A fruitful existence

Merrily we bid each other goodbye with promises to see each other soon. I passed through Anna and her grandmother's compound on my way home, and called out for my friend to come and play or accompany me back across our shared boundary of fruit trees. Invariably, we stopped to climb them or batter fruit down with long sticks when the trees were difficult to climb. In my opinion whoever decided to grow all these fruit trees: the red grape vine on the archway to vaKuru, apples, oranges, lemons, red and white guavas, and more mangoes was a genius. This was a simple village girl's favourite snack bar. VaAmaria patient as ever, was always waiting, a large and small hoe slung over her shoulders, a clay water pot on the ready for head balance, a basket with sweet potatoes and pumpkin for lunch and a grass slasher for any free hands. Our activities and diet varied in accordance with the seasons and this was the mid-summer season. We were likely to spend the day in the field halfway to St Peter's, weeding and slashing the flourishing elephant grass that threatened the young maize plants along the boundary of the field.

We had the expert services of the field extension officers, *mudhumeni*, trained by the government district officers to assist. They visited us on their bicycles or motorbikes checking to see if we have been following their advice. We were told that digging furrows was very important, for drainage and management of soil erosion. We clearly were the exception to Parthat Dasgupta's insight that 'the circumstances of poor farmers often push them to degrade their own environment, thereby increasing their own poverty. Sure, we did not appear to get richer, it was not progress, but we could feed ourselves. VaAmaria enlisted the services of strong athletic village boys, the majority of them cousins, for a bucket of maize. All that was left was for us was to pray for good rains. Some years these were bad resulting in crop failure, very little grazing for the animals and precious little drinking water. When the rains were good, that is to say, with no excessive flooding, and little damage to crops or the environment, we all rejoiced. There was plenty to eat and store in our *duras* for the near future, the red rich loamy soils of the village squelched and churned beneath our bare feet or our bodies as we mud-wrestled for fun – much to my grandmothers' chagrin. Soap was a rarity and washing our threadbare clothes clean of this abundant red dye a challenge. Often, in the evenings, as we sat around the fire, listening to the crashing cymbals and drum rolls, the splitting whip-crack of thunder or lighting and the tinkling of the spontaneous rivulets on the shower-softened grass, the older members of the family would be inspired to tell stories. Stories passed on through the generations – related to water and our bountiful environment. It is said that in the days not so long ago, before the white man came and the forest and rivers were sacred. Humans lived among forest nymphs, water mermaids, speaking to lions and other animals, and our real God sent prophets. One such great prophet was Chaminuka, who performed all manner of exploits. His powers could summon the rain, make him invisible, and hide a whole city. Harry Potter eat your heart out, and he did not even use a magic wand.

Rituals

The mist rose off the surface of the steely grey-green gurgling body of water to languidly seep through the dense green foliage in the distance below, and I imagined that the *njuzu*, mermaids, were retiring to their home at the bottom of the lake further down the concourse. They could not be seen by humans or else the unfortunate person would be taken captive to disappear forever or coerced into training as a healer or witchdoctor. The unfortunate or the chosen, depending on your perspective, could only be saved if certain rituals were performed at the site of disappearance. The most important condition, it was said, was that no one should cry or indicate sadness. I wondered what I would do were I ever in that situation. Living in water all the time and eating worms and snails. I could not even swim. There was no chance of me going to the river on my own, vaAmaria told me we were going to see an African man of God, and accepted at the highest level into the sacred place where the men and sisters could talk to God. I could not be delayed.

When the first ever African Catholic bishop, Patrick Chakaipa, was invested, several villagers including me trekked to Salisbury by foot and by bus. What a stunning, musical extravaganza of worship and devotion.

The evening before the journey, was dedicated to the preparation of our picnic basket. VaAmaria roasted nuts, boiled eggs and pot-roasted a chicken which Stephan and I chased around the yard and into the thickets, finally capturing it by using a pincer-like strategic move. I held the animal down and Stephan sliced its throat with a sharp knife. The warm blood gurgled like the water, sprayed us all with red spots and bubbled into the tin dish ready to capture it. This we diluted with water and poured into the rubbish hole to minimise incidence of flies – a real nuisance at the best of times. We already had an appreciation of hygiene and waste disposal. Boiling water was poured on the bird to facilitate de-feathering.

Kerosene lamps through light over the comforting pungent fire waiting for a smoky flavoured snack. Who needed barbeque flavours?

2449 Egypt Lines, Highfield: the house of the people

I have no recollection of my own of the transition to town. I strongly suspect that this period of my life would be best dealt with in a state of hypnosis while seated in a comfortable therapy chair. I am told that I suffered great trauma. I was due to start primary school within a year or more, having sojourned in the TTLs for the greater part of my childhood. All native children attending the Group B government or mission schools were required to commence Grade 1 the year they turned seven. In his wisdom, my father had sent his emissaries, Aunt Nurse 1 and Aunt Vee, to assist me with migration. I am told that I cried all the way to Salisbury, and vaAmaria cried for days. According to her, she remained inconsolable until I had returned during a school holiday to spend time with her assisting with the weeds in her maize patch, as we did when 'we were'.

Aunt Nurse 1 had now relocated to Salisbury's Gomo Hospital – the largest and only such institution for the 'Native Africans' living in the capital of Rhodesia, who provided the bulk of labour required in the nascent industrial sites which supported the mainstay economic activity of the country – agriculture.

The standard core house on roughly five hundred square metres of land, originally had two bedrooms, a corner of a kitchen, a sitting room/lounge of similar proportions and an outside toilet, the type where the sanitary bowl was embedded in a slab of cement and in my opinion very dangerous for small children. The shower was located on the side wall of the toilet building. This meant that showering was a delicate exercise in balance and sure foot movement.

Any sudden move could easily land one in an undignified heap in the dubious mix of urine and excrement should the bowl not be adequately flushed. Bath time was my least favourite, until the renovations of the seventies. The kitchen side of the house was neatly divided into pathways to the ablution block, the small vegetable garden patch against the fence and my favourite place during the summer, the peach tree. The adjacent house was separated by a metre wide *sendirine* – sandy lane or sanitary lane. Our pride at the front of the house was the small veranda with standing room for about three adults and large enough for two chairs. The lounge housed some brown sofas, to obscure any dirt, and a small black and white television – we were the first people in this neighbourhood to have one such. The neighbours would congregate outside the fence on the dusty street to watch *Tom and Jerry, High Chaparral, The Flintstones, The Three Stooges* and *Hawaii Five O'*. Steve McGarrett was the man! During holidays and weekend afternoons, our walnut veneer sound system, also in the lounge, would blare out music in competition with, it seemed, the entire neighbourhood, and not just the traditional African rumba, jive, mbira tunes or chorals – not at all. The music included the hottest and latest longplays – LPs and singles on the record players, which were prone to scratching and produced a repetitious sound, much to the irritation of all. It was interrupted by shouts of 'change the record' or 'put my favourite', then 'Ooooh that's my song!': Mahotella Queens, Miriam Makeba, Dobbie Grey, Percy Sledge, Bob Marley, Jimmy Cliff, Tom Jones (dad's favourite), Thin Lizzy, Tom Petty, The Carpenters, Abba, and The Beatles would do their thing in Highfields. When the artist was not known, often the case, requests for 'Leaving on a Jet Plane', 'Cat on a Hot Tin Roof', 'Fox on the Run', 'You'll always be a Friend', and what about 'Ob-la-di ob-la-da life goes on bra' Then someone would shout: 'Who is that again?'

'The Beatles!' Hands clapping and clicking and peals of

laughter would pour forth.

The next door neighbours to our right – MaJoshua and Kiri – not much to know – and to the left – tenants, the prostitute and many escapades – I did not dare complain.

In due course the house was extended, but for some time we slept under the stars as we waited for the asbestos roof sheets to arrive. Fortunately, the rains were a long way off.

Four more rooms were added, inclusive of a dining room, extended lounge and a parent's bedroom, the boys' and girls' bedrooms and a bedsit with its own door on the kitchen side of the house. Prior to the cousins moving out – as accommodation increased with the addition of more core houses in the township – at any given time, there were close to twenty family members sharing the rooms sardine style. No one seemed to mind, due to fatigue or the story time opportunity that the living set-up provided. In the yard, there was the peach tree. No matter the number of times I fell from that tree, I returned to wrestle the fruit from the leafy branches as the worms joined the fray.

The family business

The corrugated iron warehouse with cement stone slabs, shining in the hot sun, dazzling our eyes like a futuristic bunker, took its place at the south corner of the kitchen frontage in the mid-seventies – our first store. This occasionally provided us with much excitement and a brush with the custodians of the law. Intermittently, the neighbourhood hoodlums would break-in and help themselves to a variety of goods, including our precious *mahodha* delivery bicycles, for their empty hideout homes or for sale in other townships. My smart father was certain he knew who the slimy characters were, but was not prepared to point a finger without evidence. We would wake up to 'Heee today we were robbed!'

'Haaah what happened?'

The fence 'protecting' our home was breached by the use of wire cutters on the sanitary lane side. The police wearing their smart khaki uniforms, prominently displaying their handcuffs, notebook and pen in hand would arrive after my father had made a report at the station situated at the Machipisa Shopping Centre. The police never apprehended the culprits. Maybe they did not try hard enough, because they were kept on their toes by the rebellious and troublesome Africans grumbling about majority rule, freedom and some such 'nonsense'. At that time, I imagined that the people who stole from us thought our family already had too much and maybe they needed the goods like the thieves in the village who stole chickens or cows to use in their appeasement rituals. Still theft was always discouraging for my parents and older cousins who spent up to fifteen hours working at our grocery shops at the shopping centre.

My father had a vision that wealth creation would uplift the standards of the entire extended family and serve as an example for his fellow, struggling, poverty stricken black man – the ultimate outcome being an educated majority able to fend for itself. This was a good thing. Thieving was a setback, never an obstacle as *baba* would sigh and sagely say: 'That's life'. I listened very carefully and embraced the words of my hero.

Mr Machipisa, after whom the shopping centre was named, was the foremost black businessman of that era. He was responsible for the establishment of the centre by the Rhodesian government during the fifties. The curious thing about the centre was that the first place one was greeted by upon entry to the area on the main road from the white dominated city centre was the Gwanzura Stadium – where all the entertainment for the Africans were staged – and the Beer Garden next to it. Clearly entertainment was a top priority for the City Architects.

Tete Bela's marriage

In my sixth year, my father registered my sister Ruva, and myself at the City Council Social Centre Kindergarten which combined the clinic on one side, a kindergarten on the other and a canteen in the middle for the employees. The canteen was open to the general public who could afford to pay the nominal charge for a plate of government subsidised – delicious, by any standards – sadza, cabbage and stewed beef, sometimes rice, mincemeat and cabbage.

At this time, we found ourselves involved in a momentous event, Tete Bela's marriage. Since *baba* was the nearest oldest male relative representing our late *sekuru*, all the *lobola* ceremonies took place at 2449, which was generally representative of Grand Central Station. All the relevant relatives, which included the aunts, uncles and family representatives spent time with us and participated. The wedding ceremony took place six months later at the Anglican Church near Cyril Jennings Hall in the centre of Machipisa Township and what an occasion it was. Ruva, my cousin Tari and I were flower girls. I was so relieved that I did not have to be maid of honour. Let me digress a little and tell you about a troublesome event that took place in Wedza. I was only about four years old, still living with vaAmaria, when Amainini Caritas married the love of her life. Happy as I was to be a flower girl, I was stunned to find myself the maid of honour. How could my aunt do this to me without prepping me?

Tete Bela and her new husband lived in a bedsit two blocks from 2449 and a posse of children, occasionally surprised her, usually at meal times. We heard that one of the ways a man proved his love was by ensuring that there was always food in the house. Besides, our activities left us hungry a great deal of the time. Tete Bela did not seem too enamoured with marriage, and it was not long before we were all aware that something was wrong. It was only two children, two and a half years later, she returned home, with tears pouring down her pretty chubby cheeks. *Amai* was at home. It was a Saturday. She welcomed her, made some food, offered solicitous comforting words, telling her not worry and that it was not necessary to say anything. It could all be put in abeyance for later. Oh bother! I wanted to know why such a beautiful event heralded by all that preparation and fun could be the cause of tears. The call of mud games soon distracted me, and I went outside. In the evening, Baba heard how being beaten almost daily was the reason for the misery of Tete Bela. Of course, the posse sat near enough to hear a large part of the conversation. But surely not? I questioned myself. Could grown men fight with adult women whom they were supposed to be married to? I must have misheard. Many meetings between the families resulted in the two boys being taken away from Tete Bela, since she had left the matrimonial home, and customarily the children belonged to the man. Oh no! Those boys who were almost twins in appearance and size were going to live with their paternal grandmother in the village. I walked round to the back of the house and cried tears of sorrow accompanied by a low volume wail, punctuated by regular intakes of breath, in the perfectly abject position. That is face against the wall resting on one arm, with the other hand clutching the heart. Young children needed their mother.

Tete Bela seemed to take it all in her stride. She settled back to a life at the grocery shop with all the others. Having her with us was a blessing, and we became very close to her. In the evenings, we sat around in a circle in the kitchen and the storytelling of *tsuro na gudo* resumed. 'Once upon a time, the rains had not watered a very dry land. There was little food, and hunger affected humans and animals. There was a clever animal, the Hare...' This was interactive communication at its best, pioneered but not patented. Tete Bela would commence thus in Shona, *'Paivapo'*, with each of her pauses we responded *'Dzepfunde'*. She delighted in impartation; we were thrilled with the nuances, the songs and the lessons to be learnt.

Township living

Although I embraced the pacey life in Highfields Township an inner part of me yearned for the peace of the natural environment with which I had established an unbreakable bond. As a result, I did not involve myself wholeheartedly in friendships. I remained a little aloof, one might even say shy. Even then, my parents discouraged interaction or loitering in the streets, save for polite greeting and conversation with the location inhabitants. Their viewpoint was that too much socialising would result in idleness, an uptake of bad influences and a host of vice found in densely populated modern settlements. My family, many cousins old and young, and my sisters were sufficient companions. With time, however, I miraculously acquired the friendship of two girl twins Salome and Maggie; they even had a slightly older brother Manu, and I realised later on that I'd had a mild crush on him.

I met this trio at my first primary school, Chengu. The twins were in my Grade 1 group and shared a similar enjoyment of the journey through numbers and letters. Salome, the eldest twin by minutes, was tall, slim and beautiful, with long hair, she became my main competition at school over the three following years. I liked her the most, although Maggie who was comparatively pale in complexion, chubby and shy was also nice and less inclined to 'put her better foot forward'.

After school, we spent some time at the 'small items counter', of the family shop helping to sell sweets and matches. On busy days, we could be requisitioned to man the cooking oil pump. This was the least favourite chore because it was messy.

At Chengu Primary School we began each day with a line-up by grade and in chronological order outside in the parade area which was in front of the main school administration block. The headmaster Mr Zunguza and the teachers stood at the front watching us like hawks. We were not to speak or fidget as we said prayers, sang the national anthem and listened to very important notices. If it rained, then assembly was cancelled. One day in his booming voice, Mr Zunguza informed us that bullies would not be tolerated at the school, nor thieves and mal-adherents. He then, notified a boy called Isaac to report to his office as soon as possible. The whole school looked around trying to identify Isaac, and determine why he had been singled out. I was soon to find out for myself, in a very traumatic manner.

I was still having accidents of a gardening nature at night. I had progressed to owning a wooden bed with a straw-filled mattress. It was not springy or therapaedically engineered, the bed was fairly hard but it was mine, to share occasionally with any of the visiting cousins, at their own peril of course. Actually, sharing made me feel safer and I preferred this. The terror of night had me in the middle of its crosshairs. I had a recurrent dream when I was carried effortlessly by two or three little men, not dwarfs, but little men as in *Gulliver's' Travels* from my wooden bed through the dark passage, past the door to my parent's bedroom. I wanted to shout out, but the noise died in my throat because my lips could not move, I was paralysed. In the lounge skirting board was a mouse-size hole, we would enter and that is all I recalled upon waking. What took place beyond the small entrance? Either I entered into a different dimension or my imagination was fuelled by the story books I read voraciously, Enid Blyton's *Famous Five and Other Stories, Alice in Wonderland, Through the Looking Glass, Aesop's Fables* and Greek Mythology. Possibly fact and fiction had morphed into one for me.

Could it be fear of Isaac? His father, we heard, was in and out of jail for robbery or maybe it was because of politics. One could never be too sure. Isaac's mother was in the rural areas I think, and the boy had to look after himself most of the time by waylaying my two cousins, sister and I on our way home from school via the family grocery shop. His keen survival instincts beeped him directly to us after a short but intense period of reconnaissance. Our little group, were well supplied with goodies, snacks and oftentimes money for ice-cream for our lunch. Isaac picked on my cousin brother Bhudi Asa – my father's elder brothers' eldest son, I did not differ him from a real brother. He would demand that we surrender our booty. If we refused, he threatened to stab or physically assault *bhudhi*. This always broke my heart into two pieces. I did not know or understand violence of this nature until this time. I was eight years old.

The rally and shooting of people

'Vharai madoor, vharai madoor!' Close the doors, close the doors, the police are coming. Do not forget to secure the burglar bars and then all of you come into the store room, hurry! hurry! The police reserves, the anti-riot unit and pumas, their armoured trucks, are on their way. Mark, take Yemi home quickly. Do not stop for anything.' I suspect Mark was a runner, because instead of making haste to 2449, he lingered to participate in the ruckus that was about to take place. I saw thousands of people coming from all directions on foot and the police trucks snaking their way from the main section compound of Southerton, past the sports stadium. Thank heavens I knew how to get home by myself. An hour later Mark eventually found his way to us, sporting a graze as big as an orange. It was the oozing out of bright red blood from his eye that had all of us holding our hands to our mouths, and the questions pouring out of our own eyes in profusion. 'The people were chanting and singing songs and the police started firing their guns, I think a large number of people are dead' narrated Mark, eyes wide with a mixture of anger, shock and terror.

Scent of war

It was not only acceptable, but it was expected that the established *wekudhorobha*, town people, should offer shelter, food, and assistance to rural to urban migrants known to them and to friends and relatives. As such, our small home at number 2449 was a home away from home to many, as long as they did not mind sharing what space was available on the beds in the two bedrooms or on the floor, in the dining room, kitchen or lounge. A major drawback was the early waking hours, necessary to facilitate movement in the common areas. *Baba* among his many gifts was very hospitable, ably aided by *amai*. At this stage, Jerry came into our lives like a breath of fresh air. Ten years older than me, then ten, and fifteen years younger than *baba*, he became the younger brother that *baba* yearned for. Uncle Joe, Baba's real brother had survived three near-fatal car accidents and the last one had left him slightly brain damaged and a bit manic. Uncle Joe was convinced that the spirit of the ancestors wanted to manifest itself through him as the family *svikiro*. Unfortunately, no-one took him seriously even after his belching rather dramatically and claiming he was allergic to onions and anything else with a strong smell. I found all this quite amusing, but loved him all the same, because he was such a gentle, loving soul who had a special relationship with *amai* because he had finally settled down with her cousin, the gorgeous Clara.

Jerry had a job as a disc jockey at the Rhodesia Broadcasting Corporation African Radio Two, Mbare Studios – a station targeting the black Africans and their vernacular languages. The station was contracted by the largest town retail/wholesale shop for blacks called Mantos and hosted a promotional slot for the shop every day on the radio. Jerry was born for radio, his deep sexy, suggestive voice made women swoon. Men thought he was a hero for his humour. I had an eleven-year-old girls' crush on Jerry. When *baba* and Jerry took us out to movies and ice-cream, all jam-packed in the back of the pick-up truck; dressed in my trendy maxi skirt I fervently hoped Jerry would notice me –to no avail. For not only were some of my cousins closer in age to him, but they were also very beautiful. The competition within the clan could rival any pageant. To complicate matters, there was the stunning Moira. She was tall enough to rival any modern supermodel, slim, dark, gorgeous, and sculptured in heaven, with beautiful Afro hair, a university undergraduate student, who daringly wore large hoop earrings and was with Jerry. I was

7

From the Mine Up

Wynne Musabayana

I was born and bred for at least the first 18 years of my life on two copper mines in Zimbabwe's Mashonaland West Province, Alaska Mine and Shackleton Mine, which were hundreds of kilometres from my rural roots in Chikuruwo Village, Rusape. The mines were 15 kilometres apart but operated as one under the Lomagundi Smelting and Mining (LSM) Company. I was born at the mine hospital in Alaska, the larger of the two mines. Alaska was, in fact, a small town, which, after its own mine closed down, refined and smelted copper from the neighbouring Shackleton, Angwa, and other surrounding mines.

At both Alaska and Shackleton, we lived in the *komboni* (the 'compound'), a settlement reserved for black mine workers and those, like my parents, who were teachers or provided various services to the mine workers. Independence in 1980 saw us move back to Alaska, this time *kumayadhi to* 'the leafy suburbs'. The racial segregation prior to independence had meant that even though my father qualified to live in the suburbs by virtue of his rank as a headmaster, we could not actually do so because we were black.

Shackleton is where this story is set, for that is where I spent my early childhood, mixing with an eclectic array of wonderful people from all four corners of Zimbabwe, and some from outside her borders, experiencing different cultures and lifestyles.

I shared my childhood with my older sister Molly, and my mother's younger sister Mainini Monica. Our elder brother, Darlington went to Mozambique in the seventies to fight in the liberation war and our youngest brother, Great, was born after independence. Apart from taking care of us, my parents also helped to look after the welfare of their own siblings and cousins, by variously sending them to school, having them to stay during the holidays, helping them find jobs, and assisting with marriages and weddings. There were also both sets of their own parents to look after. It was a lot of responsibility on teachers' salaries, but we managed, very well.

Our friends were a cosmopolitan bunch and spoke different languages and dialects: Manyika, Karanga, Zezuru, Korekore, Ndebele, Shangaan, Ndau, Chewa, Nyanja, Zulu, Sotho, Bemba, coming as they did from Zimbabwe, Zambia, Malawi, Mozambique and South Africa. They were Christian, Muslim, atheists, and all sorts. The mine was a veritable cultural melting pot. We attended the United Methodist Church and still do today. I followed my mother's example to become a full member of the church's *Ruwadzano Rwe Wadzimai.*

Most of my days were split between school, household chores and playing. It was our duty to wash the dishes and scrub the floors of the kitchen, living-cum-dining room, kitchen and our bedroom. As we grew older, we washed clothes and ironed them using an iron that was literally made of iron, which you filled with hot charcoal embers. To keep it hot, one had to fan the embers by blowing through holes in the side of the iron. To be honest, I was not allowed to use it for long, due to the many instances when embers had fallen out and burnt holes in the clothes that I was attempting to iron. We later acquired a gas iron which was much easier to use. Many households continued to use the iron iron, though, because the overalls that the husbands wore underground needed a lot of heat to remove the creases after washing.

We were also serious farmers, with a plot of land near the school where we grew a very healthy maize crop, sweet potatoes, and cassava. There were special hoes for making the beds for the sweet potatoes and mastering how to use them was a great sign of maturity. After the maize crop was ready we sat outside with *mhai* and *mainini*, shelling the maize by hand – a process we called *kupunungura magwere*. Thereafter it was time to winnow the maize in a round shallow basket called a *rusero* to remove the chaff and dirt and prepare it for the grinding mill. When our own ground maize meal was ready, we reverted to that which was dished out to everyone at the mine outlet, where we also received ration meat. Around the house we grew green vegetables such as *rape* (strange name for a vegetable), *chomolia* and *tsunga* for every day consumption. It was quite shameful to be seen buying vegetables from the market 'as if one had not been given hands by God'.

We played a lot. Mostly out on the gravel roads that linked different parts of the compound. Boys and girls played together. In the early years, there was little danger of being run over by speeding cars as no one could afford a vehicle. So the roads were used mostly by affluent visitors who came from Chinhoyi or by garbage removal trucks, etc. Children hung out as children while the adults got on with what they had to do, i.e. work to earn money to look after their families.

On those gravel roads, we played *nhodo, rakaraka, arauru, dunhu,* rounders, *tsoro, chihwandehwande* and other games to our hearts' content. We ran in the dusty streets rolling old motor vehicle tyres and competed for positions. Old bicycle rims could only be rolled along with the aid of sticks, for fear of chafing the skin. We made *rekeni*, 'rubber slings' to try and catch birds – a task that proved impossible for me. From time to time, we watched Bruce Lee and other films at the amphitheatre. Sometimes we watched homemade films by one boy named Ngondo. In essence, they were just a series of cardboard cut-outs that he projected onto the back of a cardboard box, using candle light to make the images bigger. But we all thought he was a genius.

We went on the hunt for edible insects – *ishwa, majuru, mandere, tsambarafuta, mani'inin'i,* and locusts. Through learning from others, we learnt which locusts were safe to eat and which ones were not. There were little brown locusts and huge ones that we called *madzomba*: to catch and retain one of them was quite a feat because they had a powerful kick in their spiky hind legs. We would fry them on top of the Dover stoves that came standard with all houses on the mine compound. Sometimes, we would not bother with the frying, but just threw them, alive, into the hot ovens while *mhai* was preparing the family meal. The fact that they are highly nutritious is something I only realised later. We ate them for their taste and their crunchiness; and also because they were there to be caught and catching them was fun. The joy of roasting live insects in the oven came to an end with the purchase of a gas stove; because the insects could catch fire if they jumped onto the flames.

One pastime we particularly liked was to make 'African' bubble-gum i.e. as distinct from the one you bought from the shop. This was made from the inside bark of a specific tree. One had to work extremely hard to finally get the gum out of the red bark, which had to be chewed for long periods. Regularly rinsing the mouth with water was necessary, until one achieved the gummy consistency. It was also a very messy process because of all the spitting and spillage onto clothes. But there was kudos to be won for those who succeeded in the recognition by friends that one was the proud owner of a tough set of jaws. The resulting gum had no taste at all, so we sporadically added sugar which reduced the resistance of the gum but was worthwhile as it leant some sweetness.

At first, we received our radio signals through a transistor radio. In the evenings, we would sit around it to listen to news from Mozambique and Moscow about the war front.[1] Listening to these stations was not allowed, so it had to be achieved at very low volumes. The problem was the radio crackled and spluttered so much there was always the fear of getting caught by the compound police, who used to launch regular night raids to ensure no 'subversive activities' were going on. As our brother was one of the freedom fighters, we had an interest in listening to those channels. Besides, boastful news from the Rhodesian Broadcasting Corporation about 'terrorists' having been captured, injured or killed by the Rhodesian army always gave rise to much pain and trepidation, so the alternative stations provided a much-needed counter balance. We prayed for my brother's safety and learnt the *chimurenga* songs through listening to singers like Cde Chinx, whom I was later to work with at the Zimbabwe Broadcasting Corporation. Happily, my brother returned alive after the war, although we subsequently lost him some years later.

We later became the proud owners of a long wooden structure made of fine mahogany wood that stood on four legs which tapered off at the end and was finished off by a lovely golden edging. This radiogram could play records as well, 'LPs', long-playing records, on a turn-table. It was a beautiful work of art, with ivory coloured knobs to tune in to stations, change the volume, etc. Unlike the transistor, this item of furniture was so large that I honestly believed the radio announcers took turns to get into it before they presented their programmes. Anyway, it was from that radio that I first enjoyed hearing the velvety voices of Jane Esau, Miriam Mlambo, Philemon Jusa, Killian Butu and Mavis Moyo among others. I listened to James Makamba promoting the wonders of Brylcreem on African hair, Paul Mkondo

---

1   Zimbabwe's war of liberation or the Chimurenga war, 1967-79, was a civil war. The guerilla armies of ZANLA and ZIPRA were primarily based in the neighbouring countries of Mozambique and Zambia.

telling us that *'Upenyu hwenyu idambudziko remoyo wangu',*[2] and the songs of Safirio Madzikatire and Tinei Chikupo, etc. Looking back, I can't help but wonder if my love for that radio and those pioneers of African broadcasting influenced my destiny as a broadcaster. Added to that, my mother often told me that the choice of my first name was inspired by a BBC radio broadcaster named Miss Wynne. It honestly seems as if my career path was pre-determined.

Christmas was a particularly exciting time. Many Christmases were spent *kumusha* in our rural Chikuruwo Village, Gandanzara, Rusape. My grandmother, Mbuya Rahabi Mukotekwa was a remarkable woman. Despite the shortage of amenities such as electricity and tap water, she made the village an attractive place to visit. In the kitchen, she would have tea made the traditional way i.e. a thick and very sweet mixture of water, tea and milk. The tea always seemed to be there by the fireside for anyone who wanted it. Combined with *mupotahayi*, a locally made bread that she baked in a large three-legged pot – it was the best breakfast one could have; especially after spreading it thick with Stork or Buttercup margarine which we bought from the nearby Dziruni Store.

Next to the kitchen was the 'house', as distinct from the round kitchen. The house was where the nice things were: the sofas, dining room chairs and table, the chinaware which was kept in the display cabinet, and my grandparents' bedroom. Sekuru Nehemiah was a quiet sort, characteristic of wise old men, and was the leader of the clan. As children, we rarely went into the house. We went in there only *kuno omberana* – to do the official greetings – upon arriving from the mine, and, occasionally, to receive treats from *mbuya*. Later on, we would sit with her when she was too sick from cancer and could no longer come out on her own.

Outside in the yard, we made earthen dolls and decorated

---

2   Your life troubles my heart.

them with whatever we could find. It was always a sad moment when we had to leave the dolls to return to the mine, and took to hiding them under *mbuya's tsapi*, the granary which was built on a raised platform to stop vermin getting to the grain. Sometimes we were lucky enough to find them intact the following Christmas, but mostly we were not so lucky and had to start making the dolls all over again.

Sometimes, but not very often, we were requested by my Uncle Jeremiah, whom we called Babamukuru JB, to go out herding goats, which brought us into close proximity with some cheeky baboons and monkeys on Tombi Mountain. The baboons were rumoured to be capable of slapping young children who came too close, so we kept a respectful distance. At times Babamukuru JB would wake us up early to weed *mbuya's* groundnut field, which was just adjacent to our house. That was not fun. But we loved and respected him dearly so we were soon grumpily out of bed and on our way. I might also add that we really didn't have a choice in the matter. I had many other uncles and aunties: Babamukuru David, Tete Lydia, Tete Betty, Tete Livia, Tete Miriam, Tete Hannah and Babamunini Onisphal.

Cow herding was a man's business and there were boys who did that. At the end of the day, Mukoma Samuel would come back from the cow pens with fresh milk that would be used for the tea, to drink raw, and to make curdled milk which we would eat with sadza.

But the really special day in the village was Christmas day. Dziruni Store would be a hive of activity, with people stocking up, and the B and C, Dangirwa or Chingaira, buses regularly disgorging hordes of people returning home for Christmas. Things worked like magic. We would get up early, put on our new clothes, purchased before the big day from Edgars or Lees and Marlenes stores in Chinhoyi. Then we would have breakfast and go to church. Presents were distributed at the church. Mbuya Rahabi and Sekuru Nehemiah made sure each of their grandchildren had a ripe cob of maize, on the stalk, and a bottle of Fanta at the Christmas morning church service. All this happened against the wonderful musical backdrop provided by the ceremony. I always felt moved by the *Wabvuwi* Choir and continue to do so today. Their singing was so good, it could transport one to heaven without praying.

Christmas on the mine was slightly different. It was quite a sight watching people coming from the mine shop on Christmas eve, as they carried, either on their heads or in wheelbarrows, the brown paper bags that contained either half a dozen or a dozen loaves of hot, fresh Lobels' bread, crates of cool drinks, frozen lollipops (we called them Freezits), cans of Sun jam, margarine, chicken and rice. The Christmas bonus made sure treats were available. It was the one day of the year that everyone ate like a king. From the mine canteen, one had the option of buying *mambunyane*, a highly nutritious bun made for the hardworking underground labourers but which soon became popular with everyone, or dumplings, which we called *vetkoeks*. These were deep fried by the Women's Club, and the oil would run down your hand as you ate this delicious fatty cake.

After church, Christmas afternoons offered a time for the adults to let go and enjoy themselves, at least those of them that were not required underground. There was a lot of drunkenness at Christmas, the effects of *chibuku*, Shake Shake beer, and the more expensive 'hot stuff' which many would only afford on Christmas Day. People would take their hi-fi speakers outside the house and play music at full blast, some of them perched atop the speakers. Yes, the speakers were that big: a grown man could sit on them quite comfortably. Young adults would do their utmost to be visible, strutting up and down the roads, the men in brightly coloured bell-bottom trousers, the ladies in midi or maxi dresses. Many sported large round afros, the afro comb sometimes strategically left in for good measure. Later on, a few of the young men started walking around with large radios or ghetto blasters perched on their shoulders, listening to music at high volumes. Before headphones, the boom box ruled. The men would bob up and down when walking, in a gait called *kubhamba*, or simply 'step' to show how cool they were. The ultra-cool would tilt slightly to one side while stepping *kunge gakanje*, 'like a crab'.

On the mine we came into contact with many traditional practices. One such was called *chinamwari*, where young people were initiated into adulthood. It was a rite of passage that, seemingly overnight, transformed girls into women and boys into men. In fact, some of the boys came out of the ritual with new names, signifying the start of a new era in life. Around Grades 6 and 7, many of our friends disappeared for weeks during the holidays to undergo this ritual. To my great and abiding disappointment, I never could get anyone to tell me what exactly they were taught.

There were many cultural groups on the mine. Dances like *ngororombe*, *jaka*, *nquzu* and *muchongoyo* were my favourites among the local fare. Imported routines included *chihodha*, *gule wamkulu* and *muganda*. Mai *na* Baba Shuvai were the champions of the *ngororombe* dance. Baba Shuvai was the leader of the dance. When he danced, he wore animal skins. On his legs he wore *magavhu*, leg rattles. Mai Shuvai was the cheer leader of the women, and led the singing to the rhythm of the drum beat. But occasionally she would take to the centre of the ring to accompany her husband. Their combined energies as they pummelled the ground with their feet would shake my small world. I cannot describe the excitement I felt watching them dance.

Entertainers like Safirio Madzikatire and his son Elijah, Mai Rwizi, Zexie Manatsa and Tineyi Chikupo visited often and gave live performances. Locally, we had our own mine band led by Baba Percy who multitasked as a miner, band owner, guitar player, champion weight lifter, husband, father, and 'pirate taxi' operator, i.e. transporting people illegally between Shackleton and Alaska or Chinhoyi. He owned an old VW kombi that would often splutter and stall in the middle of journeys. Oftentimes, it threatened to catch fire at the back, because that's where its engine was placed, and we would go around alerting anyone who cared to listen: '*Mota yaBaba Percy yaa kutsva futi*', Percy's father's car is on fire again. Fortunately, he knew how to deal with the problem and the kombi would soon be on the road again.

There was also a magician called *Abracadabra* who came once in a while to conjure tricks. One day he came to the school and, as one of his tricks, asked the headmaster, my father, to give him his watch. We watched in horror as he seemingly smashed it into bits using a stone. Then he invited us all to follow him to the vegetable market which was about a kilometre away. We did this, not believing we would ever see the watch again. But he went straight to one woman's market stall, flipped over the newspapers on which she laid her fruits and vegetables, and, there was the watch. Small trick, but amazing to a young child!

There was a sewing competition for the women at the mine. My mother won many of the competitions for her exquisitely embroidered tablecloths. But I was heartbroken to realise later that the reason we never saw them after the competitions was that they disappeared, with no compensation, into the homes of the 'madams' who lived *kumayadhi* at Alaska.

There were also beauty contests held for the women though the outcomes were not always positive. While winners would be feted for being the most beautiful, some marriages failed to withstand the wives' newfound celebrity status.

One of our closest neighbours, Mr Kamanga, was a sight to behold. We called him Baba Harrison after the name of his eldest child. Here was an original *sapeur*.[3] Way back then, before I even knew there was a word for people like him,

---

3   A *sapeur* is a follower of *La Sape*. This was a sub-culture found in the cities of Kinshasa and Brazzaville. The phrase is derived from the *Société des Ambianceurs et des Personnes Élégantes* (literally meaning the Society of Ambiance-Makers and Elegant People). The movement embodies the elegance in style and manners of colonial predecessor dandies.

Baba Harrison was transforming himself from an overall and gumboot clad underground miner into a fashion icon every single day of his life. He accompanied his every ensemble with a white handkerchief which he used to swat real and non-existent flies with exaggerated hand movements. He was from Zambia and often told us this was how KK (President Kaunda) behaved. Watching him walk was like watching a film – mesmerising. As he walked, he would swing his walking stick and let it hover for a few seconds before bringing it back down with great flourish, a white fedora with a bird's feather in it perched at a slight angle on his head. He would not sit down on any old surface without first wiping it and putting a clean handkerchief down on it first. Strangely enough, in 2010, I had the good fortune of meeting and chatting with Dr KK in Ghana at a ceremony to honour late President Kwame Nkurumah. When he took out his handkerchief mid-song (he sings very well), I smiled at the memory of Baba Harrison.

Another of our neighbours had an obsession of a different kind, albeit also related to cleanliness like Baba Harrison. Mai Duduzile – Dudu – had come from South Africa and was extremely house-proud. She also had quite a temper, lapsing into her native Zulu whenever she was provoked or angry. Judging by the bemused look on Baba Dudu's face, I doubt he understood any of it, but he always waited patiently for the tirade to end. Anyway, Mai Dudu won all the housing cleanliness competitions that I remember being held. She was impossible to beat, for not only did she keep her small garden neat and trimmed, but she scrubbed herself, her children, her house and everything in it spotless. The scrubbing extended to the Dover Stove and the cooking pots, both of which were originally black but slowly turned silvery after being scrubbed ceaselessly with *muchenga* – whitish sand – which she collected from the banks of a tributary of the Angwa River. Although all of us took regular trips to the river to collect the sand, the excessive scrubbing was too exhausting for many, and so Mai Dudu continued to scoop all the awards.

Our first TV set was black and white. It came in a wooden case with doors that you could open and close, and even lock. It was rather like a TV in a cupboard. It was beautiful, but not as beautiful as the radiogram. It had long legs to raise the TV to eye level. The case was made of real wood and we would oil it with teak or mukwa oil to keep it shining and fresh smelling like the rest of our furniture. When the TV first arrived, I remember the hustle and bustle at the house as technicians and local boys set up the aerial – a very tall system of poles that ended with an antenna at the very top. It had to be taller than all the surrounding trees and houses so that it could catch the signal. As the men were putting up the aerial and connecting it to the TV, we busied ourselves preparing sadza, tea and bread, and water for the *wabasa*, workmen, to wash their hands before eating, after their work was done. All the while, we were killing ourselves with anxiety as to whether the TV would work or not, because it was not unheard of that despite all the labour, the final picture would be milky; in which case the *wabasa* would need to come back on another day to try and turn the aerial so that it faced in the right direction. Fortunately for us, it was first time lucky. We enjoyed our black and white set very much, watching programmes like *Sounds on Saturday* and *Mvengemvenge*.

The possibility of watching things in colour never arose. That was until one of my cousins came in one day with the news that a new system had been introduced in Salisbury (Harare) that allowed people to see pictures in colour. I could not fathom what a colour TV looked like, nor how much it would cost. My cousin provided some cold comfort when he advised my father: '*Sekuru*, don't worry about buying a colour TV. This black and white set can turn into a colour TV, because of the new parts that will be put in during any maintenance or repair.' Needless to say, the TV remained black and white even after repairs. Later, when finances permitted, we were able to buy a colour set.

Education, up to first degree, was a given in our house; as natural as the Zambezi River finding its way to the Indian Ocean. Looking back, I realise that studying was the preoccupation of many; either through night school which adults attended after work, or through correspondence with institutions based in Harare or South Africa. So important was it that both my parents continued studying even though both were already qualified teachers. Back then, people believed that '*kudzidza hakuperi*', one needs to learn continuously.

Every year, we had prize-giving days for academic achievement at the school, the prizes consisting of textbooks for the next grade. I always got a prize at the ceremony, which was held in the amphitheatre. The mine manager and or his wife would officiate. The two of them would stride into the amphitheatre where we would be gathered, parents and children alike. My sister and I would be with the other kids, in starched uniforms and well-polished shoes: my mother never let us out in frumpy clothes. Many of the boys would have their heads especially shaven to a glossy shine, a *zuda*, in preparation for this big day. But Maminyane would have a little patch of hair towards the front of his clean-shaven head – *kazhumu* – for that was his culture. Daiz, the mine barber was kept busy around that time.

In Grade 7, I was made a school prefect. This meant a change of colour of my uniform and made me feel very proud.

The mines were breeding grounds of great sports people, such as Charles Kawara a pole-vaulter, and the great sprinter Artwell Mandaza, who lived at the nearby Mangula (now Mhangura) Mine. It was often said Mr Mandaza could out-run a horse. To this day, I still think he could have if he had been given the chance. There was a lot of football and netball too, mostly played by and among different mine teams. It was also on the mine that I was introduced to basketball through my cousin Archibald Mukuzwazwa. At first the players looked a bit silly, because they seemed to be playing netball; only very badly as they would need to bounce the ball instead of just throwing it from one player to the other. It all looked a bit strange but eventually we got used to it. In fact, it was through the same sport that I was to meet my husband, Joni, later in university.

For tourism we visited the Chinhoyi Caves with its many stories of mysterious happenings, and places of interest in Salisbury when we had the opportunity. My sister and I also had the added advantage of seeing the priceless Honde Valley every time we visited our maternal grandparents, Mbuya Esther and Sekuru Edward Dzirutwe, who was quite a character. My cousin Patience Mutasa often recalls how he would boast as he looked at his many grandchildren, *'Mwese imwimwi, ndini Sembenedza'*: 'All of you gathered here are my progeny, me, Sembenedza'. But Christmas Pass in Mutare was always a hot favourite, with its 'Welcome to Umtali' sign etched into a well-manicured lawn and seasonal flowers on a hillside. If I am to be honest, it remains one of my favourite sights and I am happy that my own children also look out for it.

When I was in Grade 6, my father bought a car, a Renault 12. It was smaller than the Zephyr that he had had when I was a baby, but it had enough room for all of us. Soon, we were to wave goodbye to our days of getting onto the United or Matambanadzo bus or even the dark green LSM bus to go to Chinhoyi, or anywhere for that matter. We now travelled comfortably as a family unit.

At Independence, we moved *kumayadhi* in Alaska, thus saying farewell to Shackleton. It was a bitter-sweet moment. I was sad to leave my friends and everyone I had come to know, but also excited at the prospect of living in a house with more rooms than we needed: with not just a shower but a bath tub as well, lights in every room, tarred roads leading right up to our driveway, a variety of amenities to while away time, and streets lined with jacaranda trees. At the same time, I also started high school at Sinoia High School, now Chinhoyi High School.

Beyond the Mines

I wrote these recollections in Addis Ababa, Ethiopia where I am Head of Communication at the African Union Commission. I have been to and seen many places. But those years of my youth crop up in my dreams from time to time. I still have the last of our transistor radios, the one my father used to listen to in his office. It has pride of place in our home. It still crackles and spits, but it still does its job. And, YES, I still listen to the news on it.

8

Kunaka Kunonakira Anoda Zvonaka Nemwero Chigariro

Tambudzai Muzenda

Raive gore ra1981 pandakasangana navatete Mai Anna. Baba vaigorotaura nezve hanzvadzi yavo vachiti ndichambonogara nawo kana ndapedza chikoro nekuti ivo vanenge vane basa naizvozvo havakwanisi kuzonditora. Mai vaive kumusha saka zvaitora nguva kuti vauye kuzonditora nezuva rimwe chete kubva kuboarding school kwandaidzidza. Vatete Mai Anna vaigara kuMabvuku nemhuri yavo. Baba vainduudza kuti vana vavo vose vaienda kuchikoro uye vakanga vakangwara seni. Ndipo pandakatanga kubuka semunhu sikana ndichiona kusasana nekuparadzwa kwevanhu nechirwere cheshuramatongo – pasi parohwa nenyundo. Nyaya dzekuyaruka kwangu hadzipereri kuMabvuku bodo. Ndakapinda Gokwe kuna mbuya vanobereka baba, Masvingo kwaibva Sekuru Kwenda, baba vababa. Kufudziswa mbudzi nekuchereswa makugwe ndowaingove mutserendende weyaruko. Nyaya dzinoenderera kusvika kuKambuzuma kwandakambogara natete Mai Thandi. Mai Thandi vaive nevanasikana vaviri navakomana vatatu. Ndakakudzwa nemadzitete angu aive mazigadzi pese pavaimira kana kufamba. Madzimai aiva akazvimirira munguva yandakanga ndisinga mbozivi kuti mabato emadzimai akamira sei zvatakazoverenga pave paye kuti inonzi *feminism* chii! Madzimai iwaya aigara nemhuri dzavaichengeta, vana vose vakapedza chikoro pasina kana bongozozo randakaonawo semunhu akanga asingagari navo mazuva ose. Kuda pairohwa imbwa mupinyi wakavigwa. KuMabvuku ndakagara kubva 1981 apo ndaisundirwa kuchikoro chemaRoma nevabereki vangu. Baba vangu vanoiti ivo vaiziva kuti chikoro chakanaka nekuti mwana wamaiguru wavo aive muchita Sister Georgina.

Chikoro – Chishawasha Mission

Gore richitanga ini handina kufarira nyaya nemadhiri aitambwa musi wandakazosiwa namai vangu pachikoro Chishawasha Mission. Ndaive kamunhu kaduku duku. Handifungi kuti ndaive ndakareba kupfura *half* yemita chaiyo. Ndaive ndakapfeka uniform yangu yeblue ririrogwe rine kumusoro kune macheck-check egrey, *blue* nebeige. Bhutsu dzaive dzatengwa kwaBata – dzainzi maToughees nemasokisi machena, juzi reblue zvakanga zvatengwa neuniform yangu kwaENBEE. Pachikoro apa paive nemiti yakawanda yemupine, magumtree nemiJacaranda. Chikoro chacho chaipindirwa kugedhi guru paive nezichechi rakakura nemadziro aita seane mazerere. Chechi yaive yakakura, sevanhu vandakasiyiwa navo vaive mazigadzi akakurawo. Mai vangu vakati vaizodzoka vaimboenda kunobhadhara mari yechikoro. Ini sarei nemazidzimai aya kusaziva kuti mai vakanga varova pasi. Ndakaramba kubva pabhenji randaive ndasiyiwa ndakagara ndichiti mai vangu vaidzoka. Izvo ndakanga ndaitwa gara ndichauya. Ndakaridza mhere ndakananga nzira yandaifunga kuti mai vakanga vatora. Ndakanzwa nzeve dzangu kurira nemoto nekuzarirwa nehuturu hwekurasikirwa namai vangu. Ndakabatwa ndichisumudzwa sesaga remagwiri nezidzimai guru randakazoziva kuti raive hama yekumusha kwababa vangu. Sisi Constance – semashevedzero atakaudzwa kuti tiite pachikoro, vakanditora vachindinyaradza sechisvava. Ndakachema nemadzihwa achiyeredza setsime razara nemvura yemukoho. Vakanditora vakandiendesa kunorara. Kuseni patakamutswa ndakanzwa zvimwe zvivana zvaive zvakangoinzana zvichichemera vana maivazvo. Ndakashaya pokuchemera ndikaouna kuti nyaya baba dzavaindudza kuti ndinofanira kukura kana ndasvika kuchikoro dzaive pedo. Ndakanga ndawira mumukaka senhunzi sezvo ndakanga ndataurira baba kuti ini ndaida chikoro naizvozvo ndaizogara nemazigadzi iwaya dakara ndipedze. Ndaive ndisina kujaira kumukira kuseni ndichigeza ndoga. Baba na mai vakanga vaita basa rakanaka kuti ndidzidze kugeza ndoga mazuva andakanga ndiri kumba navo. Saka ndaiziva kuchengeta sipo yangu nekuyanika tauro rangu kuti riome nebhurugwa randaifanira kuwacha ndega. Zera remunhu ane makore nhanhatu harisekesi. Ini ndakaona ndondo chokwadi ndikambobvunza kuti pamwe vabereki vangu vanoda kuti ndifire mudondo here? Chikoro chaive chakaoma nemhaka yekusaziva kutevedza gumbo remberi nereshure nemaitiro anoita kuti usawe. Ini handina kuziva kuti kuseni ukamuka unofanira kunoshamba nekukurumidza kuti upfeke uniform yako wonanga kunozora mafuta, wopfeka bhutsu, wokama musoro. Kana vhudzi rarebesa raigerwa nerazor yaiva yakanyorwa kuti *Razor Sharp Lion*. Musoro wazodzwa sepa wotanga kusvuvurwa nereza, dzimwe nhambo waichekwa. Asi hapana wawaiudza. Pachikoro apa paive pamusha naizvozvo waifanira kutsvaga shamwari nehama dzekutamba nadzo. Shamwari inogara newe muclass. Mazuva akawanda akapfuura ndikatokanganwa zuva randatanga kusvika pachikoro. Vana Sisi Constance, Felistus na Elizabeth vakazotova mai vangu makore akatevera vachitichengeta sevana vavo. Munhu anokuona mwedzi mipfumbanwe achikuchengeta pagore achiona kuti wadya here, wapedza kushamba, wapfeka zvinodziya kana iri nguva yechando kana kungokumbundira kana wambochema uchiti unoda mai vako. Madzimai iwaya haana kupiwa kutendwa kwakakwana, kuchengeta vana mazakwatira vanobva nzvimbo dzakaiyana nemitemo inosiyana mumhuri. Vaigona basa ravo rekuva mai kunesu tose. *Term* yakapera babamunini vangu vakauya. Ndaive ndambovaona pavakauya nababa vangu vachiti Babamunini Ishe ndivo vaizonditora kuchikoro kana pave nehorodhi. Asi musiwavakauya ndakatiza ndichiti handivazivi. Ndakachema ndichiti ibhinya. Sisi Constance ndivo vakazondigarisa pasi vakatanga kundibvunza kuti ndaivaziva here uye kuti ndakavaona kupi. Ndakataura kuti ndakavaona pavakauya nababa vangu – asi vaive vasina ndebvu. Apa babamunini pavakauya vaive nesango rendebvu saka ndakavhunduka ndikatya kuti ndiyani iyeye. Babamunini Ishe vakatora tirangi rangu resimbi raive duku duku. Vakarisungirira pacarrier yebhasikoro ravo, ndokundinakura kubva pasi vachindigarisa pamusoro petirangi riya. Sisi Connie vakandibhabhaisa takananga Tafara nenzira yekugomo.

Mabvuka and Tafara

Babamunini vaichovha bhasikoro asi tichisvika makata vaimuruka vosunda bhasikoro. Takapfuura kugomo, nepaSilveria House. Babamunini vaindiratidza Arcturas Mine, taipfuura ipapo tonanga kumazitank aipfumbura guruva chena raikosoresa, paCircle Cement. Paive nemazitank akakura aive akakomberedza dzimba dzevamwe vanhu vaigara mujinga mematank iwaya. Miti yemihacha ne mizhanje ipapo yaive yakachena kuti mbu seyazorwa upfu nepfumbu yecement. Makore akazoteverea ndaiziva kuti tikasvika paArcturas mine kana ndikaona matank iwaya uye babamunini vakosora zvakanyanya. Taitanga tasvika kuTafara kwaigara Babamunini Ishe. Gore rechina ndiri pachikoro nekugara naVatete Mai Anna zvainakidza chaizvo. Nguva kubva kuchikoro kuzosvika kupera kwemagariro angu kuMabvuku pakaitika nyaya nen'ambo dzakawandisa. Babamunini ndivo vakanditora tonanga kwaAmai Anna. Pandakasangana navo, tete vaichangosvuta fodya yavo yebute. Vakandiona wakandisimudza vachidaidzira kuti, 'ichi chana chehazvanzi yangu uya wekuinda Hwenera makore apfura. Ichi ndicho chisikina chake, chinogara nesu kuno kana baba vake vachifamba mhiri kwemakungwa.'

Vatete Mai Anna vaiva hazvanzi yababa vangu ichokwadi. Vana mai vavo ndivo vakanga vakasiyana, asi baba varivavo vese. Mai Anna vaigara kuMabvuku, ne mhuri yavo. Ini ndakanga ndisina kumboonana navatete kusvika musi uyu. Mai Anna vaive mudzimai akasimba anofamba achitinhidza pasi. Makumbo avo aive akasviba pasi – kwete netsvina bodo, nekuti vaive vakasviba kudaro. Kana mifananidzo yandaiona yaSekuru Kwenda veMasvingo, vaive vakasviba kuti ndoo. Vatete vangu ndivo kuzotanga kuseka kuti ndakazoita chigwaya kubuda kwambuya vangu vaive neropa rakasangana nerechirungunekuti tingadero takangoti tsvaa nekusviba serima. Vaiseka vachiti baba vangu vaiva bhusumani. Pedzezvo hama dzepedo dzaiudzwa kuti mwana wabhusumani. Mazuva akatevera ndakashamwaridzana nevana vatete. Vatete vaive nevana vasikana vana nechikomana chimwe chete chainzi Shawn, ndiye aive gotwe ravo. Musikana mukuru ainzi Maria, vamwe vaive Anna, Farisai na Shingirai. Vatete ivava, sematairirwo aitwa nababa, vaive nemuromo usingamharwi nenhunzi. Babamukuru, murume watete aive akanyarara, asingatauri kana. Vainzi vanoshanda kwaigadzirwa fodya mu Harare, British Tobacco Association. Babamukuru, vaMusoni vaingotaura kana vawana mhamba. Makore maviri akapfuura ndichigara kumba kwatete pahorodhi, handina kumboona murume uyu achimwira. Anna ndiye aita zvekunyevera achivanda kana vakatarira shure vachienda kumba huru yavo. Iye fifinyika kuseka kuti, vakadhakwa. Anna aiti mai vake vaisada kuti vana vaone baba vachimwa doro pamba, saka vaivhara gonhi remubhedhuru mavo vonwa. Anna ndiye wekundiudza futi kuti baba vake vaishanda nesimba kubasa ravo naizvozvo taidya chingwa nebutter nguva nenguva. Paweekend ndipo pataidya mazai nechingwa chekwaLobels. Ini naAnna taimhanya kuseni kunotenga chingwa chaipisa kubva kuna Mr. Lobels. Amwe mazuva taita lucky kuti Mr. Lobels vaitipa *candy cake*, kwete mahara – nekuti aive mapisi e*pink icing* anenge adonha pane amwe makeke. Taifara tomhanya kunoisa chingwa kumba asi vatete vaizopenga kuti tinofanira kusapihwa zvonaka nevatorwa. Ini ndaipindura kuti Mr. Lobels ihama yedu nekuti vanoziva patinogara. Vatete vaingodaidzira vatarisa divi, 'Imi moda zvonaka muchapara mhosva pano imi, baba vako iwe maNdhlovu vanondiponda zvomene.' Vatete vangu vaifarira kufamba famba mumaraini nemadzimai *society* yavo. Vaita zve *Burial Society*. Izvi zvaibatsira kana munhu ainge afirwa ari memba aikwainisa kuwana mari yekugadzirira kuchema nhamo yemufi. Uye mamemba acho aiuya kuzobatsira nekubika nekunyaradza uyo anenge afirwa. Vaita zvemadzimai eruwadzano – vamwe vaibata munamato vose vachinamata kana kubatsira mudzimai ainge awana murume ane ziso. Makore andakagara ikoko ini handina kumboona vanhu vakafa vakawanda kunze kwababa vaTrymore ne vamwe sister vechita na Mbuya Ziguru vakanga vafa nekuchembera. Ne umwe mwana akafa awira mumvura, akabatwa nenjuzu kuti akwanise kushopera asi baba vake vakaramba nekuti vave mupositori.

Baba vaTrymore vaive vakaparika asi vasina kuroora mudzimai wavaigara naye. Vatete vaipota vachiti aive pfambi nekuti aitevedza mabhawa, ndipo paakawanana na baba vaTrymore. Hama dzababa vaTrymore dzakaramba kuti varoore mukadzi iyeye nekuti ainzi akanga aine mhinganidzo. Zvainzi kwaakambobva akanga asiya musha waparadzwa ne nyaya yedivisi yakaanga achekeregwa nayo nababa vake. Vatete vaitaura asi vachiraira kuti mukukura taifanira kungwarira vanhu vasina hunhu saSusie *and Trevor*. Susie aifarira nyoka dzemapere. Pamba pavo paigara pane mafaro vachiridza vana Jonah Moyo, Bhundu Boys ichangobva kuBritain asi vaiti vakaridza *Rudo Imoto* yaMarshall Munhumumwe, vaimveyesana vachiseka, vachidururira chepfu yehwahwa pavharanda ravo. Chapu yairohwa maiwe! Izvi vaita *every second Friday* nekuti Trevor ndipo paaitambira. Varidza *music* tichinzwa mhanzi dzese *even* malatest *albums* ana Dolly Parton. Susan aive tsikombi yakazvimirira. Aive neganda rakati piriviri kutsvuka. Mutsika patinhira chaiye. Aipfeka mbatya dzaifanirana nechimiro chake. Aive mudzimai akaropafadzwa pachipfuwa neshure. Aifanana naKatarina wavaMukadota. Aive nechimiro chinofadza kana nyama yemunhu kadzi. Aifamba zvishomana achiita searikurohwa nemasaisai edziva akapfeka shangu dzakareba dzine hiri yakatetepa sepwa isati yaibva. Ini ndaiti ndikamuona achiuya kubva kumasitoro ndomira munzira sendiri kutsvaga Anna. Ndaida kuita saye kana ndakura. Susan aitaura chirungu semunhu aneflu ne mhino yakati twasa. Ainzi akanga abva kuAmerica kwaaive agara nemurume aida kuti abereke vana asi Susie, sekumushevedza kwataita, akanga atadza kubata mwana mumaoko. Ainhuwira semafuraizi, achizora lipstick yaitsvukisa muromo wake kunge aruma munhu. Vatete vakatiudza kuti akanga asangana nebere kuJoni – Baba T avovaishura nekufambisa nyoka yavo mumakwenzi akawandisa. Imba yana Trymore vaive *number* 5 kubva pane yana Anna, *number* 11. Anna aifarira kutamba nevana vemumaraini saka ini seshamwari yake ndaingoteverawo. Taitamba, raka raka kana kuti *bakery*. Mazuva ekutanga taingotamba takapfeka hembe dzedu, asi mumwe musi vatete vakati kana tisina kupfeka mabhokadhi tisatambe *bakery*. Saka musiwataitamba bakery taipfeka mabhokadhi edu toita kunge maboys tichisvetuka sehwiza musango.

One day tichitamba ndipo pandati kuna Anna, 'Baba Trymore vafa.' Nekuti pataitamba vakanga vakangotarisa kwatiri vasinga zunguziki. Anna akati titsvage chimuti tivabaye. Pataka svika padhuze takaona vakati zii asi vachibwayira zvishoma shoma. Takamhanya kumba tichinoudza vatete kuti baba vaTrymore vakanga vafa. Vatete havana kubva chimwe chinhu kunze kwekutiunza kuti tigare mumba uyezve tikabuda, vaizotizvambura senyoka yapinda mumba. Asi Trevor paakatanga kushayika pamepu achidzoka kumba kwasviba, vatete vakati vakanga vamuona achiita sedzangaradzimu. Ini ndakafunga kuti pamwe aive akadhakwa sababamunini vangu vairova matama enzira kana vamwira. Pavakarwara zvakarwadza kuona munhu apera serutsanga. Matama avo akanga awira mukati sevanhu vataimboona vekuSomalia paTV vachinzi vari kufa nenzara. Mwari akambovazodza nyasha dzake vakaita nani asi havana kuwana rufaro semagariro avaita vachine utano hwavo. Susie akanga adzingwa nehama dzavo vachiti akanga achekeresa Baba Trymore. Akagumbuka mukadzi akachema asi hapana akamuterera. Aitaura misodzi iri mumatama kuti Trevor aimuda, asi akasiya pamba apa nerutsito mumoyo. Hamakadzi ndodzaiti kuseni voburitsa Trevor panze pavharanda paive nemushana. Vatete ndivo vakatiudza umwe musi tichiramba kudya porridge vachiti deno taiziva kuti humwe hugwere hunongoda bota. SaBaba Trymore vanongodya bota chete nekuti maronda nehugwere hwavo hwaisada kuti vadye zvinozvimbira. Takamuka kuseni tichinzwa mhere panze. Vatete vakangoshevedzera kuti maunganidze akanga auya. Takaswera mumba mazuva maviri kana matatu, tichidya, kududunura madhoiri avatete tikaenda kubhedhuru kwavo kunotamba nechioni. Anna achitarisa chipfuva chake akapfeka bodi yemazamu yamai vake. Mirror rewardrobe raive guru pa*door* rese. Takapedza nguva tichiseka tichitarisa mazino, mazamu akanga asina kuita se aSusie. Makumbo akanga akachena kuti mbu nemhororodzi, nemiromo yakanga ine mbovha dzebota ratakanga tadya kuseni. Mazuva maviri akapfuura vatete vachiuya manheru nerimwe zuva ravasina kudzoka. Anna na Maria ndivo vaitaura, kana torara, kuti Baba Trymore vaive vasina hunhu. Kana Babamunini Ishe vakambouya kuzotichengeta mazuva iwayo. Ivowo vaita sevaigwara – vaikosora ne kudikitira vachitadza kumira. Babamunini Ishe vakanga vabatwa neugwere. Kure kwegava ndokusina mutsubvu. Mai Trymore vakanga vamboramba kuzogara nemurume wavo vakazodzoka kuti vachengete Trymore akanga ave kutanga secondary. Vatete vaiti Mai Trymore vakanga vakasimba nekuti vakanga vavhara churu kuti nyoka dzisa mwire mumwena wavo.

Vaienderera vachiti taifanira kuzvichengetedza semhandara kuti tisabatwe nezvigwere zvenyika seshuramatongo. Vatete vaiti, 'Ukavhurira nyoka dzese unobatwa nebvumbi inoruma ugofa zvishomana sekudya kwehwiza.' Idzi dzaive nyaya dzakafanira mukukura kwedu. Hatina kumbofa takapokana navatete. Idzi dazaive nyaya dzaisangana nengano. 'Vasikana munofanira kugeza kwete kuita sa Dadi anogara anesvina saka aive asina mushuvi. Iwe,' vachinongedza Maria, 'ukatamba nevakomana kana madhara aya unopedzesera wodya bota. Namata nyama dzitnonhodzwe mwanangu.'

Baba vaTrymore vakashaya muna *December*, nekuti baba vangu vakauya kuzonditora kuti ndiende kumusha kunoona vanhu. Maria akanga awana maresults ake e *Grade 7*. Akanga asina kupasa sezvaaida – ndokusaka aiita sebhuru rinoda kutunga jira dzvuku. Akawana nzvimbo kuSecondary paTafara asi aida Harare High yaive mutown. Ini ndakasumudzirawo gore iroro ndonanga *Grade 5*. Ndirowo gore randapedzesera kuenda kuMabvuku kana Tafara *for holidays*. Isu taive ne *TV* isina colour asi taipota tichienda kushamwari dzababa vangu vaive nayo. Saka ndaiudzawo vana kuchikoro kuti ndino ziva colour yebhachi raMukadota kana mafurauzi ari parogwe raMai Rwizi. Kuenda kuLuna Park paholiday zvainakidza futi. Makore maviri ekupedzesera ndaikwira bhazi kubva kuna Fourth Street ndega.

Missionaries and modernisation yani?

Missionaries and modernisation yani? Makore ekutanga pandakasvika paChishawasha muna 1981 ndaisakwanisa kugeza ndega kana kuwacha, asi makore akatevera ndakanga ndave kungona kuwacha mbatya dzangu ndega, mabhurugwa ne masokisi. Ndaikwanisa kuchengetedza chikafu changu ndega nekukomora musoro wangu. MaSister echita echirungu akanga akawanda *before Independence* yabata vana vevhu. Asi makore nyika yeZimbabwe yave kutongwa nehurumende yevanhu vatema, vakawanda vakanga vodzokera kumisha yavo mhiri kwemakugwa, Germany.

Masister iwaya aigona kutaurawo chiShona saka zvainetsa kuvanyeya. Father Magaya aive munamati anenge mubrother aitura chiShona semunhu chaiye. Makore ekutanga vaiuya vachitaura ngano dzavana Tsuro na Gudo. Asi vaisimbira muchikoro kuti titaure chirungu chete kunze kwekunge tichiita Shona *lesson*. Ne nguva iri kure kana murungu asati ajairira aitadza kudana kuti Rudo kana Chido. Sekuti Chido ainzi Chidho kana Rhudho – taiseka. Tairohwa dzimwe nguva neshamhu kana taita musikanzwa. Kwainzi maRoma echirungu masister echita iwayo ndiwo vaitonga chikoro nekuti vakanga vavakira vanhu vatema zvikoro. Saka zvavaida kuti tiite kunyangwe zvaiva zvisina hunhu taifanira kutevedza mitemo yavo. Vakawanda vainzi maMissionary vakauya nekuda kwaMwari, kuti vanhu vatema vaponeswe kubva muzvivi. Vanhu vatema vainzi vaive nemoyo yakaipa saka isu taifanira kuva zvifananidzo zvaJesu aive murunguwo. Masister echita aitiudza kuti taizoropafadzwa kana tikada kutevedza chita. Mashoko iwaya akatanga kundipa mafungiro aidairwa neshamhu. Taidzidziswa kusashora kana kunyangadza vamwe asi pedzezvo vaibvunza kuti ndiyani ari kubuda mudorm pakati pehusiku kunotsvaga vakomana. Pachikoro pedu paive ne vasikana vakanga vayaruka. Vamwe vakanga vauya kuchikoro *after the war ended*, saka vakanga vatoita zvechikuru kubata bonde kunzvimbo yainzi mumatanda. Vamwe vaizoshayika pachikoro zvonzi vakanga vaita mimba, vamwe vaidzoka vasisina mimba dzacho. Vaidzoka vaizivana navana Sister vakuru pachikoro saka paibatwa basa chinyararire – asi rinamanyanga haraiputirwa.

October 1986 raive zuva guru pachikoro pedu, taive ne *parents day* yedu. Ini ndaive mu *Traditional Dance team* – ndaitamba muchongoyo. Baba namai vangu vakauya nehanzvadzi dzangu umwe akambouya kuchikoro gore ra1984, asi akatiza akwira makomo eChishawasha akananga Mabvuku nekuti baba vakanga vanonoka kuuya. Akawanikwa kuCentral. Ne lucky taive na babamunini vaishanda semupurisa vakaita kuti agariswe paStation. Futi paive ne *call* kuti mapurisa atariseri zvikomana zvitatu zvaifamba zvoga. Akapedzesera ave mu*day scholar* ku Blakiston Primary muAvondale.

Igore randakaona kukosha kwemurume ainzi Samora Machel. Samora aitonga nyika yaive pedo nesu yainzi Mozambique. Akafa mundege yatakazonzwa kuti mabhunu muAzania vakanga vapfuura kuti vavhiringe mhinganhidzo dzavaiita kuti vapambe vanhu vatema. Ini ndakanga ndisina kumbomuona asi paTV vaMugabe vaitaridza kurwadziwa moyo nekushaiyika kwaSamora. Ini vaMugabe ndakanga ndambovaona gore reIndependence ya1985 pandakaenda nababa vangu kuRufaro Stadium vachitaura nezve matongerwo enyika muZimbabwe. *Hatichina Wekutamba Naye* yakaimbwa neRunn Family – yairwadza kunzwa. *I had no idea why I cried but the song was just touching.* Aive mwana wevhu Samora. Nziyo iyi yaitaura nekupambwa kwevanhu vatema nekupondwa kwemagamba akaita saSamora, Mbuya Nehanda, Chitepo, Biko nevamwe vakawanda nemabhunu.

Makore akafamba, makore akatevera ini ndikapoterawo semusikana akanga abvazera. Muviri wangu wakanga wave kuchinjawo semusikana akanga okurawo. Ndakatangawo secondary school *and I liked it a lot.* I had the other girls I was with in primary school and it felt like a little family and we just bonded. I was aware of the other girls growing and of course the escapades of the older girls during our junior years became topical. Some spoke of boys and hairstyles of choice and after school interests. We wondered actually, on many occasions, why the other older girls would tell us we needed to become 'girls' – 'proper girls' and they would show us how to pull at the thing down there – the thing between our legs. We laughed about it and yet still asked what it was all about. I thought about asking my mother but I was anxious about how I would start the conversation. '*Mai, ndakadhonza mati…*' It was just too much. What if it was not supposed to have happened? We should have reported this behavior to the nuns. But the nuns wanted us to be pure and not desire boys so imagine what they'd say if they found out about girls desiring girls and being touched this way? Times had changed so fast. *Zvonaka zvodhura* – what is the price! At the end of my first year of high school in 1988, I went home on my own by bus. My father picked me from the Fourth Street bus terminus.

After years of going to Mabvuku and sometimes visiting my *ambuya kumusha kuGokwe. Ndakaona kuti baba vangu vaida kuti tizive magariro ese mukurarama kwedu* so that we would appreciate life even more. At the time I had no idea, as I do today as a grown woman about the messages from Vatete *vachiti imbira kusvikira nzeve dzopfungaira nekupisa kuti 'Zvinonaka Chokwadi Zvinonaka Zvinodhura Vakomana'*. It was a song by a local band that spoke of how luxurious or good things are expensive – she used this as a metaphor of life's desires and consequences of yearning after the good things in life. I heard this same song sung by my Tete Mai Magomo and *baba*.

Kobva Zera/Coming of Age

Ini mukukura kwangu handina kumbobatwa nemhosva dzaibata vamwe vasikana. Paive ne shamwari dzakasiya chikoro apo vakavhurira zvuru kuvakomana vakanyepa kuti zinyoka hari pfiri pakutanga saka paive pasina mimba. Vasikana vakasiya chikoro kunorera vana pakava ndipo pakaperera sarungano. Vakomanawo vakaenderera nechikoro vakafawo malawyers , ana tete drumming me over on how these snakes were poisonous and would ruin my life. Some girls lost their lives to *shura matongo* as young as that, just like that. *Shura matongo* did not discriminate. Even my family was maimed – Uncle Chris, Aunt Mary, cousin Henry only 25, my friends Karl, Sally, Hazvinei and too many to mention. The young, rich, old, and the educated or not *vese vakatemwa*. Some thought it was flu at the time that would just vanish one day after Vitamin C and others played roulette with HIV/AIDS. Days had gone when we could innocently play bioscope. Bioscope *iri taibhadhara 2c kupinda kuti tione.* In Mabvuku this was such a treat and *taigaraiswa muchirugwi chehuku takatarisa kadhibhokisi rinenge rine* plastic *kunge* television. *Nester ndiye waiuya ne zvidhori zvemapepa achitambisana nazvo.* There were sound effects and voice overs at the time. *Toy Story* was way behind the innovations of Nester. Unfortunately, he was not really encouraged to pursue his talent in theatre or his creative ideas come to think of it now. *Aishandisa kenduru kuti tione bioscope iri. Raitaridza vanhu vanofarirana vachizopedzesera zvotsvadana. Ini ndaimbozviona mumabhuku asi ndakanga ndisina kumbotsvodawo.* Anna and I would giggle like silly girls at this. Of course Maria never came for these bioscopes because she thought it childish. But then the time HIV hit us all, we had no idea and all these feelings of safeness ended.

We started hearing of violence, the war in Somalia, hunger, Nelson Mandela, *mabhunu* down South – trying to silence the voice of Africa, Vietnam, Pope and his obsession about sexuality, and talk against female genital mutilation. Genitals – is that what we were playing with in primary school? Information was travelling so fast and I felt congested and was feeling completely overwhelmed.

My father always insisted that I be the best and be the person who can challenge herself to be the best I could. Failure, he said, would be the medicine to success too.

During my holidays, I often would visit my *tete* in Kambuzuma. Tete Mai Magomo was always amazing – a woman so cheerful, learned and very much a queen in her own right. My *tete* had gone to school and gone as far as Form 4. She married her dear sweetheart husband who worked at the airport and would bring us jam and treats from the Air Zimbabwe flights. I felt so proud of their achievements and determination. My *tete* had many children whom she and her husband worked so hard to put in school and they have all become such great people with their own families. I was so free and would speak to my *tete* openly. My *tete* would have been competition to Monique the American Queen of Comedy herself – she was such a comedian on all levels. Sometimes I still can't tell if she is joking or being serious. *Kusasana kunoparira – nyemba dzinozvimbira kana vechita.* Even in my second year in high school, I still went to my *tete* during the holidays. I felt free with her in the townships and did not enjoy the suburb lifestyle as much. Perhaps having gone to boarding school in the *bhundus* had made me regress a bit.

As I entered my teens, I had strong opinions about everything of course. My attitude did not go down very well with many of my family members. *Baba* would try to put me in the right path, and my mother simply thought I needed more prayers for my wretched soul. My brothers, as they too entered their teens had a stench of boys who rarely felt water on their maturing bodies. My body was changing too.

My moods became erratic. My uncle would try and cheer me up by saying: 'Young wife come here and give me a kiss'. I would turn around *ndichiridza tsamwa yechiNaija chaiyo. Ndaitosvotwa navo futi. Asi musi uyu vatete vakapinda mune imwe nyaya. Vatete vakatanga kuti 'Imi mainini makatamba nevakomana here? Munenge mazvimbirwa ne nyemba wani.'* Had I been playing with boys, I looked pregnant, she asked? I laughed and replied; 'Yes. I played with boys but had not had groundnuts because they made me fart.' *Tete* got frustrated and before I could say a thing the next thing I knew a meeting was called with various women, some family members and elders I had never seen in my life. Some of the women were gentle with me and the others quite aggressive. It was like an exorsism. *Tete* got up and announced that she was going to check if I had been 'tampered with'. I asked what she was talking about. She told everyone that with my mood she suspected that I was pregnant. *Kuseka inini – ndakaseka kunge munhu abatwa neshavi.* I laughed and *tete* was completely perturbed. It was at this gathering that the women introduced me to the world of sex and started sharing very graphic details about how to please a man. I laughed at the thought of my *tete* having the power to make her husband come home when she released 'her airs'. I had been introduced to the world of womenhood.

Back at school, we realised the times had changed. Politics came to the fore. We spoke of ministers who died mysteriously in car accidents and political issues we knew nothing about but what we overheard our parents say.

We experimented with our bodies even more. A friend Majorie that I had been with in junior school went to a river and did a ritual, we heard, that if we tried would enlarge our own breasts. *Takaenda kurwizi umwewo musikana aive nemazamu akakura kupfura edu akatiudza kuti tikarumisa mazamu nezvinyurusi anokura.* And so we did. Not sure if this was the cause for growth but for a while I believed it. The bite gave such a sensation like a bee sting but tickly all the same.

We gossiped about the nun Sister Angela who got pregnant and sniggered about what she had done – speculating about her nightly walks with brother Micah and their hidden kiss we had witnessed. You see our window was situated right opposite the nunnery. Our beds received so much light late at night we could see all movements. We'd see the nuns coming back from dinner with the priests or when they went for prayers on special days like Passover. It shone so brightly there was no mistaking a kiss – a wet one for that matter. We watched with shock as Brother Micah put his tongue in Sister Angela's mouth. This we never shared despite having witnessed it three years earlier. I guess it was not significant then. *Nyama ya*Angela I guess *yakawora* after all. The sister had failed to resist temptation we mocked. The nuns used to say: '*Kana ukatadza kukudza Mwari panguva dzese kunyanya kuti utonhodze nyama kuzvivi, nyama inowora.*' Sister Angela was forced to leave the nunnery, to become a mother but Brother Micah stayed on practicing in the Brotherhood!

Gore rakapera, I decided to go and spend time with Babamunini Ishe in Tafara. *Ndakawana babamunini vakarara. Babamunini vakangomuka zvishoma vachindikwazisa asi ndakona kuti vaimanikidzira. Vakanga vaonda semombe yemashanga. Ndakavabvunza kuti vakanga vaenda kuchipatara vakati, kuchipatara hapana anokwanisa kuvabatsira. Vakanga vangopihwa mapiritsi asi pasina kuchinja in his illness. Kubva pavakabva kuhondo babamunini vakanga vasina kuita utano hwakanaka. Ndakavabikira tii.* I left Tafara and went to Mabvuku to see Vatete Mai Anna and Babamunini vaMusoni.

In Mabuku, a lot had changed. Babamunini vaMusoni had succumbed to throat cancer. Meals were rationed. Maria, their daughter was now married to her policeman. Vatete Mai Anna was sleeping in her bedroom. She called out in a whimper, *'Ndiwe here mwana wehazvanzi yangu, Zhou mauya heka. Douya kuno ndikuone mainini.'* I smiled and walked over to her bed. She said she was just so fatigued and that she worried for her darling husband and wanted to move back to the rural farm in Masvingo. I thought it a wise idea. After all she had managed most of us so long. *Vatete vakandiudza kuti baba vangu vaizouya mazuva anotevera kutonditora kuti tiende kumusha. Mazuva maviri akapfuura baba vangu vakauya kuzonditora.* Unfortunately, it was also in time to take Babamuni Ishe who had asked that he go home to rest. *Vakasiyana Maria, akabata murumo, handina kuziva kuti vakamuudza kuti kudii. Taka bata tara tonanga Masvingo. Ndakapindawo dare ravatete ndoudzwa nezve marwaro ababamunini. Urwere hwavo hwaingonzi chirwere chenyika.* The truth is that he had tuberculosis and sadly the stigma with HIV and coughing led many people to their deaths because of fear of being discriminated against. Babamunini passed on once he arrived in the village. He had seemed so much happier but soon it was again a time of *maunganidze* – a family gathering – this time I was old enough to participate. It was an extremely mind opening experience of what happens. How else would I have been able to know without these families and *vanhu vakandikudza kuziva kuti nhamo inofamba sei?* There was a sense of *kubva zera,* you know, with the feeling that I had graduated – from seeing death from the windows in Mabvuku when Baba Trymore died – to being involved now.

What I experienced close to me and life, made it possible for me to learn this and *ziviso kubva panguva iyi haina*

9

Small Town Girl

Theodora Rondozai

I was born in a tiny clinic circled by a low hedge and patrolled by a fierce pair of geese. I was sometimes referred to as a 'UDI' baby after Ian Smith's 1965 Unilateral Declaration of Independence. As a little girl, I had a vague sense that this was not a good thing. But then, life was idyllic during the first six years of my life at St Augustine's Mission in Penhalonga, *kwa*Tsambe near Mutare, where my parents were teachers.

My brother and I would disappear after breakfast, with friends and dogs in tow, roaming freely and getting into endless scrapes, and only reappearing when we needed further nourishment. There was no TV, and no concerns about safety. Everybody kept an eye on everybody else's children. At the end of the day, we would trudge home, covered with a fine film of dust, and exhausted from the day's adventures. It was here that I fell in love for the first time, and here that I suffered my first heartbreak, when Mosotho declared that he fancied Eugenia and wouldn't be marrying me after all. Later, school was to become a brief daily interruption to the fun. With my mum as my Grade 1 teacher, there was limited wiggle room.

When my father's career outgrew the mission, we moved to Zimunya African Township, also known as *ku*10 Miles. It was a dormitory town for a large leather factory, with row

84

after row of tiny houses with no electricity. Initially, we moved into one of these for a few months. Oh, the adventure of going to the outside toilet with a torch at night! I remember the commotion when our dog ate the neighbour's chicken. My six-year-old brain registered for the first time that black and white people did not live in the same neighbourhood, unlike *kwa*Tsambe where some of the teachers were white, and sometimes came to our house for tea. There was not a white face to be found *ku10 Miles.*

So, I began Grade 2 at Zimunya School with the misfortune of once again having my mum as my teacher. I quickly established myself as something of a celebrity, what with being the fair-skinned *medem's* – the teacher's child. I was extremely competitive, and took it as a personal affront if I didn't win the 100-metre sprint or come top of the class. I was also bossy, precocious and not at all lady-like. I remember my mother's utter mortification when she came around the corner one day, just as I delivered a merciless kick on the behind of a little boy who had offended me.

My parents had bought a piece of land at the top of the hill and were building their own house. Ours was the first self-owned residence in the township, and when power was connected and we moved in, my popularity knew no bounds. Other new residents followed, building what were, by local standards, impossible mansions. This area, which would light up at night whilst the rest of Zimunya flickered by candlelight, became known as *Kuma*Rich.

Within a few years both my older siblings were in mission boarding schools. Many children were sent to mission boarding schools for high school. There the focus was on academics and they encouraged independence. I would be consumed with envy as my brother and sister packed their trunks and tuck boxes. It seemed to me a very grown-up thing to do and I desperately wanted in. In Grade 6, at my insistence, I was sent to at Hartzell School at Old Umtali Mission. Sadly, the reality did not match my expectations.

The food was limited and unappealing, and the ablutions a daily nightmare. One event (although comical in retrospect) did little to help me settle in. During my last term at Zimunya, aged eleven, I had entered an essay competition administered by the Rhodesian army. It must have been a feeble attempt at public relations as the liberation war was heating up. As luck would have it, I won first prize, and an army truck with a couple of white army officers (dressed in camouflage fatigues, no less) duly showed up at Hartzell asking for me. An impromptu presentation of a brand-new FM radio followed. Pictures were taken, apparently for the *Umtali Post.* Of course, this made me look bad, and word of my 'selling out' to the enemy spread. That night a large group of furious girls descended on me, demanding an explanation and I narrowly escaped a beating. Soon I was writing dramatic letters home, peppered with hyperbole about my suffering, and begging to be rescued. I conceded this life was for girls made of sterner stuff.

So, the following term I found myself back at Zimunya School, subdued but quietly thrilled. Life was becoming increasingly uncomfortable, and the local Rhodesian news became increasingly ominous. Every evening we would also tune in to listen to the 'Zimbabwe Broadcast' on Radio Mozambique declaring confidently that 'victory was certain'. Every now and then, late at night, there would be a violent banging at the door. My father would open the door to a group of white soldiers. They would threaten to shoot Smokey, our Alsatian, as he crouched between them and the door, growling unrepentantly until my father called him off. I would cower behind my dad, stricken with utter terror as they searched the house for 'terrorists'.

A year later, in mid-1978, my father and I did the rounds at the private boarding schools in Harare, writing Form 1 entrance exams. I had my pick of offers from three schools, and Harare Convent was deemed the best fit. (They very kindly offered me a bursary).

The intention had been for me to begin as a new girl at this Catholic school in Form 1, but as I'd not previously studied French, it was suggested that I join the final term of their primary school after a crash introduction to French during the August school holidays. (This proved to be highly fortuitous. A few weeks after I left, my old school was partially burnt down and the township was evacuated – a casualty of the war. It was to be several years before I returned).

So it was that in September of 1978, in the third term, I joined Sister Vincent's Standard 5/Grade 7 class at the Harare Convent.

I spent over six years at the Convent and I am still amazed at how much I was influenced by my time there. After all, who could leave untouched by the dedication that Sister Panny, Ocky and company put into educating us. Only years later did I realise the irony of being taught about sex by a nun! I suppose you could say I 'grew up' during those years. Many lifelong friendships were made, and so many years later, unapologetically, I still have the Convent girl in me. But the beginning of my Convent career was less than auspicious. It was a different kind of trauma altogether.

For one thing, no one knew of my former celebrity status. And all of a sudden, I was surrounded by strangers, just as puberty struck. I was gauche, entirely without my mojo, in possession of that unacceptable 'African' accent that drew mirth, especially from the other black girls who were veterans of the whole interracial thing. And this time, there was no running back home, so I had to tough it out.

In Form 1, I was promoted to the A stream. I started to play sports and make friends as I settled into the hostel. How happy I was to see Wadzanai, a familiar Mutare face. Gradually, I became more acceptable, and I have to say this was helped by a popular white girl choosing to befriend me in the early days.

They were interesting times. Events were moving inexorably towards black independence, and the white children's speech often reflected their parents' dread. Occasionally spats would flare up. Black people were moving into white suburbs. A white friend of my parents had clandestinely housed my parents after they left Zimunya, homeless. When then they finally managed to rent a house down the road from her, their picture made the *Mutare Post*, above a caption about them being the first black residents of Fairbridge Park. I remember one of my white friends in the boarding hostel receiving a letter from her father telling her that they were going to move to South Africa, to a place 'where there would be no black people'!

The great thing about being up close to different races (and there were several) is that it demystified them. Generally, black people's interactions with other races were characterized by a dynamic of overawe versus superiority, which often developed into aggression, anger and mistrust. Living with them revealed white people to be 'just people' who happened to be good at swimming and bad at dancing.

So many years later, Zimbabwe has a different face. Our generation was unique in living through that period of profound change. Today, international news is all about the politics of our crumbling economy. Visitors are always pleasantly surprised to find the die-hard humour among Zimbabweans of all hues – in their defiant '*I am Zimbo*' T-shirts – a vibrant arts culture, and a new generation of black and white young people who work and play together and have no personal memory of *that* racial conflict, and who take cultural differences in their stride. Even if they may go away, they take a piece of Zimbabwe with them, and in their hearts, it is always for a little while. They are 'making a plan'.

10

Bridging Divides

Joy Chimombe

I was born at St Augustine's Mission, at a mission school run by Anglican priests, mostly English, with a few nuns who managed the church and conducted small-scale subsistence gardening. Situated in the Eastern Highlands of Rhodesia, the Mission was perched on a hill overlooking the rolling hills of Penhalonga, a small mining town, west of Umtali (Mutare). My maternal grandfather was the building and maintenance foreman and he lived in the workers' village across the little stream with a strange name – Mutora Huku (Grab the Chicken). My sister Shumi, was also born there five years later.

My parents had met in Gwelo (Gweru), a town in the Midlands where my father was teaching and my mother was living with her older sister. My father then got a scholarship to study at the University of Delhi in India. He returned to marry my mother in 1962, then travelled back to India with her. My sister, Pai, was born in India.

Back then, both my parents had British citizenship as the country was still a British colony as it was before the Unilateral Declaration of Independence (UDI). They therefore travelled on British passports. When they came home, they settled in the Eastern Highlands where my father had found work as a chemistry teacher at Old Umtali Mission, a high school run by Methodist missionaries. This is where I spent the first seven years of my life.

St Augustine's mission was 20 kilometres away. I still remember the first house we lived in, a small cottage with a veranda, where my sister and I would play *nhodo*. We later moved into a three-bedroomed face-brick house. The Mungazis lived opposite us. Their house was identical to ours. The maid would fetch us from school, make sure we were well fed, and then send us off to play with the Mungazi kids, a girl of our age and a younger boy whom we would dress up as a girl from time to time. The maid would then come back for us at 5 p.m., bath time. We would then each have a slice of buttered bread to stave off hunger until our parents came home from work. In typical colonial fashion, we had our dinner sitting at the table at 6 p.m. and afterwards read books or played games while my father listened to the BBC world news at 7 p.m. Television was unheard of back then.

My parents were both teachers. My father taught high-school chemistry. His students nicknamed him 'beaker'. My mother taught kindergarten and domestic science. I can't say we grew up in an urban environment. It was more semi-rural because the missionary-run schools were set in the Manicaland countryside with rolling hills and fresh country air. Our life was pretty simple. We walked to school daily with two and a half pence which would buy us lots of sweets.

Saturdays were town days when my parents would drive us to Mutare to shop for groceries and then take us to the park. A visit to Meikles Department Store was the highlight of the week! We always walked out with a new dress or some shoes.

On Sundays we would go to church and Sunday school. Sunday lunch was the fanciest meal of the week. My father would drive my sister and me to Christmas Pass to buy the *Sunday Mail* while my mother prepared a spread – roast chicken with roast potatoes and veggies or roast beef with veggies and rice. This was often followed by one of three puddings, jelly, chocolate or raspberry pudding, or ice-cream.

Once or twice a year the circus would come to town and our parents would take us to Mutare for this great spectacle. I clearly remember only being allowed to buy tickets for seats on the side of the ring, the seats reserved for black people. The front seats were for whites only. There seemed to be nothing alarming about it. To us, that was how it was and that was how we lived. Whites were to be respected as the 'purer' race. Their skin smelt different and even their poo smelt differently from ours – or so they said.

Whenever there was a big football match and my father's team was playing, our parents would take us to Sakubva Stadium to watch football. A stop at the fish and chip shop to buy our take-aways on the way back home was routine.

In 1972, we moved to Howard High School, north east of Harare, close to Concession. It was a school run by Salvation Army Missionaries. My father had been fond of his former work in Manicaland but made a choice to leave. You see, he was a smoker but the school authorities had decided that it was inappropriate to have a teacher who smoked as it was against their Methodist moral and ethical policies. Well, my father was adamant. He wasn't about to quit smoking. He then decided to leave and find work elsewhere, and so he took up the post at Howard. We packed up and travelled there in my father's red Opel. My youngest sister Chiedza was born there.

My sister Pai and I attended Nyachuru Primary School which was on the high school campus. We learned a new form of physical exercise. This was a well choreographed exercise routine to which we sang. We were selected into the teams that were to compete in the schools' competitions. Our parents came to watch us compete, driving behind the school lorry that carried us to the event. I remember that during the same year, I learnt how to swim as well as ride a bicycle. I also learnt how to cook sadza. I was seven years old. My mother sent us outside with pots and mealie-meal on one fine day and told us to go and cook sadza. Although the product of this first task was unimpressive and lumpy, it was tasty enough for my mother and her friends to eat for their lunch that day. I had passed my first cooking test!

In 1973, we moved back to Manicaland to St Augustine's Mission, where we lived till 1976. Life for us was pretty similar to the one we lived at Old Umtali. Going to church, to school and playing with other teachers' children at weekends and after school.

My mother would send us to our grandmother's farm in Tsonzo, 20 kilometres away, during the holidays, to get some authentic rural experience. My gran looked after a few of my cousins who went to a school in that area. She would wake us up at dawn with the first crow of the rooster to work in the fields. We would return for breakfast around 8 a.m., or rather judging by the sun's position, as my gran never used a clock. She would send us back to the fields or to help mind the cattle until midday when it was too hot to be out, after which we would be fed lunch. Our afternoons would be mostly spent wandering into the bush in search of wild berries or having a swim in the river.

Because of these regular rural outings, which were meant to toughen us up, I have tasted every wild berry you can find in the Zimbabwean bush. I have also had every tropical disease you can think of: malaria, bilharzia, typhoid, you name it, I've had it!

I also learnt how to balance a bucket of water on my head, how to fetch and chop firewood, and how to light a fire. Sleeping on a hard surface and having candles and oil lamps as your only source of light was the equivalent of one big camping holiday. Don't ask me to go camping today, I have had my fair share of the 'bush' experience, and I don't wish for another holiday without running water and all the other goodies that come with a luxury holiday again.

Once a year, my father would take us on a long trip to Fort Victoria (Masvingo), to visit our paternal grandparents. It was a four-hour journey and my parents would make it worth our while. My mom would pack a picnic basket and we would stop at the lay-bys along the highway for a meal. A scenic stop at Birchenough Bridge on the Sabi River was the highlight of our trip. The bridge was named after Sir Henry Birchenough, whose claim to fame was apparently the fact that he chaired the Beit Trust, which funded and planned the construction of the bridge. The bridge was designed by Ralph Freeman, the man who designed Sydney Harbour Bridge in Australia. My father would always tell us the facts about the places we visited. One year, the car broke down on our way back from a trip and we pushed the car to Birchenough where we spent the night on a shop veranda as it was too late to find a mechanic. All I remember is how cold it was!

Birchenough area, apart from the bridge, is also well known for its mangoes. We always stocked up on mangoes to take back home.

Christmas every year would be celebrated at our maternal grandmother's home, and always on Christmas Eve, when my grandfather would put a big tree in the middle of the living room. Presents would be piled under the tree. He would play some dance music and we would all dance around the tree. Then he would stop the music and we all had to look for our gifts under the tree till the music started playing again. Those were memorable Christmases. On Christmas Day my father would drive us to Nyanga for the day and take us up to World's View from where we would see 'the entire world', as my father would tell us.

The Chimurenga war had begun in the early seventies and by 1975, my father was losing his students one by one to the armed struggle. They were all joining the freedom fighters, though the Rhodesian forces preferred to call them terrorists. The leaders of the freedom fighters or guerrillas would call secret meetings to which my father and other teachers were summoned. The school heads later got wind of this and my father had to move schools for our safety. He moved to Bulawayo to take up a teaching post at a township high school in Luveve, but decided to leave my sister Pai and me in Mutare for language reasons. Pai was put into boarding school at Old Umtali Mission and I was left with my mother's younger sister in Sakubva Township in Umtali.

It was a completely different experience for me – the change from country living to township living. People walked the streets freely at night, children played in the fields and parks, though football and other games were often played in the streets. Tuckshops and markets could be found on street corners and under street lights at night where people bought bread, roasted mealies or roasted peanuts and fresh fruit. The streets were alive day and night. Neighbours could be heard shouting across the streets for the latest gossip. People would come to your home to ask for salt or maize meal when they had run out. There was music everywhere, coming from people's homes, one did not necessarily have to own a radio. The township streets were our airwaves day and night. There was never a dull moment for township people. I did not, however, enjoy the experience very much. I was homesick.

Later that year my parents moved me to Chishawasha, a Catholic boarding school about 20 kilometres north east of Harare. Every child in that school came from a township in Salisbury. They spoke Chizezuru – a Shona dialect very different from the Manyika that I had grown up speaking. I suffered a culture shock, but within three months I had adjusted and could speak fluent Chizezuru. I spent the next year at Chishawasha. Then, in 1977, my parents moved to Salisbury. My sister Pai was now at the Convent High School. I joined her the following year. On his high school teacher's salary, my father was able to put all his four children through six years of private education. To this day, I have no clue how he did it!

Before I started high school, the nuns at the Convent recommended that I attend private French lessons so that I could catch up with the other girls who had been studying the language in Standard 5. I had written an entrance exam earlier and I must have done well because I was put into the A stream in Form 1. From the stories my sister had told me about the Convent, I could not wait for the first day of school. There were just three black girls in the class: myself, Faith and Tsitsi, who had also come from Chishawasha.

Shona was taught as a second language, which seemed a complete joke to me. What was even more of a joke was the fact that Mr Patsanza, the Shona teacher, would give me 98% for tests and exams and yet I would not have gotten a single thing wrong, having come from a school where Shona was taught as a first language.

I was immediately selected for the basketball team once I told the teachers that I played netball in primary school. The sport took me on my first aeroplane trip to Reunion Island on a school basketball tour. My father bought me a second-hand tennis racquet so I could learn to play tennis, but I found the sport so boring that I quit.

I will never forget my first swimming lesson. The teacher asked if I could swim. I said I could, but she still sent me to the baby pool and ordered me to swim the doggy paddle. I found that very embarrassing and demoralising. She would always tell us that Africans were not made for swimming as their bones were only designed for running. That immediately dissolved any hopes I had of becoming a swimming champion. I never made the team. I did, however, make the choir and the drama club.

High school was the first time that I experienced being taught by white teachers. I found it very difficult to understand them. As a result, my year-end results were not great except for maths which I loved. The teachers then suggested I move to the B stream in the following year. I wasn't too concerned about this since it only meant that I wouldn't study physical science. I spent the next five years at the school and by the time I left, I had lost my African accent and became a certified 'coconut', or member of the 'nose

11

Snippets of my Life

Wadzanai Valerie Garwe

I am the first child of four girls. I was born in Bulawayo on 18 August 1966, and I was much loved. Even though I was one of four I was also part of an extended larger family. My father had seven brothers and sisters as did my mother. In Zimbabwe, your father and mother's sisters and brothers are also your fathers and mothers. In essence all my dad's sisters and brothers are my uncles, whether male or female, and they are called *babamukuru* – older father, *babamunini* – younger father and *tete* – paternal aunt, to distinguish them by age and gender, however their functions are equal as they represent my father and are my father in his absence. My mother's brothers and sisters are my mothers: *maiguru* – older mother, *mainini* – younger mother, and *sekuru* – maternal uncle. As the first girl child and first female grandchild I was much loved by all.

I was born during apartheid and my parents, who both did their post high-school education abroad in the United Kingdom and Scotland, were determined to give their children as broad an education as possible. In Zimbabwe, my father had excelled at school and thus education had been his stepping stone to the external world. My mother had been sent to the United Kingdom to study nursing by her father, a journalist who also believed that education was the key to freedom. It should be understood that during my parents' formative years, the regime only allowed them to pursue professions in two areas – education and health. A man could become a teacher or a doctor and a woman could become a teacher or a nurse. That was the extent to which Africans were allowed to aspire or dream. The Rhodesian government was producing a number of Africans whom it could use as civil servants who were civilised and educated enough to communicate with the indigenous population but would spare the existing administrators the onerous tasks that involved speaking to the natives. They created native administrations so that they would have to speak to the bare minimum of Africans. I was conceived in Scotland and I believe something in my makeup is uniquely Scottish even though I have yet to visit the area.

My parents were nationalists and returned to Zimbabwe after their studies. Once they had me, they decided that I was to go to the best schools in the country which were mostly the religious institutions, however they also decided that I would go to a multi-racial school. In Zimbabwe, during the 1960s and early 1970s there were a number of religious schools but they were segregated by race. My parents, who were Anglican and Methodist (father, mother) respectively decided that I would go to a Catholic, predominately white religious institution and thus begun my journey. To understand what a complex situation this was I will articulate the hurdles they had to overcome: (i) Catholic schools generally only took Catholics – I was not Catholic I was Anglican; (ii) Catholic institutions in the city generally only took whites – I was very African and I could not claim a drop of mixed blood; and (iii) Catholic institutions had a quota – one African or coloured (mixed race) or Asian child was admitted to the institution every year. To further complicate the equation, we lived in a small town, Gwelo (Gweru), actually we lived in Umuzingwane which was about 30 kilometres away from Gweru town. Small towns as you can imagine tend to be more conservative than the capital cities, in this case Salisbury (Harare) was the capital.

I believe at the time the Regina Mundi Convent had never taken an African child. My parents blithely ignored these impediments and duly registered me for the 1972 intake. I was called to an interview and was accepted. However, the Catholic sisters (nuns as we called them) erroneously read my maiden surname. They thought they were admitting a European child because the surname was Garwe, which they seemed to think was Irish. Needless to say, there was a lot of consternation when I arrived at the gates of the convent on the first day of school, African as ever with my hair beautifully plaited and riddled with blue ribbons. My mother was somewhat of a perfectionist (nursing does that to you) and appearances were everything – she has traits of Mrs Bucket in the English television series, *Keeping up Appearances*. As a Catholic establishment, they could not turn away a child – Christian charity, especially one who needed conversion from the Anglican faith and legally I had an acceptance letter. So, I became the very first African child to go to school at the Regina Mundi Convent in Gweru and that year the Catholic nuns had to extend their quota to two – I believe the other child was Indian but do not quote me on that. I have no idea whether taking me prejudiced the next year's intake of students but given the Rhodesian government's mentality at that time, I would not be surprised. I should also note that the quotas of children of colour attending predominately white schools were weighted with the Asians having the highest weight (considered the lesser of three evils and Africans the lowest weight). Thus, began my journey through the Catholic system. The beauty of the Catholics is once they have you, they will not let you go, so when my father was transferred to Mutare (Umtali) as a schools' inspector (he worked for the Ministry of Education initially as a teacher and then as an inspector for the African schools), the Dominican Convent in Umtali was forced to take me – that school did not practise the quota system and I was the first 'person of colour' to enter that establishment. In Mutare, I was the only African child in all seven junior school grades – special indeed.

Thus, began my educational voyage which has taken me to various countries. One incident which has always struck me as being a classic example of racial stereotyping in the educational system is the awarding of the English prize to the child most proficient at English. During my penultimate high school year, I was the best student of the English language in the school – I was now studying at the Dominican Convent in Harare. Every year the nuns granted a prize for the best student in each academic discipline. My parents were surprised to be summoned to the headmistress's office because I was generally an obedient child keeping my proclivities generally below my parents' radar. I was also clueless as to why they were being summoned; I could not think of any gross infringement that warranted parental intervention. Thus, I was much shaken by the summons. However, the nuns were calling my parents to the school because they had a somewhat delicate situation on their hands. In so far as they understood it, the Rhodesian government's doctrine did not allow that an African child could speak English better than a white child. Thus, the nuns were in a quandary. I was clearly the best student in both English literature and language academically. Even though the nuns had tried to discourage my obvious desire to excel in the language, I had proved my prowess both internally (examinations and homework) and externally (Eisteddfod, the Allied Arts[1] competitions and external high school examinations) so the evidence was overwhelming.

---

1   The National Institute of Allied Arts was established in Rhodesia in 1913. It runs annual competitions with external examiners in Speech and Drama, Literary skills, Visual arts, Vocal and International. The latter, is called the Eisteddfod is a competition originating in Wales. < https://www.facebook.com/groups/niaazim/about/>

Sister Pancratius, our draconian headmistress, was in the unenviable position of telling my parents that even though I was the star student, government policy did not permit me to receive the prize. So, in an effort to appease everyone, the nuns decided that a white would receive the English prize and I would receive the History prize (depriving a more deserving History buff – history was never my passion except, of course, the more racy bits). Thus, I have the dubious honour of being the best History Student for 1983 instead of the best English Student. I love my country.

I think my life is particularly unique because of my parents and the circumstances under which I was socialised. I was born during a period of apartheid and my parents only spoke to me in English, refusing to teach me the vernacular language, Chizezuru (popularly known as Shona) as they wanted me to excel and wanted me to speak without a traditional Shona accent. I occasionally spoke in Shona to visiting relatives. Inevitably, this differentiated me from my peers. I lived with Africans but went to school with whites and this should explain my somewhat schizophrenic view of the world. During this period, Africans lived in high density townships. As the liberation struggle intensified, the Rhodesian government began to make certain concessions to the Africans, to appease the tethered beast that desired freedom, and one of these concessions involved creating a more middle class, less highly populated neighbourhood in which the Africans of a professional class could own larger houses with internal ablutions. The standard high density township house would have between two and four bedrooms and a toilet, which was outside and was a hole in the ground. As part of my father's refusal to be daunted, he built us a wooden platform such that his relatives would not have to squat when they went to the toilet, so our toilet always had a raised wooden platform with a seat – many of my friends used to relish going to the toilet at our house. This facility was also kept pristinely clean and disinfected under the guidance of our germophobic mother.

I was called *murungu* (the white child) by my relatives and my peers because my parents insisted that I speak Shona or English properly (not abuse either language) and as my first language became English, which, by default, I spoke extremely well. Even though my relatives loved me, I was always placed a bit apart because I was different. I spoke to everyone in English, and I was allowed to be precocious, because I was the first child, but also because I was studying with 'white people' so some of my behaviour was discounted as being 'white'! I also viewed my African life more as an observer rather than a full participant. My mother as the quintessential middle-class working woman brooked no dissension when it came to etiquette. I was allowed to play outside only because the houses where rather small and my mother could not keep me isolated at home, but I strongly believe that if she could, she would have had me tutored and kept away from any negative 'African' influences. I learnt to communicate in the vernacular through my playmates but I must say that to this day my spoken and written Shona is fragmented and atrocious. I can barely complete a sentence in Shona and it is often grammatically incorrect. My ex-husband always used to tell me when we went to the local market: 'Point and keep your mouth shut, because once you open it the price goes up'. 'A tourist in my own country.'

As a first daughter, I was under a lot of pressure to set the example academically and socially so I had to be the 'perfect' child. My constitution was such that I could be moulded and once my mother had a second, more demanding, child, my sister, less attention was directed at moulding me and I had more freedom to play. As I now know, from having children, the first child is given more attention and receives more discipline, because the parents are keener. As the other children come along, the parents delegate this responsibility to the older child(ren). Even though it is every Zimbabwean male's dream to have a male child, my father was blessed with four girls. As the first, he chose to ignore gender and treated me as he would have a son, thus I was socialised to fix and repair mechanical things, bicycles to begin with and vehicles as I grew older, assist him with the gardening, and accompany him to drinks with the boys on those nights when my mother was on night duty and my father had to baby sit. My mother worked equally hard to impart some feminine skills, specifically those that would render me capable of being a 'good wife' – namely the domestic chores associated with running a household. Thus, I could capably change a tyre and buff the parquet floor until my face could be seen.

During my younger formative years, my time in the township was spent playing with my peers so I did learn the games of *pada, dunhu, nhodo,* playing house and other childhood pursuits. We lived in towns and cities and rarely visited the rural areas for any extended periods, largely because my paternal grandmother loathed my mother so our visits to the rural area were infrequent and truncated. I only remember one occasion when we spent a week with my grandmother, which opened up a whole new world of fetching water, cattle herding, swimming in the streams, and telling (or rather being told) stories under the night skies. The majority of my young life was spent in townships.

Kindly remember that up to Standard 3 (fifth grade), I had never gone to school with African children and it was when I reached this level that the Zimbabwean liberation war intensified and my parents were forced to ship my sister and I to the capital city, Harare, where my maternal grandparents lived. Here, everything was different. The township that I moved to, Highfields, was larger and more cosmopolitan with people from a class that I had never known before – a black entrepreneurial middle class. I suddenly came into contact with the children of African businessmen, a whole new animal, and in Harare there were many more multi-racial schools, so many more children attended them. Please note that prior to moving to Harare, I had been the only child who crossed the racial divide, with my parents having to drive me 40 kilometres, one way, to take me to school. In Harare, we were enrolled in the Dominican Convent (we being my sister Chipochedenga and I) because, as I said before, once the Catholics have you they are obliged to keep you: (You can check out any time you like but you can never leave). Also, to my surprise, we were picked up by bus – Mr Chiweshe's bus; a bus in which there were several African children going to similar multi-racial schools, so my horizons were widened. However, the African girls largely went to St Martins (before coming on to the Convent) so I was still in the minority, that is from Standard 3 to Standard 5. At this stage (now seventh grade), a lot of the African children moved to the Convent, as it also had a high school.

One of the most traumatic occasions that I can remember is when the St Martin's girls who accompanied me on Mr Chiweshe's bus moved to the Convent. I was happy that they were coming, but kindly remember that I already had my little circle of friends, a little clique with whom I was used to spending my school time. Remember, I was a master at separating my school life from my home life and may the twain never meet. I had also been a big fish in a small pond for many years – the only African girl in a sea of white faces. Needless to say, on the first day of school, when it was time for break, as I always did, I dutifully took my sandwiches, lovingly packed to my taste, to the quad (a large macadamed playing area where we used to sit in front of the statue of some wonderful patron saint – maybe Mother Mary) and sat with my usual suspects, Margaret Reeler and Aline Hall. My African friends where scandalised! After all it was their first day at a new school and I, the veteran, had abandoned them. Suddenly, I was the subject of much discussion and you know girls can be particularly spiteful. Luckily, I had back-up, my maternal aunt(s) – *mainini(s)* had also transferred to the convent and they were able to calm the waters, but I faced strong resistance for the first week or two. I remember feeling particularly bewildered as I could sense some hostility but was not sure why people were being hostile. In the bus, my aunts would sit next to me until the storms calmed but it certainly was the first overt experience of racial profiling that I had ever experienced. In my calm little world, the ripple of racism had reared its ugly head.

Now you may be surprised that this is one of the first times that I ever sensed racism given that I was going to school with people of a different colour but children do not see colour. The only time I can recall that I experienced the colour barrier in my schooling life in Umtali (Mutare) was when I invited my best friend from school to come to my birthday party. Please note this was unusual because essentially my interaction with my schoolmates was only within the school premises. I did not sleep over because they never thought to invite me and I never thought to invite them. Africans do not generally do sleep-overs anyway unless they're related to the person in whose home they are spending the night, and usually go *en masse* to visit. All this sleep-over culture is a very new concept and I must admit even I have problems coping with the reality of little girls wanting to sleep over – my parents would never have countenanced it. The logistics of arranging a sleep-over would have seemed insurmountable and it would never have occurred to my parents or I to suggest it. In fact, most birthday parties during my young existence were held at school. I do not know if this was to prevent the Caucasian parents having to deal with an African child coming over or whether it was just more practical to take a cake, drinks and a few eats to the school during school hours. As a working mother now, I find it is easier to have parties at school so I assume this was the case for most of my friends' mums. Anyway, with typical Wadzi blinkers I circulated birthday cards because my parents had completed building a lovely home in Zimunya Township – a new middle-class neighbourhood – and we had a large home with a garden and an internal toilet.

My best friend at the time had a father who was in the Rhodesian armed forces, fighting the terrorists/guerrillas (African insurgents we would call them now) and it was inconceivable that she could come to my party. A few mothers were brave enough to RSVP and make their way to the party but the majority made excuses. My lovely friend threw a tantrum of such mega proportions that her mother was forced to telephone my mother during the course of my party and request directions. The mother drove the distance as the township was ten kilometres outside the city of Mutare and finally made it to the party. To say she was surprised is an understatement. I am not sure about the propaganda that the Rhodesian government circulated at the time, needless to say it was along the lines that we were savages who lived in huts barely removed from the apes. I did not fully comprehend the political undercurrents that were swirling around us, but I must say that I remember my mother and my friend's mother having an intense discussion during the party and they stayed much longer than the other children. I got huge props at the time because it was the first time that a party had been held with multiple races in Zimunya and I do not think I ever lost the mystique. In fact, to this day my relatives still say 'Wadzi and her white friends'. In a lot of ways, as strange as it seems, I feel a lot more comfortable in mixed race company than I do in African company because my formative years were largely spent with people other than my own race.

I do remember that because our parents were investing so much in the education process financially, emotionally and socially, they demanded a lot from us. I had to excel at everything I did whether academically or otherwise and I remember being in the swimming, tennis, hockey, debate, choir, basketball and drama teams – being an all-rounder. I was lucky to be someone who could manage the academics and the sports but I remember being dragged by the lower lobe through the quad after a particularly gruelling parent/

teacher discussion in which my mother was told by my German teacher, Sr. Anselma that I was a 'little madame' with an attitude. I remember my parents' disappointment when I could not do physics and chemistry (they were bundled together) which were 'A' stream (first stream) subjects because I had a terrible allergy to a number of chemicals and used to have long hiccupping/sneezing fits which incapacitated me for days. As I had to drop physics and chemistry, I was forced to drop into the 'B' stream. My parents were devastated. They did not make a huge deal out of it in front of me but given the immense pressure we were all under, I can just about imagine their disappointment. I must say that moving to the 'B' stream was most liberating for me. There are certain hidden pressures associated with being in the top stream that fall away in the lower streams. Needless to say, because I had been subject to the pressures I was still highly competitive, but the pace in the 'B' stream was so much slower and seemed more relaxed that I was able to read my romantic Mills and Boon novels and take myself away to far off lands with beautiful, tall, dark and handsome strangers during the course of my lessons. One of my classmates wrote to me a few months ago and said she actively hated me because I would read a novel in class and still make straight 'A' grades, but what she did not understand was that for the African children we had no choice academically. We were not allowed to get anything less than an 'A'; a 'B' was barely acceptable and a 'C' unknown – at least in my family. There was absolutely no room for mediocrity and perhaps this is the hidden cost of racism – the Africans felt that they had to excel in order to gain acceptance.

I think I was destined to end up in the United Nations system because within myself I am a unique blend of African with multi-racial socialisation.

12

'Born Location'

Isabella Matambanadzo

I am what is called a '*born location*'. The term is used, sometimes with affection, sometimes with disdain, to identify those who were born in the urban, black working-class suburbs of Zimbabwe, that is, the locations. It is one of those labels that I have learnt to embrace because I often sense some sort of veneration about it.

So, I arrived on this side of the world at 4.20 a.m. on 5 June 1973 at Harari Hospital. At that time, Harare was called Salisbury, and Zimbabwe was known as Rhodesia. My birth occurs nearly a century after Europe's mega-project of colonial expansion into other parts of the world. The empire's search for geographic territories, additional trade markets and wealth drastically altered and affected the lives and realities of the citizens in the regions that were forcibly placed under various forms of racial domination and resource control. While the name Rhodesia was derived from Cecil John Rhodes, and reflected the role he played in securing territories for Britain, it is a name that is very much synonymous with racial and material oppression. At that time, the country was deeply segregated on racial, class and gender lines. Remnants of these racial tensions remain in various forms today.

My name, Isabella, is in honour of my grandmother. She

had benefited from mission school education through the United Methodist Church. Racial discrimination limited and restricted, by law and through policy, educational and employment rights for rural, poor and black women. Her brother, Ebson Zimondi was a Reverend at the United Methodist Church at Nyadire Mission, and this had enabled especially his younger siblings to have access to education, which was very rare then for rural black children, let alone girls. She completed her high school and teacher training at Hartzell, in Mutare in 1947. At that time Mutare was called Umtali, it was a fort town located in close proximity, about eight kilometres, to the border with Mozambique, which was under colonial management of the Portuguese.

These days, it takes just a few hours to drive to Mutare from the capital city, but in those years my grandmother's journey from Uzumba involved walking long distances to the station and then arduous train rides and hitching rides on freight trucks. I have always marvelled at her pioneering spirit and great sense of determination. I think I get this travel bug from her, because in many ways much of my life has been spent on the road.

After graduation, my grandmother took her first job at Mutambara Mission School. She preferred to work as a teacher at rural primary schools in the villages she had been raised in and the villages she had come to know as home through marriage. She taught throughout her adult life. And even when she met and married, in 1950, my very dashing grandfather Amon Kubvoruno. They had their family, and she kept on working and teaching, which was rather unusual because marriage can mean women put their careers on pause, voluntarily or otherwise, in the interests of family life.

He was a very dapper sort of chap, my grandfather. He smoked proper cigarettes, his preferred brand was Kingsgate. Smoking was apparently rather fashionable in those days, and the hallmark of a gentleman. He always wore a tie, jacket and fedora felt hat. He is also of the Rozwi group, who had political and economic aristocracy and are known for their battlefield prowess. We spent many vacations with them in the village in Murewa and it was always such an incredible adventure for us. He had a *party line* telephone installed in their home in the village. She had a bicycle that she would ride to and from her schools with her exercise books loaded into a basket that was strapped onto the carrier of the bike with a rubber noose. She taught right up until her death in the 1990s. Initially, she used to receive her salary in cash in a brown envelope with her name marked on it. And then after petitioning the Commissioner for Native Affairs, an astounding title for a black, African, woman to confront, she opened a bank account. She did not have an identity card and had to have black and white mug shots stapled into her bank account book as a form of visual recognition.

My grandmother gave this appreciation for education to not only her children, but also all the families in the communities she lived and worked in. This is a very strong pattern in my family, of working women, giving women, conscious of community service.

December 1973 to 1975

Bulawayo was my home in my early years. We lived in Pelandaba, a township near a cemetery that influenced the name Pelandaba which means 'the place where everything ends'. After I was born, my mother, who is a nurse, had decided she wanted to add further skills and qualifications to her training. The nursing school was at Mpilo Hospital in Bulawayo. It was incredibly arduous for her being a working mother and student, but I do not remember any complaints. Some people will attribute that to my very young age, I have a different view. My mother has a remarkably resolute character. She was following her passion, her desire and her calling. And she was securing her independence and autonomy, in a world and at a time when black African women did not have the rights to selfhood. So, she put herself on a very gruelling regime of family life, work and study. Her attitude exuded sheer inexorableness.

My mother had night shifts in the hospital wards, daytime studying, homework, the family and a fun social life. It was after all the seventies, the years of bell-bottoms and Afros and Afro-chic tie-dye attire. The smell of imminent freedom from colonisation was in everyone's stride. I remember a significant amount of travel during those years because my father's career was also very much on an incline. My mother was relentless in getting her academic proficiencies and qualifications lined up, and building her family, all of which speaks of remarkable support from my father. I still see this in her to this day. She is well into her sixties, but is very much a woman with, and in full charge of her own mind. A woman with a very big, considerate and caring heart. She has always loved to travel. When we were young it was road or bus trips to Botswana, Malawi and Zambia.

Old Canaan, Highfield

By the time my younger brothers, the twins were born, in April of 1976, our family had relocated to the capital city. We moved into Old Canaan, Highfield. Our home was near Mhiza School in the black working-class township of Highfields. It was a little difficult for me at first because I spoke mostly Ndebele, having lived my formative years in Bulawayo. But the other children in Highfields were very friendly and accommodating. They would stand at our gate and call me out to play. We hung out on our township streets. We played games like *pada, nhodo* and *ara uru*. These are the township versions of hopscotch. We also played *amina kadeya*, the hand smacking rhythmic game that is all about ambidexterity. We played in the dust roads with rough stones and pebbles and marked out the course with sticks.

Highfield is a high density ghetto, located to the south west of modern day Harare, the capital city of Zimbabwe. Highfield was primarily set up by the white settler colonial government as a residential zone for workers in the neighbouring industrial areas of Southerton and Workington. It is affectionately known by both former and current residents as *kuFio*, and home to the Machipisa Shopping Centre, a hive of entrepreneurial black-owned businesses. Our collective admiration and respect come from having been ensconced in the heart and soul of the urban freedom fighters.

The war years

My earliest memories of the independence war are from this era. Not only did we have relatives coming from the villages to live with us in the city but my parents were contributing financially though their business to the liberation and resistance movement. So, there was always the backdrop of working for the liberation war effort in our home. Matambanadzo Bus Services was among the network of African-owned transport businesses that included Kambasha, Ruredzo, Kumuka and Tavengwa and many others that made a selfless and very generous material and financial contribution to the liberation war effort. Every revolution needs resources. Thinking back, this is one of my earliest experiences of home grown philanthropy, and it has sunk something into my brain and soul about charitable works. It wasn't by any means the glorious, red-ribbon-cutting picture as it is sometimes said to be. Great sacrifices of human life were made. My uncle Edmund was arrested for being a recruiter and mobiliser for the black underground movement. My other uncle Ernest drove a bus over a *chimambaira*, a landmine and his leg was blown off, and he lost an eye. He was in hospital for months thereafter trying to get rehabilitation of both physical and psychological wounds. He walks on crutches today from those injuries, and ingeniously rides his bicycle in the village pedalling with one leg.

Farai Tama Kubvoruno, who died recently, was plagued by various addictions related to his years as a *gandanga*, a freedom fighter, I think this is also the time that I remember the shadow of sadness falling over our family because another uncle, Makuwerere, disappeared. He was the go-between, smuggling shoes and denim trousers to the comrades. We were very, very fortunate that his body was found and we were able to give him a decent funeral. Many others passengers, staff members of the bus company perished in landmine and other attacks. And their remarkable contributions to our freedom has left a deep desolation on all of our family.

Still, life in *Fio* was made memorable by other exciting things. There were the shops at Machipisa and Gazaland, the hustle and bustle at the nearby Mbare market, which remains a massive space for all forms of African inspired entrepreneurship to this day. And there were the heroes: the leadership of the liberation movements had homes here and went about their organising and mobilising in the neighbourhood. President Robert Mugabe's house, which was blasted at, is a major monument of this time and can still be seen in Old Highfield, where it stands. The walls remain riddled with bullet holes.

We had fire drills at schools sounded by a blaring siren and had to learn to hide under our desks because there were raids and bombs. You can imagine being a child and growing up in the midst of it all. And the shortwave radios with political news that Independence, with a capital 'I', was coming. And Bob Marley and Prince Charles were going to be there too.

Bob Marley and my wailing.

So, I got all dressed up for Robert Nesta Marley and The Wailers. I figured if the man had occupied my eardrums all these years, with my parents blaring reggae in our home, well, I had better look my best and go and meet him. I had a pair of very snazzy blue wrangler jeans that were the vogue, and baby platform sandals and a woollen Rasta cap in maroon knit that would convince Bob Marley to leave Rita for me and take me to Kingston, Jamaica. So, my heart broke into little pieces when my parents said they only had two VIP tickets and children were not allowed. I had the biggest tantrum this side of the universe. '*Saka Muri kundi siya kwa Bob Marley?*' I asked them, indignant as my whole six-year-old self could be. And indeed, they left me at home, to watch the raising of the Zimbabwe flag on black and white TV. I cried enough tears to fill the Zambezi River to bursting point and refused to speak to my parents for days afterwards.

The Avondale years and multi-racial school system

By this time, we had moved to the northern suburbs which had become recently accessible to black families with Zimbabwe-Rhodesia and imminent independence and the official end of segregation. Our parents were granted a loan by a building society where a gentleman who worked there as a clerk said my father had done him an incredible favour in a time of need. I was still very much a boisterous ghetto child, and my youngest brother had just been born. Our play, as with all healthy children, was loud and energetic. Bud Spencer and Clint Eastwood television shows meant we spent a great deal of time re-enacting elements of the spaghetti western *The Good, The Bad and The Ugly*.

Although I was initially enrolled at the all girls' school, the Dominican Convent for KG 1 and KG 2. My closest friends at this time are Sally Bhajila and Carmen Moodley Bennet. Carmen had been with me at the Arcadia Nursery school, at a time when I missed my brothers desperately and was rather sad at the prospect of a separation throughout our junior school life. My brothers were always very much my first friends and ideal company. We also had a much-loved dog called Tigger. The boys had picked this name up at their nursery school, Pooh Corner, which was modelled on children's fiction writer A.A. Milne's *The House at Pooh Corner.* Our Tigger resembled the one in the children's book.

Our parents enrolled us into a co-educational environment

at the nearby Sharon School, in Milton Park. I moved there for Grade 3. Our motto was 'Let there be Light' which are the first words that God speaks in the book of Genesis. The school believed in providing knowledge and enlightenment. It was a marvellous multi-cultural and academic experience. Not only were there many black African children enrolled there, but there were children from the Hindu community, who spoke of grandparents who had come to Africa from Asia, and children from the Muslim community. The teachers were devoted to their young pupils not only in the classroom but also on track and field, and in the delivery of extra-curricular activities.

Being a very small school, we counted on some of the community infrastructure for our school sporting and extra-curricular needs. We would cut through the back route to the Old Hararians sports club, where we had our tennis lessons, our annual theatre and end of year events were held at Harry Margolis Hall, which is currently a popular venue for weddings.

We knew no boundaries in Avondale. We felt sure-footed and safe. We rode our bicycles and climbed trees up and down the cul-de-sac we lived on. We quickly became friends with the late Olley Maruma's stepchildren: Elizabeth and Jonathan Graves who had just moved to Zimbabwe and lived a few houses down from us. For some reason, we never used the main gates to go into each other's homes. We climbed the trees, and swung over the hedges and fences. Olley, a recent returnee from Britain, was very debonair, he was quick with his smile and had a fascinating mind. Although we were children, he insisted we call him Olley. He wore fashionable leather jacket and platforms and was working on films. He identified with revolutionary politics, and spoke endlessly about Black Consciousness and Steve Biko, Karl Marx and socialism... He was also passionate about making films that portrayed Africans in a constructive light. He worked for the Zimbabwe Broadcasting Corporation (ZBC) as a television producer. He was also a lecturer in television production at the Harare Polytechnic's Institute of Mass Communication. He would, much later, be among those people who would nudge me to follow a similar path of work and study.

Up the road, at number five, were Catherine and Christopher Read. They had a swimming pool that all the kids would jump into. Their father John worked at the University of Zimbabwe and drove as many families as could fit into his station wagon to the *Drive In* for a monthly outing at the cinema. We were introduced to the Boy and Girl Scouts movement by them and joined the club on Kerry Road in Avondale.

Evans Muchetu is another friend from this era with whom I continue to enjoy enduring amity. I do not think there is a single road that our curious feet left unexplored in that neighbourhood. We would walk the length of Lomagundi Road to Greencroft, take a left turn and back track to Strathaven, lumber up and over the hill of Argyle Road and end up at Avondale Shopping Centre. Our favourite place to meet friends was the ice-cream parlour at Happy Days, and the pool at MacDonald. We also spent a lot of time hanging out at Reps and the shops at Second Street Extension.

Everything had the flavour of an adventure. It was a time of great celebration, there were parties and festivities everywhere, and the exuberance of being a brand new, free nation was in the lightness of everyone's step. Long playing (LPs) records with the Harare Mambos, Zexie Manatsa and the Green Arrows, and Safirio Madzikatire was the order of the day and night.

In addition to the Maruma family, and the Reads, Mrs Mary Stumbles, from next door gave us a very warm and friendly welcome to the neighbourhood. All the kids on the street called her Ambuya Stumbles, her contemporaries called her Molly. She was the widow of the late Honourable Albert Rubidge Washington Stumbles, former Speaker of Parliament and a former minister of various portfolios in the pre-Independence governments. We had unbridled access to her immaculate garden and her well-stocked pantry. There were always treats there for the children from the neighbourhood. Her husband had established the law partnership Stumbles and Rowe, and her now adult children had left home for tertiary education in other countries, so she always welcomed our company. Mrs Stumbles, who was the elder matron on our street and herself approaching retirement insisted on interacting with the other women on the road and regularly asked them over for her luxurious afternoon teas.

High-school years

The letter of acceptance from Arundel School came as something of a pleasant surprise to me in 1985. I had found the entrance examination very cruel, some of the questions bordered on abstinence. I had, in fact, prepared myself and my parents for the receipt of a short, politely worded letter of regret, one that is associated with the delivery of bad news, and for rolling out a plan B. Suffice it to say that our home was abuzz with joyful anticipation that I would go to this remarkable institution of higher learning for Form 1 and that many of my childhood friends from Sharon had also been accepted. So, there was a sense of collective jubilation about this new chapter in our lives.

Arundel was very much a traditional institution, with routines that had been established since the laying of the school's foundation stone on 27 May 1955. It is highly regarded both inside and outside the country, so the longer-term promise of even better things to come is always on the horizon. Yet, I found it gruelling. Perfect performance was expected inside the classroom as well as outside. Given that facilities for all our academic and non-academic endeavours were top of the range, there was really no escape. The teachers were the finest possible: leaders in their own disciplines. They were both gifted and demanding. It is clear that we were being prepared. Quite for what, I was on that journey, and yet to discover.

Our Headmistress, Mrs Dorothy Twiss, who had been at the helm of the school since 1969, ran a very tight ship. Dealing with a contingent of pubescent girls must have been a work of art. She expected, and certainly got, results. She, together with Mrs Rose Cochrane, has recently published a book entitled *Grace and Learning from Africa*. It chronicles the Arundel School story with the superior style she demonstrated in her years there.

My mind grew in leaps and bounds in the Arundel environment. And new, fulfilling friendships were made. My grandmother's sudden death was a very big blight on my Arundel years. But that is a story to keep for another season. My spirits were somewhat lifted by receiving the award of the Philipa Wheeler Trophy for academic achievement, an unexpected distinction, given the sense of struggle I had within.

College and university

My most recent studies in an academic environment have been at the University of Oxford's Said Business School, where in 2008, I took the Advanced Management and Leadership Programme, an Executive Education course designed specifically for professionals working towards finding solutions for the world's complex challenges. Oxford is mind-blowing. It is a cosmopolitan campus, extremely well endowed, with humungous libraries and a culture of reading and learning. Prior to that, I had graduated with a Bachelor of Arts (cum laude) at Rhodes University in Grahamstown, South Africa. I managed to study for three majors, English Literature, Journalism & Media Studies (with Distinctions), Theatre Studies (with Distinctions) I am also the fortunate recipient of two scholarship awards without which I would not have been able to be at university. In 1997, through the generous efforts of Mrs Mazorodze, I am one of several recipients of a scholarship from the Sally Mugabe Foundation. And in 1998 – Reuters' Foundation Scholarship. Because both of them are merit based, the priority is really to get excellent grades. But university life is also about having social experiences. So while I graduated in April 1999 with Dean's List Student Recognition and received Academic Colours, I was also able to be active in the Student's Representative Council and to work on the campus news paper and radio station.

I was at Harare Polytechnic's Mass Communications Department for two years, between 1993 and 1995 where I was heavily influenced by the teachings of Dr Tafataona Mahoso, who was the head of school. He had texts such as Walter Rodney's *How Europe Underdeveloped Africa*, on our course work, Frantz Fanon, Karl Marx and Kalil Gibran. At night I studied with the Zimbabwe Institute of Public Relations and attained my Diploma in 1995. In April 1995 I was awarded my Mass Communications Diploma, with Academic Awards:

1. Best Feature Writer and 2. Best Interview. My parents were incredibly proud of this moment.

Career path

I now have extensive experience working on issues of development and human rights in Southern and Eastern Africa, with a specific focus on women's rights and the media. As a journalist I reported for the global news agency Reuters, from the bureaux in Nairobi and Johannesburg. My main mandate is for the Pan-African television show *Africa Journal*, telling stories for and about our continent. Our work is broadcast across the world and tries to achieve some of what Olley Maruma spoke to me about all those years ago, convey Africans in a favourable light. Nairobi is a brilliant posting; I love the work and the friendships that we make. Our office is a cultural melting pot, and I enjoy working with our tightly knit team of news-makers. It is not easy being away from my family, but I am received into many families both at work and outside. The otherwise vibrant experience is blighted by the deep wounds left by my father's sudden illness and death during this period.

In Zimbabwe, I enjoy working at the national broadcaster ZBC, as both a producer and a presenter on Radio One. I love radio. It is instant and incredibly participatory. My supervisor, Orbert Mandimutsira, gave me a slot for a show called *Women's Half Hour*, and we discuss some rather controversial women's rights topics. Lilly Mandimutsira becomes a close friend and colleague, who is selflessly devoted to mentoring my professional broadcasting style and voice. I could not have enjoyed broadcasting as much as I did were it not for her incredible support, and the phenomenal input of our audiences.

John Masuku, who is Head of Radio at ZBC, is a dynamic trainer, who gives us tutorials in radio producing and presenting. We later work together when he asks that I join the Board of the independent Radio Voice of The People (VOP) project. This lands me in very hot soup, because in 2005 the staff and board members are arrested on trumped up charges of owning and operating illegal broadcasting equipment. The case goes to court at Rotten Row Magistrate's court and we are ably represented by leading human rights and media freedoms attorney Mrs Beatrice Mtetwa. The magistrate is a very professional person, who also looks at the case in terms of the evidence that the prosecutor puts forward and he throws it out as 'a circus'.

My journalism and women's rights work would not be what it has been without the mentoring I received from Mrs Patricia Made. She opens many, many doors for me, and I am always grateful to her effortless and unconditional support. We work together at the SADC Press Trust, publishers of the Southern African Economist magazine. It is a remarkable time for me learning by her side. Her ability with words is fascinating, and her delivery is of outstanding quality. She leads from a place that is deeply influenced by humility and the principle of doing no harm. I do not think I have ever met another person who has opened so many opportunities for other people without expecting anything other than that they do well, and achieve their fullest potential. At SADC Press Trust, the volume and quality of our work on women in the SADC region is really ground breaking, because it is at a time when there is very scant information. I remember spending a lot of time creating tables and charts from data gathered through the Central Statistics Office and UN agencies to make a case for women's human rights. During this time I get the opportunity to write numerous news led features for development news agencies such as Inter Press Service (IPS), the New Delhi based Women's Feature Service (WFS) and Africa Information Afrique (AIA).

The combination of journalism, information and communications enable me to join the Zimbabwe Women's Resource Centre and Network (ZWRCN). Here I keep learning new things about the segregation women continue to face, the areas of opportunity and how to contribute strategically to women's human rights advocacy and lobbying initiatives at the national, sub-regional and continental levels. The work focuses on fiscal governance and gender budgeting, accounting for the contributions women make to the budget through care and unpaid work. Dr Theresa Moyo, one of Zimbabwe's few women economists is a great influence to my thinking here. Her writing and academic research push my mind to begin to think about women and resources. I also learn, in more depth about grant-making and fundraising experience, from both ends of the market value chain, as the team leader of grant recipient institutions and the portfolio manager in resource administering private foundations. This knowledge has continued to deepen over the years.

In 2004, I begin experimenting with working in a consulting capacity. It has been a journey to enable me to put all I have learned and continue to learn into a vehicle that joins up my various interests in women's human rights, the mass media, civil society and the creative arts sector. Part of the flexibility of consulting is to learn through those experiences that fall outside the parameters of job descriptions, and part of it is to have liberation, a sense of my own agency and autonomy. It has meant sacrificing certain things that being in the formal market place provide. I am privileged to keep building a portfolio of published research on women's rights, and on the media for publications administered by the Institute of Development Studies (IDS Bridges) at the University of Success, the United Nations Food and Agricultural Organisation, the Commonwealth Foundation. I am also very fortunate to get work in institutions where I continue to join the dots of experience and exposure, of learning.

My portfolio includes Virgin Unite, the Nduna Foundation and Humanity United, who have structured jointly an initiative for Zimbabwe called Enterprise Zimbabwe. And there is also the six or so years as Zimbabwe Country Programme Manager, Open Society Initiative for Southern Africa (OSISA). Established in 1997, OSISA works in ten southern African countries. It is part of a global network of autonomous Foundations, established by philanthropist George Soros.

Family and the future

In 1999 my father went into a diabetic coma. He died that July after a really harrowing time in intensive and critical care. My father's business had also undergone severe shocks. I know, from the conversations we had, that it was very painful for him to live through the losses of his most productive years. He was very much a self made man. Born in or around 1934, his birth certificate is dated 17 January, but he always said that was a guestimate. He came from Kachuta Village in Goromonzi. And spoke of incredible family poverty during his childhood that prevented him from going to school consistently and certainly beyond early primary education.

As such, this was one of the things he was very particular about. Bringing home school reports showing sub-standard performance, or less than favourable remarks from teachers never really sat well with him. He wanted nothing short of academic performance.

He grows up farming, and on the side, picking oranges in the Mazowe Valley with his father and siblings, as a casual labourer. They used to refer to it as *ku*Citrus. As a young man he finds employment as a domestic worker for a family whose name I never found out in the capital city, and begins to save his wages with the vision of establishing his own business. He then moves on to become a bus conductor, earning a little more and still saving. He has his sights set on purchasing a bus and establishing a rural transport business to service disenfranchised Africans and create jobs.

His first attempt fails because a trusted interlocutor takes off with his savings. At this time black Africans are not allowed to operate bank accounts and do not have ID books so he has saved all of it as cash. So he starts saving all over again, and this time develops temerity about handling his business transactions directly. He grows a business that has both local and regional routes into the southern African states, negotiating transport permits for frontier territories. Mangwiro Transport goes overland between Harare and key cities in Malawi. Mafenyatsela Bus Services crosses the Plumtree border into Botswana.

Not only had he survived colonisation, a world war, the liberation struggle and many other forms of trauma, but he knew how to live this life as if it was the only one he had. For me, this is part of the legacy he gave me, to live full and strong.

He also gave me an unprecedented love for family. We are a very big tribe in our family. This had meant we come together and support each other in times of trouble and need. I live with my mother who is in her 60s, and she still goes to work. It is one of the daily delights of my present life to be able to enjoy a very close and loving relationship with her and to harmoniously share a home with her. Some people find it strange, but I think for me, any other arrangement would be quite odd. My mother, through the magical space of her womb was my first home. I am privileged that she is my present home. It has not always been that way, given my career and academic movements, and I am grateful that we have been given this time together.

My nephews and nieces take up a big chunk of my heart and soul, as do new and longer-term friends. Some may share this life with me for a lifetime; others may only be here for brief interludes. As the saying goes, you can take a girl out of the ghetto, but you can never take the ghetto out of the girl.

I have always nurtured an interest in reading, and writing poetry and fiction. In 2011 I was pleased to be published and look forward to continue devoting myself to further writing and reading. In my spare time I love gardening, painting and making jewellery.

I look forward to the time when this contribution, can grow and fully recognise the various generosities of the many individuals in my family and beyond who have, drop by drop, contributed to any goodness in my character.

13

Raging Silence

Nyasha P. Katedza

In our innocence we played in a world that we
   thought belonged to us.
We ran in freedom and abandonment.
The dust settling on our youthful legs
As we picked it up with our rushing feet.
Joyfully fleeting from home to home
Unaware of the worries that creased our parents'
brows.

The bombs came with suddenness
The sound of gunfire splitting the silent nights.
The windows darkened.
The lights extinguished.

Hush Children, don't make a sound.

The nights of noisy family dinners and shrieking
   laughter
Forever lost to the unseen battles raging.

Our lives were measured in home, school, hospital,
   church.
Beyond that we were unaware.

Raging Silence by Nyasha P. Katedza

Hush children, be silent!

On holidays we went to the Tribal Trust Lands – oh
    yes, that's what 'they' named them.
We went to our ancestral homes to visit the great-
    grands, the grands and the cousins.
We spent the days in the sun, in the fields, learning
    about our heritage and our ways.
We picked corn, we sowed the fields, we used the
    tools that our grandfathers had made
    with their own hands.

And the guns came,
And the bombs fell,
And the roads were not safe,
And anticipation became mixed with dread.

Finally, the worried faces began to seep into our
    childish consciousness.
Why can't we talk?
Why can't we play?
Why do we have to sit in the dark?

Hush children, not a sound!
The bad men will come and find you!

In our childish innocence we chafed at the restric-
    tions,
Adding to the creases appearing on our parents' faces.

Hush children!

And the bullets rat-tat-tatted.
And the bombs dropped.
And our parents' frowns became our own.

And the silence grew.
Entering our souls and forever destroying
The safety we felt in the familiarity of our surroundings.
Hush now. Turn off the light!

… And our parents, who had struggled and studied,
Our parents who had fought battles against the sta-
    tus quo, the village elders, and, at times, their
    own parents;
Our parents who had forged into an unknown
    world
In order to achieve the most they could, under the
    repressive system they'd been born into;
Our parents turned to us with angry faces
At the slightest sound
Their anger not strictly directed at us,
But how, in our childish innocence
Where we to understand?

Hush now, be quiet!

And the silence grew
And the battles raged
And the guns rat-tat-tatted
And the bombs dropped.

In the silence we also grew.
We went on with our lives
Our parents fought their battles,
Punctuated by the country's struggle.

…And some of us left the raging battles of armed
    men,
For countries we'd never heard of.
We learned new languages
and learned new cultures.

Raging Silence by Nyasha P. Katedza

Our parents' struggles, now punctuated by new battles,
Became those of displaced peoples.
Now not fearing we'd be taken by freedom fighters,
Or shot down by flying bullets
They settled down to the task of raising immigrant
    children
Who would not forget their ancestors.
And the battles raged
And the bullets flew
And our parents spoke of the struggles at home
To whomever would listen.

Hush children! Don't speak out of turn.

And the silence settled into the separateness of the
    immigrant,
Joining with the silence of those not-so- long ago,
    dark nights.

And the voices at home joined with those that had
    left.
And pressure was brought to bear.
And the bullets stopped flying.
And the bombs stopped dropping.
And a country was born.

And we went on with our lives...
Wondering at our beginnings
While we flew across an arctic highway
Covered in snow.

14

Memories of the Transition

Rutendo Hadebe

The story of the build-up to my transitional experience begins in 1976. I was a Grade 3 pupil at a Roman Catholic school in a black high density township called Mkoba in the Midlands province town of Gweru, known then as Gwelo. At that time, my father who had been in partnership with a former schoolmate in a construction business was facing challenges in obtaining a job. The main reason was that white residents (the target market) were not building houses, thanks to the volatile war-torn environment. The ripple effects of the economic uncertainty resulted in a lot of adjustments to our household. One of these included abandoning our prestigious weekend grocery shopping trips to OK Stores or Desai supermarkets. These weekly trips had earned me a superior status within my little Mkoba village peers' hierarchy. I was the envied child from the grey-and-green house (a ridiculous combination) on the corner where the OK delivery van delivered groceries, including goodies such as chocolate, yoghurt, ice-cream, sausages and bacon which were not the contents stocked by the general dealer in the nearby township. So, yes, I was also that child who was privileged and whose mother oversaw a vegetable garden that always had colourful flourishing peas and carrots, in addition to the staple leafy *chomolia.*

By the beginning of 1977, my father was working on an ad hoc basis because hostilities between the Rhodesian Front and the nationalist liberation armies had escalated, which continued to affect the economy. Remote as the war seemed, my small being's ego took a knock. I felt I had been demoted from my superior social status.

But no matter how desperate things became, my parents were not about to let it affect my education. 'Education was sacred'. They pushed me to stretch my imagination by continually telling me that the sky was the limit once I was educated. And I did. I always had the most interesting professions to offer in class as part of our English lessons. Our teacher would prompt with, 'What would you like to be when you grow up?' Animated clicking fingers sounded as the hands of all 48 children would shoot up with cries of 'teacher', 'nurse', 'driver' and 'doctor'. Then, choosing my moment, I would provide the required spice, by stating that I intended to be a lawyer, an architect, a banker or an air hostess. Seeing my classmates' perplexed faces, the teacher would ask me to tell everyone what my chosen career entailed. I basked in the attention, enjoying the process of 'opening their minds' and because this happened so often, school was certainly an affirming space for me.

Although I oscillated between many future careers such as pharmacist, news' reader, and engineer, for along time, I was sold on the idea of being an air hostess, thanks to the black and white Air Rhodesia TV commercials which boasted beautiful black and white models dressed as air hostesses emerging from the national airline. There were always flawless, tall, with very fine features and I wanted to be just like them. And, of course, the black models had stretched my imagination and broken boundaries in our racialised environment, making my dream a possible reality.

The politics of the day was very clear to me, for I believed everything I heard on radio and read in the newspapers. So, I understood that the Ian Smith regime were the good guys, and the terrorists referred to as *matororo*, 'the boys' were the baddies. After all, they killed women and children, the radio told us, information reproduced by the national broadsheet, *The Rhodesia Herald* and reinforced by the alternative newspaper strictly for Africans, *The African Times*. At that time, none of my relatives had joined the liberation army so the good and the bad were clear in my mind. Interestingly, my parents seldom discussed politics with us, and very rarely did I catch them discussing the subject between themselves.

In 1976, the support for a Methodist bishop, called Abel Tendekai Muzorewa became very strong. He was Christian in his approach and certainly exuded an air of peace and confidence, and judging by his clean-shaven spectacled face, I was convinced he could end the war. To my naive mind, he was a saviour. His slogan symbolised by a closed fist (similar to ZANU-PF's slogan today) was accompanied by a loud mouthing of *dzakutsaku, dzakutsaku* ('heavy-heavy').[1]

The contesting opposition group was led by the veteran black nationalist leader in the country, Joshua Nkomo, whose loss of favour from the majority of the population was purely based on his Ndebele ethnicity. His group and party ZAPU's slogan was an open hand, (almost similar to that of MDC today) and was accompanied by the enunciation of *'Zzzzzz'*. The two opposing parties consumed the township. At that time my group of friends, which included Christina, Wellington, Kundai and Violet, often walked around imitating elders and shouting 'heavy'. One day, however, my best friend, whose parents were Ndebele, told me quietly and innocently that her parents had told her that when other children started to go 'heavy' she must open her palm and say 'Zzzzz'. Most of my friends did not know the significance of these slogans. However, I believed I was a bit more enlightened on issues of the politics and told

---

1   The UANC leader, Bishop Abel Muzorewa, addressing a rally, would raise a rifle in the air as he shouted *dzakutsaku, dzakutsaku*. The heaviness or weight of the gun symbolising the weight of the struggle.

my friend, *'Zvinoreva kutimuri vanhu va'Ngomo',* that means you are Nkomo's people. As I remember the exchange was flippant and we continued being each other's best friend. It really did not matter; we were just children.

As the war hostilities escalated, I began to pay more attention to the radio news which always entailed a security forces communiqué naming and numbering casualties in combat exchanges. In 1977, my father, through a friend acquired a fish and chips restaurant in order to make up for his lost employment and income. It was prestigious to be a businessman, but I still struggled with the uncertainties, which came with transitioning from being an ordinary girl to a businessman's daughter. All businessmen in Mkoba lived in a secluded, prestigious section of the township that had huge suburban houses with tiled roofs and neat gardens. I was not sure I would be able to pull off the transition, since my parents and our lifestyle seemed incompatible. In fact, at this point we did not even have a family car – my father rode his Samson bicycle to open his restaurant at six in the morning and returned after midnight. So, for the first few months, I did not disclose that my parents owned a restaurant. I was scared to become an outsider among my long-time friends, while not fitting in with the children of other business families.

One man one vote

However, before I knew it, the politics changed towards the rhetoric of 'one man one vote', as black people were going to vote for the first time. I knew that Bishop Muzorewa was contesting. I liked him because he was clean-shaven and had an Afro. To my mind, he occupied the same place as the 'cool', famed Afro-wearing singers such as South African Richard John Smith and American George McCrae. I had heard him on radio promising to end the war. So, when I said my prayers, I simply told God 'make him win, so the war can end'. Yes, although by staying in the city, we were distanced from the war hostilities, I was scared for both sets of my grandparents who lived in the rural areas, of Mhondoro and Wedza. The day I heard that terrorists had been shot in Wedza, I had a nightmare. I was particularly scared for my grandparents on my father's side who lived on an isolated plot within the Chemanza Methodist Mission land. I became obsessed with the idea of the Afro bishop ending the war.

The run-up to the election was quite exciting. For the first time in my life, I learnt the *toyi-toyi*. The bishop did not really have competition. Among the urban working class who intended to vote, many were already sold on him, especially since his only credible opposition, Joshua Nkomo, had refused to participate and recognise the 1978 Internal Agreement. So that left another man of the cloth Reverend Ndabaningi Sithole and two traditional chiefs, namely Jeremiah Chirau from Zvimba and Khayisa Ndiweni from the Matabeleland region to stand against him. My parents were excited to be voting for a government as full citizens of their country for the first time in their lives and passed on that excitement to us.

Of course, while the selections continued, very little was publicised by the local media about the debate taking place internationally about the representativeness of this election. The likelihood of it being inconsequential because of the failure to include key civil war stakeholders, such as the leader of the ZANLA forces, Robert Mugabe, and the leader of the ZIPRA forces Joshua Nkomo. This critical discourse was happening far away from my little world and was unknown to me.

As expected, and according to the media of the day, Bishop Muzorewa won with a 'landslide victory'. As for me, I expected him to use his magic wand immediately. In my child's mind, I wanted the war to end. I was scared of visiting my grandparents and being attacked or abducted by terrorists. I was scared of being involved in a landmine accident. The dangers of the war were numerous and occupied a dark place in my imagination.

The war did not end. The country became known as Zimbabwe-Rhodesia a compromise indeed. Weird – 'a country with a surname' – everybody said. However, instead of the war ending, there was an addition to the war between the 'terrorists' and the Rhodesia Front, when Bishop Muzorewa's auxiliary force, *Pfumo Revanhu*, The Spear of the People joined the struggle, which only intensified the fighting on the ground.

I guess I'll never know what the intention was, but I remember watching a 'Face-To-Face Encounter with a Terrorist' on TV. This entailed the then Prime Minister Muzorewa trying to persuade the 'former ZANLA commander' Comrade Max to join him in his mission for peace. I was conflicted because the former looked scary but was also charismatic and spoke well. Even now, I remember the disappointment and emptiness I felt when the discussion ended without anyone categorically declaring that the war would end immediately. Instead, it escalated and casualties increased on all fronts. And then a lot changed in my life.

A move to the suburbs

Immediately after the bishop came into power, black people were allowed to move to formerly all-white suburbs. My parents started looking for a house. My father had bought a car, an immaculate brown and beige Datsun 120Y station wagon. All that what was missing to qualify for businessman status was a suburban home. We also needed a larger house because my father's brother and his family had moved in with us from Mashava, a mining town, in the wake of combat exchanges in that area. While I was happy to have my cousins around, I missed having my space and being able to make personal requests to God: (I was at that point in my life when I continually confronted my God in prayer with a long list of requests before going to bed).

When my parents told me that they were looking for

a house in the suburbs, I was ecstatic. I was going to be a businessman's daughter whose father owned a car and a big house; this time in a white man's neighbourhood, what more could I ask?

When my parents finally identified a house, it had three bedrooms and a tiled roof in a suburb called Windsor Park. It had servants' quarters and beautifully manicured gardens. We moved in and I imagined having blonde white girls as my friends. I would speak like them and become superior to my township friends. My dream looked about to happen when I realised that our neighbours, a Mr and Mrs Skeen, had two daughters. I spent the first few days rehearsing how I would approach them. However, it did not take long before I saw Mr Skeen, working with his gardener to erect a barrier between our house and theirs. It closed us off from seeing their porch and their veranda. It was a good enough sign to tell us we were not wanted. I hate rejection and this was the first time I experienced racial discrimination and being blatantly 'othered'. My dream and ego were bruised.

On the other side, there was an Afrikaner couple, the Van der Merwes. When we moved in, the wife was pregnant and temperamental. If we made a noise next to the fence, she would shout out something, which I am now certain were obscenities in Afrikaans. So, yes, the transition provided a lot of adjustments, and pain, emotionally and physically.

As soon as my school community heard that we had moved house, both the teachers and my peers expected me to move schools. I must admit I was impatient to do so and to become a part of an almost all-white cast in a school play and appear in the city's newspaper, *The Gwelo Times,* as had happened to my friend Josephine. She was lucky ... all those white friends around her, I had mused as I paged through the newspaper's entertainment page.

My teacher had tried hard to convince me not to move. I was, after all, the brightest student among all the Grade 6s. Although a few other students made it into the top ten over the years, I permanently occupied the number 1 spot, saving him and the class's face. If I left, my class would be in trouble and this would reflect badly on him. So, when he talked to me about how the transition might not be so great, I disregarded any advice he gave me for I had my own views.

A suburban school

I was one of the three African girls from so-called affluent families who in 1979 had heeded the call to enrol into 'whites only' schools as the country took its last steps towards black rule. My parents, believing in everything white, enrolled me into Cecil John Rhodes Junior School (CJR).

The first day was challenging, I could not understand what the droves of white children were saying, and they could not decipher what I was saying. Although there were two other black girls in the class, not one of us understood what was going on and continued to whisper among ourselves right through break time as we were not sure whether talking was allowed or not.

However, if the first day was challenging, then the second day was tragic. The teacher, who could have been straight from 1969 Woodstock Concert, with shoulder length hair, a rather tight psychedelic shirt and flared trousers told us to give a one-minute impromptu speech. I was the first black pupil to be picked for the task. As I walked to the front, I remember trying to stop my heart from racing. It felt it could easily fall out of my mouth. My title was 'food'. Finally, after what seemed like eternity, I managed to say in my heavy Shona accent, *'FOODHU...'.*

The class roared with laughter, with some of the pupils repeating what I had said. As the class went into a frenzy I became even more terrified. All the food facts that I'd tried to sum up, evaporated, and my eyes started stinging. Finally, after repeated 'settle down' commands from the teacher the room was restored to sanity. I gave it one more go, this time making it just above a trembling whisper, *'Foodhu* is *Goodhu',* and, as predicted, this was followed by an uncontrollable wave of laughter and mockery. I could have fainted. My brain froze and this time the teacher having read the horror on my face took my hand and walked me to my chair.

This particular incident silenced me. I resolved to not discuss or answer questions in class, opting instead to wait for an opportunity to put all on paper. The teacher was gracious enough not to push. I never shared this painful event, or the many more that reflected racial prejudice, with my parents. Instead, I chose to live it alone. This, I did, because I knew my parents' decision to move me to this white school had earned them a favourable status in the community. They were revered, and they saw themselves as pioneers. The whole decision was also a financial drain on them and I was not about to tell them that I hated the school and missed my simple township friends.

Instead, I swaggered past my old school in my CJR uniform, basher and all, pretending to be on top of the world evoking, envy among my lesser friends. The truth of what was happening became the stuff for my journal which I hid under the mattress. In it, I bared my soul, my pain, my confusion and most of all, my encounter with racial prejudice and blunt unfairness.

However, after a whole term, a lot of listening and practising in front of the mirror, I gathered enough guts to converse: first, with my teacher; then, gradually, with the Italian girl who also seemed to be struggling with the English language and accent, and, finally, with the judgemental close-cropped Caucasian boys. The three of us black girls stuck together. Once, when I strayed into the white girls' camp in my effort to be closer to 'whites' as advised by my parents, I spent the two following break-times alone, as the white girls had decided I was past my best-before date, and my two black friends decided to punish me for wavering loyalty.

The new school also gave me a sense of abundance in comparison to my old school. At the latter, all 1,030 students shared one source of drinking water which we fought over during recess. Now, as I watched the garden-spray over the vast green school grounds, I wished my township friends could share in my experience and my new world – so many toilets, so few pupils in a class, a film room and even a radio and record player to serenade us during our art class. It was too much for me to enjoy by myself, it had to be shared with my township, but how was the question.

There was also no corporal punishment. The white boys in my class answered back when the teachers asked them to do something. Years of regarding teachers as the leaders of the community, adults who often used violent methods to educate children and whose decisions could not be questioned, made it difficult for me to rationalise and reconcile these differences. To me these worlds were too far apart. I concluded that I was better off keeping them compartmentalised. The irony of it all is that as more black children started coming to the school, I was not warming to them. In fact, my personal politics got complicated. Somehow, I felt my privilege and exclusivity was being encroached upon and threatened. I so much wanted to identify with my white friends and perpetuated the demarcation between 'them' – the new, still-heavy-Shona-accented black newcomers – and me, who was with the white majority of the school. My new goal was to show my white friends that I was not like these black newbies, who spoke 'funny' and in return drew pleasure from hearing my white friends say; 'You are not like them'.

Although I initially struggled with the transition, by the end of first term I had made my mark as a kickass scholar among all my peers in their different races. I discovered that intelligence transcended race, gender or class. I was clever enough to do anyone's homework for the price of homemade marmite sandwiches or a pouch of marbles.

But as I slowly began to settle down and identify with my schoolmates, the politics of Zimbabwe continued to change, elections were held in February 1980 and the results were announced on a school day that I will always remember. Almost every white child brought a hand-held portable radio to school. By this time my political loyalty had leapt from the Afro'd bishop to liberation struggle leader Robert Mugabe, thanks to a cousin of mine, Monica who had come to stay with us for a holiday. She continually preached how cool the liberation forces were and how she had so much wanted to join them but had missed the opportunity. She even had a ZANU-PF shirt with an image of an AK47 printed on it.

The other side of this cousin of mine was that she had been attending a white school longer than I had and was not intimidated by white people. A few days before the elections, she had taken me to the park, she in her AK T-shirt of course. When we got there, we found two white boys sitting on the swings and as much as we waited they seemed to have no intention to give us a turn. After waiting for what seemed like an eternity, Monica walked up to them and in a very white accent said 'Okay you get off it's our turn now, GET OFF'. The one white boy could not believe what he was hearing and answered with the expected 'no ways'.

To my horror, Monica immediately yanked his body off the swing. When his friend saw this, he voluntarily handed over the second swing to me. I was impressed. To me Monica was radical and, after that, whatever she said was gospel. In fact, I became so obsessed with the liberation heroes that even at that age of twelve, I was prepared, one Sunday morning, to make my way by bus to the township just to hear Robert Mugabe speak. I was sold on the idea of liberation heroes and the struggle.

So when the announcement of election results came on a cold school day, I was certain that ZANU-PF had won. However, my white friends certainly looked as if they had no idea what was coming. I could hear them in their little anxious groups alluding to the fact that they were certain no one had voted in a terrorist (the terrorist being Robert

Mugabe and his ZANU-PF party). No one in their right mind would do that, instead the bishop would win, they concurred. I gave them a knowing smile making a mental note not to miss out on registering their priceless reactions when the results finally came out.

When the deliberate voice on the radio finally announced Robert Mugabe as the victor, I certainly got the show I had been expecting, there were lots of 'no ways man', and 'we are definitely going down South'. Even my teacher who generally took things easy was bit apprehensive and made an effort to calm my classmates. Because of this, my other two black friends and I could not openly rejoice. Instead, we had to go to the toilet and laugh so hard while musing at how white people had read the politics so wrong.

Of course, in the next few weeks some families moved to South Africa. However, many white people had fallen under the spell of Robert's Mugabe's appealing reconciliatory speech which included the following lines:

> *I urge you whether you are black or white to join me in a new pledge to forget our grim past, forgive others and forget, join hands in a new amity and together as Zimbabwean trample on racialism, tribalism and regionalism and work hard to reconstruct and rehabilitate as we reinvigorate our economic machinery.*

In my last months at this junior school, not much else changed, the teachers more than the pupils tended to be racist. In the mid-year, Grade 7 exams I beat both sets, coming top in all the common subjects. Normally this would mean that I would automatically go into the A-stream which was reserved for top academic students. Still, I found myself in the B-stream because it had become school policy to use it as the entry class for all new black children until they had proved beyond reasonable doubt that they were academically savvy and had unquestionable aptitude of the English language. I met all these expectations but Mrs Smith would not take me into her 7A class, meaning I never got to study French at junior school, a privilege reserved for Grade Seven A.

Strangely enough, although I knew I was being treated unfairly, I never shared this challenge with my parents. Instead, the only person I told was my brother who was in Grade 3. I am not sure why I did not push my parents to confront the school; perhaps because I understood how small my family and I were in the face of the dominating white institution, the school, and took a strategic decision not to mess with the existing norms.

By the time I left the junior school, I bagged every academic subject trophy there was – except French, of course. My parents were continually busy like most typical black business couples, and hardly had a relationship with the school, and in fact they hardly attended any of the school functions. I know that today this is seen as unforgivable, I realise now that they could not identify with the culture of white schools, which asked them to be part and parcel of my learning process. In my township school, learning was left to the teacher and the school, in fact we were not even allowed to take our books out. Reconciling these two cultures, was a major challenge for me and my parents.

I am glad my parents stepped up to the principle of playing an active part in a child's school life for my younger siblings, but for me everything was trial and error.

Looking back

Although there was pain at an individual level, in retrospect, the years of transition are framed in my mind as the years of national glory, years of plenty when everything worked. They are locked in my memory as years of high standards of service delivery and represent a benchmark for what Zimbabwe could be.

The country has gone through a metamorphosis since that time. I am, however, grateful for those painful but challenging years of transition. They shaped me and taught me that being an expert at something gives a person leverage. They also provided a profound understanding of power dynamics. It was also a period that taught me to move away from mediocrity and to understand the politics of difference and belonging. Zimbabwe's irony is that although white people were in the minority, they created a mainstream to which we all wanted to belong. Our minds were sold on whiteness, and those who did not make the grade, due to their heavy accents, or insistence on traditional values, or seemed stuck in their backwardness became the struggling outsiders.

Over the years, having travelled and lived in different countries, I now realise how our transition experience did not include a revaluation of who we are. I lost my language and a piece of my African identity and history. However, I know as a people we gained a lot of trans-national positive qualities. We became Africans who could make it on the international stage, because our politics was simple: 'simple' because they were steeped in a black and white world view. If you worked hard at school and got a good qualification, you would get a good job; then you would channel those rewards into family to ensure that those behind you, siblings or cousins, walked the same path. Ours was not a nuanced success doctrine, (but rather a 'suck it up' one) meaning there was no room for arguing structural imbalances based on race, gender or ethnicity. So, we burst onto the international scene with no expectation of any concessions, but a goal to work hard and take care of family, both immediate and extended. This meant success for us was a necessity and never an option. And when we did encounter concessions (such as first preference based on our gender or race) we seamlessly snapped up those positions.

Were such experiences good or bad for me? My experience is lost in ambivalence A transitioning Zimbabwe was definitely a learning ground in negotiating skills and for that I am grateful. The lessons of difference and belonging have been instrumental in enabling me to adjust to different communities and societies with ease.

Retrospectively, I realise that in an effort to make the new Zimbabwe work many of us suffered humiliation, ridicule, and sometimes loneliness and those situations demanded that we found survival strategies and we did. Our transition had to fit into the normative Independence narrative which was that something good was happening. The bad and ugly that came with it remains the stuff for reflective analysis today. After all, what was important was to obtain an education, which would open many doors, and that it surely did!

15

British Africans

Tsitsi Elaine Tsopotsa

'We want you to choose how we travel back to Rhodesia.'

My dad addressed my brother and me.

'By plane!' I blurted. I couldn't wait. I knew nothing about the country except that it was home. The place where the sadza we ate came from. The land where they said words like *makadii* and they actually meant something because they were deeply rooted in the culture.

'We want to think about it,' my brother had interrupted. I suspected that he wanted to persuade me to his way of thinking. I was pliable when we went to our shared bedroom.

'It's silly to want to travel by plane, because in a few hours we will be there and then it will be all over.' He advised with his eleven years of wisdom.

'But I can't wait to get there.' Me, wild-eyed and bewildered.

'It will be more fun on the boat.'

'On the boat? You mean a small one? Won't we drown?' My countenance shifting slightly, I was now more open to persuasion.

'No stupid. Look at the brochure, there are loads of swimming pools and ice-cream.' He pointed at a picture of a kid enjoying a large cone as she navigated the ship's enormous deck.

'Ice-cream? As much as we want? But mummy will never

let us have that much.'

'Do you see any mummies and daddies in the picture?'

'No.'

'Well then, we can eat as much as we like. So, we're travelling by boat, okay?'

One morning our remaining suitcases and family of five piled into a black cab heading for the train to Southampton to board the ship. I scrambled for a seat by the window. I watched the blurred steely images slide past as the rain spat at the window. I wound it down.

'Goodbye silly old England. I won't miss you at all!' I remember my mother's astonished look. Had I really hated it so much?

We arrived in Cape Town after fifteen days with a ceiling and walls of light blue and delightful sunlight. I drank it all in with the numerous ice-cream cones. I became apprehensive, what was it really going to be like? I saw more black African people than I had ever remembered seeing in one place, the sight of whom kept me pinned to the window seat in the train to Salisbury. With it came an overwhelming sense of belonging. They wouldn't ask me silly questions about my hair or stare curiously when I cut myself and bled red blood.

Prior to this, the largest gatherings of black Africans that I had ever seen were the ones that came to the ANC meetings in London, usually at someone's house. Many of the exiled people passed through with their families. The gatherings weren't political all the time but just get-togethers. I got to play with their children, made life-long bonds with the girls and fought with the boys, because that's just what you did with them at that age.

I initially thought that it was all going to be different, but as we got nearer to the border I started to worry. My Shona was limited to a few words like *handei, majita, chaya* (when we were naughty).

'When we get back, you'll learn it right away. After all it's your mother tongue,' Daddy had told us, convinced that they had made the right decision to focus on our learning the Queen's English all the time we were away.

Because of father's lecturing position at the university, the authorities gave us permission to live in the whites' only suburb of Mount Pleasant. All those years of mother working as a nurse, whilst father finished his PhD. were finally paying off. But those heady months of idyllic living with both parents, new playmates – the only other black children in the area, from the Chavunduka family, soon came to a giddy halt.

Father developed cancer of the oesophagus, one of the worst kinds. Within a year of our return to Rhodesia he was dead.

I was devastated, my best pal was gone. I also had to grapple with a whole new world. We were told that we were no longer welcome to live in Mount Pleasant. We stayed with family friends the Munyaradzis whilst mother got the family in order. She moved heaven and earth to build a home for us in Westwood. It was 1970, black women didn't exist then, but she did it anyway.

In the meantime, we embraced our culture with holidays in the Tribal Trust Lands, the TTLs. Our paternal relatives were out of the picture, so we were ferried to Chiweshe to mother's people, for two weeks of every holiday.

'Mother, these children need to know their culture. No English, and they should do whatever the other children are doing.' Mother had instructed our grandmother.

It was an adventure and I worked hard to fit in.

'Go with her to the *tsime,*' grandmother encouraged my female cousins, pushing me towards them as they looked on, dubious of my skills.

'Will you manage?' The older one had asked.

I remember nodding confidently, wanting desperately to be one of the girls. Halfway back to the homestead, I was grateful for the sunshine as it dried my dress yet again after stumbling and being rewarded with a large shower down my front.

'Merryln is better than you, but she's younger than you.' One of my middle cousins had unhelpfully pointed out. They all stood around laughing at me. I defiantly blinked back the veil of water and tears from my eyes. The bucket on my head shifted releasing most of the contents, this time down my back.

'Well, she gets to do it every day, so she should be good. I don't have to carry water at home!'

Ambuya as usual had kind encouraging words. I obeyed the unspoken rule of not 'squealing' on the others for laughing at me. I found consolation closer to the fire with my cup of tea and a *vetkoek*. I was unprepared for the hot enamel, as it touched my lip my tears brimmed. Partly because of the pain on my lip and partly from the pain I felt that I really didn't belong anywhere.

On our first evening, I recall being called outside to sit in the dark around *ambuya's* kitchen with all the girls.

'What is that?' I screamed, the fear raising me off the ground ready to run back into the kitchen.

'Shh, shh sit down! It's the twins with scary masks.' Sisi Tendai had whispered.

I've never had the constitution for horror, I sat through it all hoping that *ambuya* would come and shoo us all to bed.

School presented bigger challenges. Father had always looked for the best schools – that is the multi-racial schools, as they thought that would be the best fit for us. The other children weren't as accepting as I thought. I had learned some rudimentary Shona. The response to which was more taunting as my English pronunciation of Shona words were met with muffled giggles or blank expressions.

'Do you think that you are European or British?' one of my classmates had asked. I hadn't dared to answer as she had a small posse behind her.

She reminded me of a large family of seven children who always walked around together bullying other children, especially black children. They all had a squint so it was always difficult to know if you were the victim of the hour. On one occasion the youngest had been sent forward to hit me, so I had pulled her into the bushes and hit her really hard then ran for dear life as fast as I could. That was the main reason that I wanted to leave London, I lived in fear that they would one day find me and all pile in to give me the beating of my life.

Those first years back in Rhodesia my brother spent fighting anyone who upset me and I had a few rounds in the sandpit myself. It took a lot out of me to fight back. By my teenage years, I had become withdrawn and had lost all of my confidence. I stopped speaking unless I was spoken to and even then, it was only to my inner circle of friends. People called me snobbish, the hurt inside and the shame of not being able to quite make the grade with the language silenced me.

I did, however, have a few really great friends, one of those was Mary. She was the first friend I had ever made. Her parents were missionaries in Umtali (Mutare) where we had first met as babies. By the time we got reacquainted, they had moved to Nyadire Mission. We were an odd pair of twelve-year-olds bonded by our deficiencies in our respective languages – people didn't quite know how to take us. One day we had a few minutes alone in Cecil Park.

'Let's sit down on the bench over there.' I had said, as we got nearer. 'What does it say on the back there?'

'Oh, it says nannies and whites only.'

'Why does it say that?' I still hadn't grasped the depth of racism in Rhodesia.

'Well black people aren't allowed to sit where white people sit.'

'That sounds silly.'

'I know, let's just sit there.'

A group of black men paused to speak to me and then smiled kindly.

'What did they say?' I asked a red-faced Mary.

'They said that they're proud of you because you've started working at an early age, so that you can help your parents – they think that you are my nanny.'

I was horrified, the colour-bar thing was starting to show-up in my life. My parents and their white friends had always shielded us from racism in England – but here it just crept up on you unexpectedly and just found you wherever you were. The excitement I had felt on coming home was wearing thin. Where then was the benefit? If father had still been alive, I would have asked him. That was the kind of question I could ask him. Our trips to the library to get more books had provided a captive listener, counsellor and friend for me. What would he make of all this? Had he known that it was like this? My young mind wondered which was worse – this or England?

Mother had turned into sterner stuff. She had had no choice. Being mother and father to four children in a world that didn't have a role for black African women, she turned into an amazing human being. It meant that she was always busy. Either she was at work at Harare Hospital, or travelling to South Africa to buy fabric to sew and sell in Botswana or talking to *mukoma* in the garden about the chickens and vegetables that they would sell or talking to the builders about her property portfolio in Zengeza and Harari.

She also had her fair share of abuse: at work, she was known as the British African, maybe because they didn't know where she had come from. My grandfather had sent mother to South Africa at thirteen for her secondary education, followed by nursing and midwifery. Soon after her return, she had married and then moved within a few years to England. I guess her colleagues just sensed that in some ways she was different. To make things worse in Zengeza, her tenants refused to pay rent to an African woman. She had to recruit her brothers to collect the rent for her. But she knew how to slap down a racist. Many years in South Africa had taught her what they were capable of. I learnt those amongst other skills when I finally found my voice some years later.

What was interesting though was that they backed down. These people who hated blacks. If you confronted their behaviour, they backed off and grudgingly showed you some respect for not taking it lying down. I learnt that early on and packed it away for a rainy day.

In the following years, I withdrew to the shelter of my best friend, Mary. Then, as we approached Form 1, her family was deported after her father drew a cartoon character sympathising with the 'blacks'. My study buddy left town – another big loss for me – and my grades suffered. It was not significant at first, but mattered nonetheless. I found new refuge with my buddies from primary school, Fikile and Perpetua. We became known as the three musketeers. I still love them today because they accepted me, teased me when I got things wrong, but buffered me against the rest of the school.

I played in the first hockey team, first netball team, was athletics captain and was part of the second and first couples' tennis for the school. When we played European only schools, we weren't allowed to play the away home in their school ground so a 'neutral' place was chosen. I still fail to understand the logic. England had been racist but that was their country, and this is ours; yet we allowed them to belittle and abuse us anyway they could. And receiving it first hand was pretty tough.

I desperately wanted to be a journalist and write when I left school. Mother had the last word. I had to do something in the hospital, something that she knew would give me a job – after all the profession had sustained her pretty well.

I began training as a nurse, first in Bulawayo, then in Salisbury (Harare). I was amongst the first black Africans to train at the Andrew Fleming Hospital. The taunting began again in earnest, not from the white girls, but from the other blacks, I didn't really have friends, but I found my tongue. I had to.

The white girls were not overtly racist, in fact some of them were really nice, especially the crowd in my class. But, no matter how nice they were, it didn't eliminate the disparity in pay. Whites on the top tier followed by coloureds and Indians and then us Africans at the bottom. To top it all, we had to be good, really good in order to get by.

Independence found me in the middle of my training. I was excited but not sure what the changes would mean to me as an individual, apart from equal pay. I knew that it would benefit the general population, I liked the idea of fairness that it implied.

Despite my father's death, we wanted for nothing. We lived and ate well. I was always up-to-date with the latest fashion. I personally wasn't at a disadvantage. It was just the behaviour of some of the white people that I wanted to change. We heard the stories.

'Three of my friends are in hospital,' my brother rushed through his lunch,' I'm going to see them.'

'What happened?'

'They were walking home from a nightclub last night and were attacked by some white boys. They stopped their pick-ups and beat them up. There were about ten of them.'

I felt the indignation. Roll on independence then. The police would be able to do something about this at least. These incidents were painful for all of us whether we knew the victims or not. We had to stand together to topple the government to feel at home.

But looking back now, perhaps our expectations needed to have been managed better. Whatever happens now, we must handover the benefit of an organised society. A place where things work, where people are reliable, and business, government and municipalities deliver the service and goods that show that we as a people value each other. But above all that what we do is for the greater good of all of us.

16

Battle Maiden

Matilda Madekurozwa

I was named Matilda, an Anglo-Saxon name meaning 'Battle-maiden', by my father.

I am the third child of six sisters. I was born on 5 November 1965 in Lusaka, Zambia after what was described as a 'very difficult pregnancy'. My mother had been on phenobarbitone during the pregnancy because she had suffered from convulsions at some point.

I arrived looking very 'odd' they said. My mother told me that although my cry was that of a normal baby, I looked just like a monkey. I was very tiny and I was covered in long downy hair. However, the opinion was that I was fine, so I was sent home.

One of the other things that happened when I was still an infant was an anomaly with my immunisations. (I still have the immunisation card as record). In those days long ago, we were given a few vaccinations which included a smallpox jab and a BCG.[1] Being a nurse, and what with me being the third child who could be experimented on, my mother decided that unlike my two older sisters with normal vaccination sites on their left upper arms, that I had to have mine done on the under-surface of my left foot. I don't know what happened

---

1 Bacillus Calmette–Guérin (BCG) is a vaccine primarily used against tuberculosis.

after that, but from all accounts the local reaction was not good; the wound took a very long time to heal. (This may explain why I later developed primary tuberculosis).

I was breastfed until my mother went back to work, then I was started on S26 milk formula – they still sell the stuff in some supermarkets. My older sister once told me that of the six of us I was the only child who took to S26; she said it tasted disgusting.

Cerelac was the baby food for all healthy babies and that is what we were all fed on.

The Nestle jingle on TV sang to us every day: 'Cerelac makes your baby healthy and strong...'

My siblings and I eventually all grew up healthy and strong, and although I grew very slowly, I don't think it was the lack of Cerelac, just something in my genes. I was a difficult one to feed and I used to get force-fed every morning with the option of Jungle Oats or Veetbix until I would almost throw up.

I was a sickly child. I developed malnutrition and primary tuberculosis in Grade 1. My mother was very upset – for imagine a nursing sister with a malnourished, tubercular child? I also frequently got abscesses on my knees and legs this went on forever (surely that wasn't the Cerelac ?) I was put onto a feeding schedule at home that mainly consisted of Milo and Choc-milk, which my eldest sister would dutifully buy for me from the vendor at school.

I was always taken to the university teaching hospital where my mother worked in the Outpatients Department. I was there so often that when I was in my early grades I told all my teachers that I was going to become a doctor.

Home

Around the time that I was born, my family lived along Wallis Road in Lusaka but they then moved a few streets away to 2927 Zimbwa Road in a suburb called Madras which was surrounded by the working class townships of Libala, Kabwata and Kamwala. Neither of our homes was in a township, nor were any of our houses uncomfortable although they were small.

Madras was a low density council suburb inhabited by professional people. There were many Indian families in the area. I remember the familiar call to prayers from the local mosque every day at noon. I don't have many unhappy memories of my early years there. My sisters and I spent many happy days playing in the streets. One of my closest school friends grew up just across the road from where we lived. In those days we would play and then go and watch television at our friend's house until 11 p.m. I do not remember ever hearing about so-and-so being abducted or raped.

We used to play jumping games with our mothers' old stockings, and we were so fit from playing with those skipping ropes. One girl would stand on each side and we would jump until the rope caught us and the next girl would have a turn.

I taught my daughters one of the songs we used to sing:

> '*All in together just* takawena;
> *I saw a beauty, beauty in the river;*
> *Shooting, fire, burning;*
> *Fish, fish turn around;*
> *Fish, fish touch the ground;*
> *Fish, fish point to the sky;*
> *Fish, fish and away you go*'

We apparently did not have issues that our children today have. We played freely. We were happy. We resolved conflicts among ourselves. I do not remember a single one of my siblings or even my friends being sent for a psychological assessment for aggressive behaviour.

We would drop in at our friends' house unannounced (we had no landline or mobile phones) and our mothers would not grumble if we or our friends dropped by unexpectedly for some food. If and when we were hungry, we walked across the road for food. I would visit my friend at any time of the day and we would sit on their kitchen floor and eat *mpunga* – rice with sugar and milk which her mother had prepared for us.

We had no palisade fences or walls around our houses – just wire attached to a few thin iron poles. We would go through the gaps in the wire to the house next door – no one got scolded for trespassing.

The biggest influences on my life

Although I grew up very close to my father, my mother brought me up because my father passed away when I was nine years old. It is very interesting for me to think back now about what or who had the greatest influence on me. I think it was probably both my parents. My father was always very political. As a result, my early days were spent going to political rallies in Lusaka at the State House. My father was working as a laboratory technologist in Lusaka and he would work night-shifts. He would get called out at any time of the night to analyse samples in the laboratory at the hospital. When he finished work he would pick me up from home (I had not started school yet. I was about four years old). We would proceed to State House and sit on the lawn with masses of people. Kenneth Kaunda would come out and address us and we would chant political slogans 'UNIP! POWER! POWER! POWER!'

In those days, Zambia had more than one political party so there was still a lot of rivalry between them. The country only became a one-party state in February 1972.

At lunch-time, we would go to the University Teaching Hospital to pick up my mother. My father would listen to his tiny transistor radio as we waited in the hot sun in the car park. He always tuned into the Rhodesian Broadcasting Corporation. The man on the radio would say: 'This is the voice of Rhodesia'.

My father disliked Ian Smith intensely. He always told me stories about how bad he was. I got the impression that *all* white people (... they were related were they not?) were bad, cruel and had to be treated with suspicion. It came across very strongly in the conversations I had with my father. I am sure that was not his intention but that is how I understood it from what he always told me. So, I grew up being made politically aware and I sometimes wonder if it had anything to do with having been born six days before the Unilateral Declaration of Independence by Ian Smith in Rhodesia. My mother always reminded me of this, perhaps my father reminded her too – I will never know.

My father always made us aware of race and racial issues. He probably did have white friends but I never met any of them apart from an Australian pharmacist married to a Rhodesian. They were close family friends. My older sister was once invited to a birthday party. She was the only black child there and when my father picked her up later that day, he laughingly commented. 'So, you were the only *darkie* there!' At the time, she did not know what a 'darkie' was and it was only years later that she finally understood the meaning and probable implications of what he had said to her.

Zimbwa Road's most well-known character was Gurumasaka. He was one of the most influential people in our neighbourhood. He taught me 'stranger–anxiety' – and how to run. He was a vagrant and no one knew where he slept, but he always came around unannounced. He wandered around the streets and helped himself to whatever was left outside. No one dared stop him. One day he came into our yard and took off with my father's lab coat. He wore it for many years after that. When we saw him, we would tell our friends, 'That's our father's coat!'

School

I started Grade 1 at Woodlands Primary School which was quite a drive from home. I will never forget the first day. My father came with me. We stood in a long line in the hall and they called our names out one by one. When it was my turn, I started to cry. The teacher, Mrs Skills led us to the classroom. After that I was fine, tiny but fine. I loved school and I was very competitive at school work. The only thing I did not enjoy was sport.

Youfi

As we were growing up there were many political rallies. The youth would come around from door to door forcibly taking people to the rallies.

They would trot up and down the streets singing:

> '*Open the door* tarara,
> *Open the door* tarara,
> *Open the door for me* tararararara,
> *If you want to hear my story*
> *Open the door for me,* tarara'

I suspect that they successfully dragged people off to their political rallies. I don't think that they ever took children, but our maid would scare the living daylights out of us by telling us that the *Youfi* were coming to get us if we did not behave ourselves. The only thing in my mind that was scarier than Gurumasaka was the *Youfi*. Even now in my middle age, the thought of them makes my heart skip more than a few beats.

My favourite shows on television were '*Kimba – The White Lion of Africa*' and '*Casper the Friendly Ghost*'. I never missed them.

At noon every day, the familiar chant in the nearby mosque would begin. On hot days we would go to nearby homes where Indian families lived and we would call for someone to sell us home-made cent-a-cools from over the back walls of the houses.

Poetry

I have loved poetry since my childhood. I still enjoy reading it. It was first introduced to me from an early age by Uncle Chairman – the late Herbert Chitepo.

He used to recite to my sisters and me, the traditional Irish lyric which Thomas Makem's of the Clancy Brothers used to sing:

'Ahem, ahem, me mother is gone to church.
She told me not to play with you because you're in the dirt
It isn't because you're dirty it isn't because you're clean
It's just because you've got the whoopin' cough and eat
margarine.'

In my eyes, Uncle Chairman was both soothsayer and prophet. He predicted my adult height accurately and he also taught me my early poetry. The poem 'Matilda' (who told lies and was burned to death) by Hilaire Belloc (1870-1953) from *The Cautionary Tales* was one of his favourites. I did not like it, but I listened quietly as he recited it.

17

Township Girl Made Good

Farayi Mangwende

I am what I am
A product of fusions
A tapestry of languages, cultures, continents
Different, but all of them defining
A divergence of beliefs, united by one cause, one goal
To be the best that one can be
My journey is that of a township girl
From Africa to Europe
A transition from sunny Africa
Not by choice, but by design
To a land where the cold was so cold it fell down as a
tangible mass
A land where they could not pronounce my name
A land whose language I could not speak
A land that embraced me, formed me, moulded me,
A land where I learnt the colour of your skin does not
define who you are
A land that allowed you to excel as long as you could
master the queen's language
I longed for home, but Africa became a distant mem-
ory
The transition complete, my language a distant past
English befitting the queen became my norm

Only to be reversed in one fell swoop
Political freedom achieved – Independence
That event determined the return back to the motherland
The euphoria, the joy
The return to my home where my language I could no longer speak
The adjustment, the teasing and taunting of my own
A reverse journey, back to the beginning, to re-learn what is my own
This township girl no more
Now a resident of the leafy suburbs
The benefits of independence
Full access to what was reserved for a few
Another piece in the tapestry
The journey remained the same
To be the best I could be
Taking advantage of what was now available for all
The experience, the joys, the challenges have made me who I am
A successful career woman, a mother, a friend, a sister, an aunt
One who adapts to all
A colourful tapestry of experiences, a fusion of cultures
A hybrid
The result: township girl made good!

18

Culture Shock

Chiratidzo Zhou

If one was to say that my life was a series of culture shocks, they would not be far from the truth.

Born a black African in Rhodesia, the British colonisers had for decades managed to convince the African in Zimbabwe that their culture was uncivilised.

As a middle child raised by a Sotho *momma* and a Mukaranga *baba*, I learned earlier on that different traditions, languages, and peoples could love together equally in peace. My ebullience knew no bounds as the contagious clicking and laughter of voices filled the home whenever my mother's sisters would arrive. My dad's fire-side conversations with the youth, some of whom are now our national heroes, intrigued me. These are some of my fondest memories of my early childhood days.

Looking back now, as I reminisce, it was such a blessing to feel the warm sun on my bare skin as I chased the chickens in the yard and picked fresh mangoes from the orchard that Bhudi Benny had religiously tendered and watered to fruition.

In pre-school, I now appreciate all the Catholic nuns who disciplined us with a spank or a pinch, making it easier to learn from fear rather than from pure curiosity. I marvel at the ease with which I could move effortlessly from momma's

Sotho and Ndebele to Baba's Shona depending on whose side of the family was in the house.

As beautiful and as my life seemed to be, it was a rude awakening to be made to believe that I could not speak my own language in a school that tried to 'civilise' me. The white and brown kids in my primary school were to be admired as their language and culture was 'better' than mine. 'English only!' was the rule in school, to strip us not only of our mother tongue, but our beautiful culture. Hence began my introduction to self-hate.

Until that blessed day, even as a barely ten-year-old child, I felt the freedom in the air. There were celebrations on TV. Our television, though black and white, seemed to permeate bright colours of black, red, yellow, and green. Black, was to celebrate the beautiful skin with which we are blessed. Black power if you will. Red, was the blood that so many had shed to gain this freedom from colonialism. Yellow was to symbolise the gold with which our country is blessed, and green is the abundance of agriculture that is our potential.

It was in front of the Swedes, the Danish, the Finish and the Norwegians, that I soon found myself reciting these meanings of the flag, together with my brothers and sisters later that same year. My first contact with these Scandinavians made me proud to be Zimbabwean, to be African and to be black, as I was yet again entering another session of culture shock.

19

Embracing My Culture

Debra Patterson

It was a typical winter's day in the small town called Enkeldorn, (Chivhu) on the 12 June 1969. You may not know this, but in the 1950s there were several sightings of UFOs over the skies of Zimbabwe, and particularly over Enkeldorn. This was a little before my time and this detail only contributes subliminally to this story.

A lot was happening in Rhodesia at that time. Prime Minister Ian Smith had declared unilateral independence from the United Kingdom. Sir Humphrey Gibbs, a British national, was still the governor of Southern Rhodesia, but his position was fast becoming untenable following a referendum held later that year, in June. Although some people want to believe that corruption did not exist during this time of our history, one of the stories on the front page of the *Rhodesia Herald*, on that particular day, was that, the then Minister of Commerce and Industry, Jack Musset, was vehemently denying allegations of malpractice by his ministry – hawking projects to certain known parties.

We didn't live long in Chivhu before we moved to Gwelo, now Gweru. I don't remember much about living there. It was a sleepy little town and I lived there from the age of eighteen months until I was four. We lived, as the vast majority of black people did, in a high density suburb. These were areas designated to blacks by the white government. Everyone knows the system of apartheid in South Africa but of course in Rhodesia we had our own system of 'separateness'. There were low density suburbs for the white people, mid-density suburbs for the coloureds, people of mixed race, and high density suburbs for the black majority.

When my brothers were born, they were pre-term and they had to stay in hospital in incubators for over a month. During this time, I was sent to live with my *tete*, my father's sister, for a few weeks. Living *kumusha* at our rural home in Domboshava was actually wonderful, with lots of fresh air and other little people to play with. I had to go with my *tete* to do all the normal chores, such as fetching firewood for the stoves, metal grills over an open fire. We had to walk about ten minutes to the stream or well for fresh water. Later, when I was a bit older, around five or six or seven years, I would get my own small bucketful of water, tie a cloth and put it on top of my head to act as a headrest and walk home. Most of the water would have slopped out of the bucket by the time I arrived, and my neck would hurt for days afterwards, but to me it was an important achievement.

The social and family life was brilliant. I remember many nights sitting around a fire with family and friends listening to scary stories or just singing and dancing when there was a full moon. During the day, we would get up to all sorts of outdoor adventures like chasing after cattle, swimming in the river or climbing trees to pick indigenous fruit like *matohwe*, and *tsubvu*. Even funerals were interesting and rather fun gatherings, as you would get to meet a whole lot of cousins and other relatives who would gather at the family home for days, sometimes even weeks. I was content and had a happy childhood.

We moved to the big city of Salisbury, Harare, when I was about five years old. The Shona language does not have the letter 'L' in the alphabet so wherever there is an 'L'; we put an 'R' so Salisbury became *Sosberry*. My parents managed to get a loan to buy a house in Kambuzuma Section 6. This was a high density suburb to the south-west of Harare.

My sister and I went to Kurai Primary School, the local school. We walked there and back with a bunch of other kids. We had to cross a piece of marshy ground and a railway line. I remember that, sometimes, after the rain, it would be quite muddy and some of the children were not fortunate enough to have shoes. Occasionally, as a sign of solidarity, we used to take our shoes off once we had left the house, just to be like some of our schoolmates.

I loved living in Kambuzuma as we had friends on the street in close proximity. No one lived behind walled and gated premises. Most families could barely afford to make ends meet, let alone put up walls and gates. We played all sorts of imaginative games and we were allowed to be out until it was dark, which in the summer, was around seven in the evening. We played games like *pada, bakery, rakaraka, dunhu, nhodo,* which is similar to Jacks, and *fish fish,* a skipping game. In the evening, we would be allowed to watch TV which in those days was black and white. I don't remember there being more than two channels. Not many people had televisions and the neighbours would come and watch the set at our house, which was great fun.

At school, there were 49 children in my class! That is a lot of children in one class but of course the Rhodesian government was not going to spend too much money on providing an expensive education for the black people. My class teacher was Mrs Bakasa and all the kids who received good marks became the teacher's pets and were given the privilege of being allowed to go to our teachers' homes to clean and tidy them up. I am not sure just when we performed this extra-curricular activity, or if our parents or the school knew about it, but it was certainly an incredible badge of honour to be able to tell the other kids that you'd been given the key of the teacher's house so you could go and clean!

My parents had been looking around for a multi-racial

school to send us to, as they quickly realised that in order to get any chance in life, we would need a better education. Some schools were reserved exclusively for white people, and so they finally settled on St Michael's Preparatory School, the prep school of Hartmann House and St Georges and a co-ed at that time. Having said that, I don't think there were more than a handful of girls in my class and we were only two black kids in my class.

It was definitely an eye-opener to be in a school where whites were in the vast majority. I don't recall actually having any problems with the adults, but I do remember a classmate of mine. He was blond and had a startlingly large number of freckles on his face. If any black person accidentally bumped into him, he would rub the point of contact on his body and then blow away the contamination. I thought it was rather amusing and I would often shake my head in bewilderment; I had the distinct feeling that he didn't actually realise how offensive he was being, but only copying what perhaps an older sibling did.

I then started Grade 4 at the Harare Dominican Convent as St Michaels was closing its doors to girls. Going to a girls' school was great and the fact that we were about eight black girls in the class certainly helped.

I have a feeling that our parents were the ones who were worried about race issues. We just went to school, enjoyed ourselves, tried to learn and be good girls. Unfortunately, we lived at a time when being black meant you were at the bottom of the food chain. I know some black families that changed their names or put an 'h' at the end of the family name in order to make it less 'indigenous'. So, for example, you would spell my surname Gonye as Goyne or Gonyeh! The liberation struggle was going on but I don't remember being affected by it in any material way. Occasionally, we would hear of villages being burnt down or people going to war but that was mostly in the rural areas.

On special occasions, it was very important that we were

properly dressed and well-groomed. That is where the *stretching comb* came into play; it was a horrible stout metallic comb which you put over an open fire to heat. Mum would then put lots of Vaseline in our hair before taking the stretching comb to our tresses. Oh, what a painful experience! Sometimes when it hurt too much, she would use a *dombo* – a flat smooth granite stone which, like the stretching comb, would also be put over an open fire and then used to smooth our highly Vaselined hair. Now my mum wouldn't hear of straightening our hair with chemicals so that once it rained or became humid, our hair would return to its furious curl which one of my uncles called the 'hard Mashona style'. So already, way back in the early seventies, we black women were struggling to straighten our hair. I am not sure if it was done to try and copy the smoothness of white hair or whether we were just following a trend set by other black women in the USA or England.

In the meantime, we had moved from the high density suburb of Kambuzuma to the suburbs. We had finally arrived. We were now living in the area which just a few years previously had not been accessible to black people. We were the second black family to move in and the one thing which I loved about living in the low density suburbs of Harare was the huge gardens which were not just for planting maize, tomatoes and other vegetables. Instead, there were large areas of lawn, and in our case, we had a huge orchard where we didn't just have mango and paw paw trees, we had peaches, leeches, and an apple tree. We even had a swimming pool ... oh the joy!

Our neighbours, the Fredikssons, were Danish and worked for an NGO. They were very kind and as they didn't have children themselves, they kind of adopted us and we were often invited over to swim, to have drinks or to play. It was interesting to note the cultural differences. When they came over to our house, my sister and I would go on our knees to offer them water to wash their hands. They obviously found us and our culture intriguing and were truly interested.

Mum had now started working for the Medical Council and I remember her always being very smartly dressed. It would never do to go to work looking less than perfect. Years later, she often told us of a certain white lady at the Ministry of Agriculture, where she later worked, who always wore really frumpy homemade shift dresses and the same black shoes – whether they matched or not. But the one thing this lady did was to save enough money every year to take herself on holiday abroad while my mum and her workmates spent all their money on looking good.

Returning to Zimbabwe many years later, I went to a hairdresser in Harare and an incident really saddened me. There was an eight- or nine-year-old black boy who was about to have his hair trimmed by an elderly black barber. He was explaining to the barber how he wanted this done and his tone was so reminiscent of how some white people used to talk to their black housemaids and gardeners i.e. as if it was beneath them to be talking to the 'lowly uneducated people'. All this went on in English and I could see the elderly gentleman was struggling to understand and express himself. What the mother said saddened me even more. She said in very loud and proud tones: *'Hahaha my son, you know he doesn't speak Shona'*. I looked at her and felt so much pity for them both, aware that she had made a conscious effort to deprive her son of something very special, his mother tongue.

At school, Shona had become one of the compulsory subjects but of course it was taught as a second language, so it wasn't very useful for those of us who were native Shona speakers. However, it certainly was fun listening to the non-native speakers trying to say the Shona letter 'D' which I realised later in life is a difficult sound to pronounce for other Africans too. My daughter is called Danai which is not an easy name for her to pronounce.

As I grew into my teens, western culture seemed so much

more inviting than our own culture. I felt that as a Shona girl, life was very restrictive. I had to greet relatives who came to visit whether I wanted to or not. I had to curtsey when I greeted older people. I had to go on my knees and ask after their health. I had to dress in a manner befitting a good Zimbabwean girl. I was madly in love with the singer Madonna and thought that she was the bees' knees. I wanted to be free and gay like her –'gay' in those days meant 'happy' – I dressed like her and loved my short skirts and ripped T-shirts. I guess, as teens, we all go through the same phase of trying to find out where we belong.

When I left Zimbabwe in 1989, I went through a period of self-discovery and found a renewed interest in my own culture. Meeting people from many different countries in the world who were so proud of their own heritage made me realise that many of us Zimbabweans had too readily discarded our own culture in favour of western ones. The older I get, the closer I feel to my roots. I have perfected the English language as well as Spanish and German and I always have a Shona-English dictionary nearby. I am finding so much joy in improving my vocabulary.

The biggest challenge for me as the mother of two biracial children living in Germany is to give them a true sense of identity. When people ask my daughter where she is from, she gives them the whole spiel. 'I am half Zimbabwean, a quarter English and a quarter German'. What a mouthful but that is exactly what she is. It's a continuous challenge to speak to the children in Shona when the rest of their world is either English or German but my heart fills with pride when I hear them actively say something in Shona like 'Mummy *huyapano!*'– or some other command.

How to retain our core identity in a world where we live between our culture and the western culture? How do we adopt western ideals but still maintain our true selves?

Having lived outside my own country for over 24 years, which is more than half my life, has made me appreciate my country and my culture a lot more. I no longer take it for granted. I research and try to learn more, so I can pass traditions on to my children. I didn't realise how important my own name was until I got married and the question of what name I would take came up. In the end, to keep the peace I went for the double-barrelled Gonye-Patterson which I kept for just over a year. I felt that as I did not have a Shona first name, I needed to keep my own, as I did not have a sense of who I really am. Now I am just Debra Patterson and I am okay with it because it's a name that connects me to the wonderful man I married in 1999. However, I feel a bit sad when I hear people who have beautiful local names turn them into English names, for example, Tafadzwa becomes Taffy or Bakhile becomes Baks. If I had a local name, I would cherish it and make everyone say it correctly!

I realise that it is so much harder to be 'Zimbabwean' when we are constantly being bombarded through TV and social media by much more lenient and perhaps more attractive cultures. Hopefully, one day, when those who are still in their teens or early twenties, have their own children, that they will go back to roots, to the beautiful values which make us Zimbabwean. Respect for our elders, respect for self and respect for the environment.

20

My Life Story: Still Standing

Spiwe Kachidza-Mapfumo

Ten years after my brother John was born, and years of trying to fall pregnant, my mother Lettie Kachidza felt as if she had won the lottery when was told she had conceived.

Eight months later I was born. Her joy at having a little girl was jolted when the doctor told her that I was in perfect health but that I had a club foot. They suggested they put a cast on my tiny foot to correct the congenital deformity, advising my parents that this could help to straighten the foot since the bones were still soft. That was the initial intervention.

I left Mutoko Hospital a few days old with a cast on my tiny foot. My mother told me many years later that she had prayed 'unceasingly' to fall pregnant. After I was born, she said that she took me home and 'spoke to God' every day praying for my foot to get better, so that I would be like every other little girl.

My mother believed in miracles and her wish was granted.

I had two older brothers Lincoln and John. When I was born, my father worked as a long-haul driver with Swift Transport. The job saw him ply the Rhodesia–Nyasaland (Zimbabwe–Malawi) route where he made another life changing decision. Malawi is famous for its flourishing fish industry. This was a commodity not available in Salisbury or the country as a whole. He started buying the fish in Nyasaland, packing bags of the dried fish between the articulated cabs of his Swift lorry. The business flourished and he then found a niche market for the Nyasa reed mats. So it was that he saved penny after penny to start a business in Mutoko, which is still going and still well known by all in the area.

His business boomed and he employed a young Mozambican named Pedro (everyone in the hood called him Peturu) from the Mwanza area. He became the neighborhood's fish salesman in the Egypt and Engineering areas of Highfield. He rode around the suburb on his 'order bicycle', which had a big square metal container, selling dried fish. People in that area knew Peturu with whom they would make an arrangement to pay for the fish at the end of the month when they received their wages.

Peturu had a notebook that he cared for like a Bible and in which he kept the customers' names and addresses. Believe me, he knew them all by name and he always got his money at month end. People back then were reliable.

I remember vividly when, at month end, the money was counted for my father to take it to the bank.

We would sit around the table with a kerosene lamp in the centre. My father and mother and sometimes my brothers (if they were not in boarding school) would all sit around counting the copper pennies, tickeys,[1] sixpences, shillings, and the half a crown[2] coins for my father to take to the bank. This is how I learned to count – with money. (I am surprised I did not become an accountant seeing that I grew up with coins around me.)

When I was four years old my father decided to build a store in the Mudzi area. My mother kept shop. I was only

1 Silver threepenny bits.
2 Half a crown, two shillings and sixpence, a large silver coin.

five when my father opened his first rural store at Suswe Township, a remote area on the Nyamapanda Road. My father had a vision and nothing was going to stop him. He was born into a polygamous family with not much money to talk about. He worked hard and after basic primary education he had to leave his village to look for employment in the city. He told me later in life that after leaving for the city to find a job he knew that only through saving his money would he become a businessman. That is exactly what he did with all those pennies and tickies, he built a thriving business in Mutoko. Fifty years after the one counter store was opened, a number of supermarkets still exist in Mutoko.

When I was five, my father gave up his job as a driver to fully focus on this business. We lived a simple life but by far better than most Africans. I grew up behind the counter in our rural store. My mother worked in the store most of the time and my father went out to order goods. I spent most of the day hanging around my mother.

My foot did not straighten out as doctors had hoped. After several failed attempts to straighten it with casts, my parents accepted that I had a congenital deformity, though my mother never gave up with her 'interface' with God through prayer.

I was a bright happy extrovert little girl. My mother just could not slow me down. My father, who adored me, always told me that I could do anything I wanted and I believed him. I do not ever remember feeling sad, or insecure because I walked with a limp. I had everything I wanted. I was never treated as a child with a handicap.

One day, I was six years old, an angel stopped by my parents store in Mudzi. It was Father Giovanni, an Italian Roman Catholic priest, on one of his many trips to the remote Nyamapanda area. He was one of the very few white men who ventured this far into the African Tribal Trust Lands for any sort of business. He and old Mr. Goddard, a miner, stopped by often to buy corned beef, condensed milk and a few other goods.

Each time Father Giovanni came by in his green Land Rover he would stop and chat with my mother who would make tea and ask Sisi Agnes, the maid, to bring it out on my mother's only china tea set. I would never miss a chance to run into the store to greet Father Giovanni and obviously to show off the little English I knew. On this particular day, Father Giovanni asked my mother about my club foot. My mother explained how the doctors at the hospital had tried the cast method, but that it had not worked.

Father Giovanni asked where my father was that day and my mother told him that he had gone to Salisbury but would return in the evening. The good priest told my mother that he would stop by on his way back from Nyamapanda and that he would talk to both my parents about the possibility of having my foot corrected by an orthopaedic doctor that he knew in Salisbury.

At nightfall, Father Giovanni came by told my father and mother that he would make the arrangements and he would return with a letter giving the appointed date to go to the city.

The day for me to go to hospital for the operation arrived. I got up early. The 140 kilometre drive from Mudzi to 'Gomo', as the hospital was known then, was not quite like any other day. The doctor came into the room wearing his pristine white coat and introduced himself. He was very pleasant and he gave me a small doll with straight hair. Each time the doctor asked my mother for my name, age and address I would shout out the response and the doctor was impressed by this little African child from a rural area who could speak English. (Back then all children in rural areas learned English when they started Sub A which was first grade.)

I had x-rays of my foot taken and, afterwards, the doctors explained that my parents would have to bring me back some weeks later for the surgery. I was a bit disappointed as I was expecting to have the operation on the same day. We went home and waited until the appointed date arrived. My parents then took me back to the hospital and were told to return the following day to check how the surgery went.

The operation was a success and after a week I went home. I had a cast which stretched from my foot all the way up to the knee. After six to eight weeks, the cast was removed. It was my first time to see my corrected foot. For the first time, I could stand with my foot flat on the ground. I still limped a bit because I needed physiotherapy to get used to walking on the foot.

That day was also the first time I saw my mother cry. They were tears of joy, disbelief and gratitude. However, the months that followed were months of excruciating pain as I undertook physiotherapy. After a few weeks of walking on crutches, I had orthopaedic shoes fitted and I walked around with these correctional shoes but with no crutches.

That same year, 1962, I started school at Sub A which was the first year of formal school at Nyandoro Primary School. At that time I had moved from Mutoko to Salisbury so that I could go to school there. I was always one of the top five children in my class of 30. Though I did not participate in any sport I excelled at my school work and I did not feel like the odd one out despite being identified as 'that girl who wears a shoe for the handicapped people'

During those days, the welfare services provided a small bus that went around the African townships to pick up children and people who needed to go for physiotherapy. Most Africans did not have cars. Christmas time came and all the children who had any form of disability were picked up by that bus and attended a big Christmas Party. There were balloons, cakes and drinks and every child received a Christmas gift and a 'real' white Father Christmas was in attendance at Mai Musodzi Hall in Harari. By far this was the highlight of every year

By the time I was in Sub B, I was wearing normal shoes and the slight limp was barely visible.

Life has been good to me and thanks to the Italian priest who happened to come my way and changed the trajectory of my future.

I wake up every morning and think 'I'm still standing', recalling that it had to be my mother's prayers that got me

21

A Hybrid Heritage

Nomsa Mwamuka

I was named after my paternal grandmother – a proud and robust Xhosa woman. She drank tea religiously, prayed fervently, gardened green and had a penchant for singing and humming holy hymns and spirituals. In spite of her religiosity she always spoke about *'eClaaass'* (class). She was amongst the league of the first black nursing sisters in southern Africa – the generation after Cecilia Makiwane – and hence her sense of pride. One of four sisters, the Bottoman girls, as was their surname, the elder girls married into prominent South African families, the Makiwane, Piliso and Mabandla lineages; while my grandmother daringly ventured out, emigrating and finding home in the then Southern Rhodesia where she met my grandfather. He was the son of an early Christian convert named Taiwa Bernard who was a 'farm demonstrator' – a position which guaranteed a degree of privilege to him and his children. For that reason, my grandfather – a village-born boy, got access to education – going as far as Adams College in South Africa. He became a teacher, a headmaster and, later, was amongst the first black people to be granted an official business license in Rhodesia. My grandfather's people remained rooted in their culture, greeting each other with the totemic name *Makombe*, yet feeling somewhat 'superior' that they could trace our roots back six generations to Kuwutsi, a chief from Sena, who had rebelled against the Portuguese settlers in Mozambique.

On my mother's side... *ambuya* was an astute and perceptive woman. She was Karanga but of Sotho descent with, as family legend goes, a mix of Arabic blood. This family line and heritage is something I am currently collating. By the time I knew my grandmother, she was elderly but maintained her bright eyes, chiselled features and clear, dark complexion. She always welcomed guests and was always curious; sitting around the fire in her round hut or cooking for people. A warm hospitable woman. *VaSekuru*, my grandfather, was a humorous, passionate man who lived to over a hundred. An industrious farmer with a large family, he had a strong religious calling, which saw him establishing mission stations and churches in Serima and Gapare villages. He had a magnetic personality and was a powerful and dramatic orator. I vividly remember an anecdote about him climbing a tree from which to more eloquently preach to his ardent, prayerful congregants and followers.

From both sides of my family what stands out is their pioneering spirit. They were intrepid, fearless, driven individuals, never afraid to break boundaries, cross borders and cultures, to be different or to be the 'first' to do something. Thanks to that spirit today we can reel of the names of an uncle who was the first black architect in Southern Africa, an aunt who was the first black female high court judge, the first black Drs, PhDs, mining executives and even a university graduated brew master. While they bettered themselves, they were also philanthropic, community-conscious people; educating and supporting families, individuals and children beyond their own relatives. Visionaries, activists, creators, teachers and leaders, with such a spirit, there was no way my forebears would let me be.

The seventies – Rhodesia

My years would be marked by irony, dichotomy and duality.

I grew up in Marimba Park, a 'suburb' for blacks to the south of Salisbury city, it was the product of white liberals. Far enough away from the white suburbs so as not to intrude upon their lifestyles, but defined enough for middle-class, aspirational, intellectual blacks to feel 'exceptional' and to set themselves apart from the 'majority'. The first black doctors, teachers and business people made their lives in Marimba Park, after, of course, moving from the townships of Harari (Mbare) or Highfield where my grandparents made their first home and started their businesses and where my father was born. Marimba Park bordered on (or was actually a sub-section of) the high density suburb of Mufakose with its government-constructed, semi-detached, four-roomed 'box houses'. The only thing that really set the two neighbourhoods apart, was our larger architecturally inspired and designed homes with sprawling yards. For my grandfather, ever the trailblazer, his home became the physical manifestation of his highest ideals. It was a double storey house on a hill with large verandas, balconies, and even a pergola. The expansive garden burst with the colours and scent of roses, daisies, bougainvillea, and lilies and at the back of the yard an orchard brimming with succulent mango, guava, peach and pawpaw trees. We even had a mini grapevine. Indoors, one of my favourite parts of the house was a library section, a bookshelf filled with largely religious texts. One book that haunted me had a cover depicting 'the Rapture' and images of 'good souls' being lifted heavenwards. There were children's books – *The Children's Story Hour Collection,* a set of red and black *Collins Encyclopaedia Britannica,* and the one book I would cherish in my later years and honour as an heirloom, the 1930 edition of Sol T. Plaatje's book *Mhudi:* An *Epic of South African Native Life – A Hundred Years On.*

Reading and prayer marked our lives – prayer before meals and prayers before bed. So 'pseudo-elitist' was this neighbourhood and our lifestyle that on occasion white tourists would be bussed in for us to wave at them and smile for their cameras. Some would even stop by to drink tea with us. We, in our neighbourhood, offered an example of colonial progress and liberal race relations in Rhodesia – propaganda that suited the Rhodesian government.

However, inflate or colour-coat it as we tried, Marimba Park would always remain a *township* – our nearest shops, churches, clinics and recreational facilities were in Mufakose; and my family spent the weekends and much of our time in Highfield. The *location* was our reality.

Family

My parents were young when they had me, barely out of high school, so I was raised as a sort of community project, everyone played their part. My family was colourful, cousins were more like sisters and brothers and my grandmother, aunts and uncles – played the parents – with my Aunt Nozipho, Aunt Sally and Uncle Paul at the forefront. My sense of self also took on new dimensions through my name. Early on, the family stopped calling me Nomsa. It was too discourteous to reprimand a child with a grandmother's name, so I became Noma with two syllables aka... NO-MA at home. When I started school my name changed again and I became 'NORMA' – an Anglicised change of pitch and intonation. Even my surname was altered to fit into a new, multiracial world; one, I was about to discover through school.

School

The school, 25 kilometres away from home, was a 'good' school. An all-girls private school where we were taught to '*annunciate*' and '*sit up straight*', '*pull up our socks*' and '*don't be cheeky*'. We were being groomed to become young ladies. We were taught rules, regulations and of places that were *out-of-bounds*. The school was exclusive – 99.8% white.

However, the irony was that 90% of the girls were the

children of rich farmers, often closer to their maids and 'nannies' than their suntanned and pool-drenched mothers; closer to the 'garden boys' and cooks than their khaki-clad and veldskoen-wearing fathers. The other 10% were made up of town-based white girls, the largely polyglot children of foreign diplomats, girls from the Asian-designated upmarket suburb of Ridgeview, and then the two of us, my West Indian descended cousin and little me.

Dichotomy

With our bottle green, white-bubble-patterned uniforms and dark green floppy hats we were the same or adjusted to sameness on the surface and externally – until sports day, of course, when in our 'Houses' we competed for colours and awards. As children, we established bonds. Largely colour blind, but with wide-eyed curiosity, my little friends would ask, 'Can I feel your hair?' I looked different, definitively. To fit in, aside from my name, my attitude, my behaviour and even my accent began to change; we were a school unit but, in reality, our lives were far apart.

In class, I was an enthusiastic student, constantly vying to be the 'teacher's pet'. I determined to prove myself in everything I did: I was from Marimba Park after all. I loved art classes and I excelled in history. I could tell anyone, anything about European history: the Greek gods, the Roman Legions, the Battle of Hastings … (I never even imagined Africa had a history!). What a miseducation. Maths tormented me – the times tables, fractions, and long division. My nemesis, however, was the English class. I loved reading and stories but I was overawed by poetry or creative writing. Invariably the topics would include: 'What I did on the weekend?' A Monday morning horror. 'Write a poem about snow'. Snow?! Or 'My favourite pet'. Really? And the topic 'My holidays'. What a nightmare!

Reality

While the other girls had evidence of their holidays – new 'neos', fizz pops, Barbies from 'Down South', or news to tell – a visit from grandma in England, a litter of kittens, or a new horse. Mine, was hard to write. Playing *rakaraka* or having singing competitions with people named Joyi, Feta, Suzi or Juli just didn't seem worthy? Climbing trees to eat *mahabros kwana malodger*, mulberries at the lodger's, or cooking and trying to eat *mbewa* (field rat) or *itshwa* (flying ants) in tin pots in the back yard wouldn't gain approval. Walking *kumagrocer*, to the grocery store with our housekeeper, Sisi Tau, to buy '*nigger balls*' and '*candy cake* didn't sound right? Going to Highfield where we would visit an Aunt Faith after having our hair painfully *washed, stretched* and *plaited* for a new week of school seemed incongruous. A gift of mealies and *nyimo,* groundnuts, from a *sekuru,* who was actually not my grandfather but my mother's brother was too hard to explain. The excitement of being allowed to carry my own bucket of water on my head from the *tsime* on a much resisted visit *kumusha* in the TTLs, the Tribal Trust Lands, the reserves, just didn't seem the kind of thing my teacher Miss Hunter would want to hear. Where would I begin to share the story of the *dare,* the traditional ceremony at home, where a cow was slaughtered, a headless chicken ran amok, traditional beer was brewed and sipped from *hari* and calabashes and the music of the *ngoma, mbira, nehosho* with feet thumping and dancing all night went on. God and the ancestors... how could explain traditional mores against Christian ways when both were part of my reality? How many times could I write about receiving an aerogramme from my mother who was studying in India at the time? How often could I repeat anecdotes overheard about aunts living in the UK and New York, or an uncle Caiphas teaching at Makerere University in Uganda? How many times could I retell the story of relatives visiting from the Transkei and what they brought with them? Lost in socialisation! It was a kaleidoscope of adventures for me, but I was always stuck. My reality just couldn't and wouldn't translate – language and culture was a battleground. These were curious and confusing times for me. English... I couldn't wait for the next class to start, or even better to become the class monitor and ring the bell... I was always saved by the bell.

As the seventies progressed, the texture and the hue of the school began to change. No longer just my cousin and I as 'the first' black pupils, suddenly there were more kids with names that teachers would stumble over – 'Mukura who?', 'Matamba what?' they would ask. I was no longer subjected to being the only one at slumber parties where my friend's parents looked at me askance, and the uniformed maids and gardeners would stare at me in wonder, muttering from afar what I would pretend not to understand. It was a world of extremes, a straddling life, a double life and hybrid existence. We were the guinea pigs, the experimentals. Our parents wanted the best for us, but was it really the best?

Rumblings of war

It was around this time that the whisperings started. School assembly briefs about the 'terrs'; fire drills, Sellotape-sealed windows to protect against a bomb blast, a K-word incident that my feisty Aunt Nozipho, beret on head and hands on hips, came to sort out, and always the caution 'to beware'. There were the subliminal tensions, between teachers and ground-staff, and a genuine fear between the town and farm dwellers. But still the tennis, swimming, ballet, piano, and recorder lessons continued, choir, stamp club and much vaunted Brownies met every week. At year end, prize-giving and Christmas carols, when we sang 'Oh Come All Ye Faithful' with gusto, knowing holidays were around the corner.

Home remained another world. There different whisperings... mumbles in the background about the *'vakomana'* and *'majiba'.* Extra boxes of food carried out the back door. Strange men staying the night in the *'boy's khaya'.* Clothes being shipped off to people in Lusaka, Dar

181

es Salaam, Nairobi and Chimoio. Clandestine drives into the townships at night, and nights spent away from home. Our own whispers amongst ourselves, the children, that so and so had a gun – was that a gun? Shock and tears when we heard our Uncle Xola was car bombed and killed in Zambia. That Aunt Julia, who was once was a nun, was now a combatant. Uncle Mzwai from South Africa... hush... Odinga's daughter for lunch. 'Just don't talk about it'. The radio crackling in the background, tuning into BBC and other news' stations. The names not to be mentioned out loud – Chitepo, Sithole *shuuu...* a world of secret and shrouded lives. Through my grandmother's people our awareness of the struggle in South Africa was acute – we understood the reference to *mabhunu*, through broader activism, we knew about the nationalists and broader continental struggles from an early age. The backdrop though... church every Sunday, Sunday lunch with its roasts and salads, juxtaposed against the afro jazz sounds of Dollar Brand's *Mannenberg*, Letta Mbulu's, *There's Music in the Air*, the songs of Miriam Makeba, Hugh Masekela and Dorothy Masuku. We knew Fela's high-life and the Motown hits of Dianna Ross and Marvin Gaye and who could forget our root sounds Oliver Mtukudzi singing '*Nyarara Mwanawe, Nyarara Kuchema*' and Thomas Mapfumo with his mellow Chimurenga beats – these were the soundtracks of our times. Behind the music, the news and the newspapers, politics pervaded our home.

Independence

Then Independence came. Elections, the right to vote. Rhodesia became Zimbabwe-Rhodesia, and Zimbabwe-Rhodesia became Zimbabwe. What marked the transition? Was it the 'celebration and jubilation' at home? Was it the helicopters flying overhead dropping pamphlets with Sis Tau rounding us up to collect them? Was it *'nyore-nyore'* commercials on TV? The *Harmony* advert and jingle? The first black Miss Zimbabwe beauty contest that township girl

Shirley Nyanyiwa won? Being taught '*Ishe Komborera*', the new national anthem a rendition of Enoch Sontonga's '*Nkosi Sikelel'iAfrica*' at school? Black newsreaders on television – voices and faces that would in later life inspire me to take up a career in the media? Or was it that towns now had new names – no longer Umtali but Mutare? No longer Gwelo but Gweru? The new emblematic flag with its gold, black, red and green and, the prophetic Zimbabwean bird? Was it that so many white families and school friends were relocating and fleeing 'down South'? Was it the new Shona teacher at school? Or was it that I could at last reclaim my name and surname and freely and confidently write my truth?

Whatever it was, the transition of the country coincided with my transition into adolescence. I reached puberty, had my first period, got my first bra, shoes with a slight high-heel, stockings and had my first 'could he be my boyfriend?' thought. I started high school.

In high school, I now had more black friends, many whose parents had studied and lived overseas in exile from the war. They twanged away their experiences of growing up in America and England... lifestyles again far away from the life that I knew in Marimba Park. But there was also a girl called Loveness, a township girl like me, who smiled and said very little. I don't know where she came from. I don't know where she went to. But I know she smelt the deep-down township in me and we became friends. This was what independence enabled – integration. I wondered if Loveness was the pride of a rural family who sent their child to town? Would she become the first senior high school graduate of her people? The first in university? By the time I got to the University of Zimbabwe none of that mattered. There were 101 Lovenesses for every one of me and my conflicted education. The sense of '*eclass*' that grandma spoke of didn't matter and certainly never should. I understood the vision behind my private education but university with its openness taught me adaptability and humility. While I revelled in

183

my social life, I was surrounded by more purpose-driven determined people from diverse and varied backgrounds. No longer a battleground of racial identity, class dynamics reigned, the tussle between the *petite bourgeois* nose brigades and the SRBs, those with a 'strong rural background'. One could laugh about this and embrace the best of both these worlds.

University also opened me up to the wider continent – reading the literature of Chinua Achebe, Wole Soyinka, Ngugi wa Thiongo and Pepetela, Ama Ata Aidoo and Mariama Ba. Through life and time, I have come to appreciate my rich and multi-faceted experiences and heritage, to embrace my identity, my culture, my traditions, and my Africanness, an Africanness grounded in my roots and the legacies and visions of my forebears, worthy of being emulated.

22

Area E and Beyond

Tsitsi Stella Dangarembizi

'MaBorn Location'

We are the children of the sixties and seventies, commonly known as 'MaBorn location', as the older folks refer to most of our generation! The majority of my generation's parents were born and raised in rural settings. With the arrival of churches in the then Rhodesia, many of our parents received improved education compared to their parents, thus they were able to migrate to urban areas in search of work and an improved standard of living. I was born at the Mufakose Maternity Clinic, in Harare and am the fourth born and the only girl in a family of five.

A tight-knit community

Mufakose was a well organised township with municipality-assigned similarly designed semi-detached houses that were all painted either in baby-yellow, blue or green with a black portion from just below the window level. The majority of the houses typically had four rooms: a lounge, kitchen and two bedrooms (one for parents, one for children) but there were a few, mostly at the corner stands that had six rooms. These generally had three bedrooms. My family had moved to Mufakose, from Highfields before I was born.

I recall the well-maintained narrow tarred roads between rows of houses. Each 50 to 100 homes had a recreational centre which was usually the 'nerve centre' of the community. Our centre was named 'Area E'. These centres, dotted around the whole township were similar. The major structure would be a multi-purpose hall with recreational and sports facilities at each, where community activities took place. Most toddlers and pre-school children would be dropped off there by parents, older siblings or child minders every day, to attend nursery school and play. It was at Area E that I learnt to play tennis and netball. Youth and un-employed adults, would play darts or table tennis, learn how to cook or sew; ballroom dancing and other life skills were also on offer. The highlight of these community activities for me and my peers, was being asked to help when the older children or adults had activities at the centre, for we'd be given free sandwiches for doing so. My fondest memory was when my maternal Uncle Freddy, who taught ballroom dancing, would ask for me to help make sandwiches and tea for those who participated. I not only learnt to make tasty sandwiches but ate a lot in the process.

As children we loved playing for hours on the swings and slides at Area E or in the streets with balls made of plastic; '*play button*' was a game which got us into trouble because we would take the buttons off our clothes, especially the big ones from coats, as they would 'fly' further, which is how the game was won; '*pada*' was a game which involved hopping on one leg and kicking a flat stone across squares that we drew on the tar with a stone; and ' *nhodo*' was a game mostly played by girls sitting in a small circle, around a shallow hole in the ground. We'd place some stones in the hole then with one hand toss a smooth stone in the air. Whilst it was in the air, the same hand would try to remove the stones from the hole, catch the stone in the air, and toss it it up again whilst trying to return all but one stone to the hole. We would also play hopscotch, and skipping games using old nylon panty hose. We were often found dodging and ducking at sunset came when family members or child minders came to fetch us to bath before settling down for the night.

Although we were young children in the sixties and seventies, I fondly remember being raised by the community. Neighbours were your parents eyes and ears in their absence. We could never be naughty without a reprimand, a hiding, or guidance. Every child's worst nightmare would be if the 'caretaker' parent(s) reported some mischief to one's parents. Depending on the gravity of the action, it could easily earn one another hiding. A child punished for wrong-doing by another adult would never report or complain to their own parents, for fear of being doubly reprimanded. That Area E community functioned like a well-oiled machine; and, looking back, it was a very caring one that moulded me into who I am.

The political climate and its effect on the family unit

Most parents had not grown up in Salisbury but started living there after secondary school when they began work and had families. They were also the 'newly politically conscious' black Rhodesians. Some, unbeknown to us as children, were political activists and key players in aiding and abetting the Liberation Struggle. The then colonial local government, which had a presence in the township through a municipal office, used to carry out spot checks at night to ascertain if each family had the correct number of people staying, as was recorded in the family records. At that time, relatives coming from the rural areas or other towns had to seek permission to visit, and householders had to inform the municipality if visitors arrived. The raids also provided an opportunity for the police to do security checks because the government knew that blacks were organising themselves to fight colonial rule. Some of our parents would be detained for long periods of time and we would not know where they were. Many of them travelled a lot on business so we would always naively assume that any parent away for a long period was 'at work'. Oh, what innocence. During those long periods of detention, neighbours shared responsibilities, so that any family where an adult was detained, would not bear the brunt of the detentions. For example, helping in the lift clubs which dropping children off at school. When many of our father figures were detained, mothers became multi-taskers and were the role-models for all of us young girls. After all, many of our mothers were in traditional jobs that many young girls aspired to at that time: nurses, teachers and Domestic Science teachers.

In many of our families, mine included, mothers often found sponsors sympathetic to the struggle, who gave them the opportunity to study nursing abroad. Our mothers often went for what seemed a lifetime (five to ten years) because after acquiring their qualifications, they stayed on to work, help support their families and, in many cases, then started hosting their children and other family members so that they could study abroad as well. In our case, my father did not wish my elder brothers to be drafted into the Rhodesian Army, so two of them left in 1975 to study in the UK. However, just as my parents were planning for their third-born son to join my mother and the others in the UK, the war of liberation came to an end.

When mothers were away studying, this meant a shift in roles with fathers multi-tasking, and playing the role of both mother and father. Sadly, however, some of those well-meaning efforts, split families and family bonds were broken over the long period of the armed struggle.

Post-Independence & leaving the township

In 1980 the struggle for Independence was over. I vividly recall the euphoria, although I did not really understand what it was all about. There were celebration rallies and parties that the adults attended at the township football grounds and township halls such as Rutendo Hall in Mufakose. During this period, a number of relatives who had been liberation fighters came home to visit and celebrate with our parents during the demobilisation exercise. They looked unkempt and some of them still had their ammunition, as they were 'fresh' from the bush! I was afraid of some of them, because of the negative propaganda from the colonial government, who referred to them as 'terrorists' and 'guerrillas'; besides it was my first time to see guns! I would hide in the bedroom under the bed and freeze if they were invited to stay the night, as is our culture. Only much later did I truly appreciate their hardships and the role the freedom fighters played in liberating Zimbabwe.

After liberation, many families that were once tight-knit began to move apart to other formally whites-only suburbs with bigger homes known as the 'Northern Suburbs'. These houses comfortably accommodated families and provided symbolic and visible proof that the bonds of colonialism were truly broken. We, as children, did not appreciate the move to the' leafy green' northern suburbs, as we were leaving behind our 'comfort zone', our many parents, friends and familiar playing grounds. No longer could we play games in the street or call friends to join us by screaming out their names from our own yard to come outside and play.

23

Finding My Voice

Jacqueline Rugayo

A product of mission schools in Zimbabwe, the first time I ever visited Salisbury, the then capital city of Rhodesia was in September 1977 on my way to the United States to join my educationist parents. Togged up in an orange polyester mini-dress and cream and brown platform shoes I bid goodbye to a city I had never known and to fond memories of a childhood spent in the Eastern Highlands quaint mission neighbourhoods where mothers knitted jerseys and held potluck dinners and baked the most delicious cakes ever! Where children went to schools with names like Big Tree, and spent glorious afternoons playing *water*, and where Rhodesian farm-owners with names like Houston, always managed to break the peace by trying to run us off the road with their trucks in which dogs sat in the front and workers in the back. Where we lived in houses with beautiful gardens, which acted as safe storage spaces for my father's banned Communist or Marxist books. Where I developed a healthy fear of police uniforms and soldiers whom I understood had issues with *magandanga* and *vanamukoma* and forever breaking my little bubble of a world where a person's colour did not matter. Where I called my elder black and white sisters Sisi Lynette and Sisi Lindiwe.

What a rude awakening! For the first time I became aware

that the world defined me by the colour of my skin. I learned that I was black and not only was I black but I was darker than my sister, that my forehead was rather large and so were my eyes. I want to believe that I learned these facts from well-meaning observers who would out point at my forehead and exclaim with stifled giggles how different I looked! 'Are you really Lillian's sister? Same mother, same father?' I would meekly answer yes to all the questions because I knew I was different. Why couldn't these people see it?

I remember inspecting my body and seeing the darkness with their eyes and tried to scrub it off with my bathing *dombo*. I carefully wiped away that soap and smeared on the trusted Vaseline Petroleum Gel. Vaseline could make anyone shine. Indeed I could swear my skin got lighter and off I went to play. These questions from well-meaning observers followed me. It seemed I was too dark to be black!

The news of my father's successful application for a scholarship to study Theology in the United States was met with jubilation. We celebrated not only the opportunity, which many cavorted, but I secretly celebrated that the Rhodesians could no longer throw my father in jail and beat him for reading Marxist books – whatever that was. He was going to be safe although he didn't seem to care one way or another. Within a short time my mother and young sister joined him and I found myself in boarding school, living with other girls like me. I found friends and lost my childhood. When my period came, I was so shocked that for a long time I couldn't tell anyone.

Learning was an exciting and yet frightening experience. My seventh grade teacher, a black Zimbabwean, would walk up and down the rows of our class as we did our assignment. He had told us to write a story, any story and as I started mine...' Once upon a time there was a girl...' I heard a loud WHACK!. Followed by another and another behind me. My hand froze and soon enough I too received a painful whack on my hand. Confused tears overflowed out of my so called big eyes. Our teacher stood in front and threatened that if he ever saw any of us beginning a story with 'Once Upon a Time' he would skin us alive! As I searched for better words to start my story I was certain that I could not survive Grade 7 and started to plot my escape across the border to join the *magandanga,* like many other Hartzel Mission School students. The romantically brave stories of young girls and boys dodging the soldiers' bullets as they successfully crossed the border into Mozambique to fight for freedom captivated every student's mind and kept me awake each night.

A few days later we were not surprised to learn that my fifteen-year-old brother, Sam, had skipped the high school fence and crossed the border into Mozambique. My parents were even more alarmed to learn that my sister and I were planning to do the same. Plans for family reunification were fast forwarded and visas prayerfully applied for and within a few weeks I learned that I was going to the United States. My uncle asked if I wanted to continue in school until my departure date. Memories of my Grade 7 class teacher's famous bamboo stick encouraged me to decline the offer and with a big smile I politely declined.

Culture shock took on a different meaning in my life. The changes were unimaginable, from sun to snow... my mother wept when she saw me emerge from the flight clad in my soul train outfit in the middle of the coldest winter in Massachusetts. I was speechless for most of my junior high and high school. I mean, if I was to dare speak who would I say I am? I seemed to be caught up in a whirlwind, a kaleidoscope of events over which I had no control. Again the issue of colour continued to plague me. The black Americans found my black Africaness too strange and I found it odd to only have white friends for the first time ever in my life. I was more accepted by a race that rejected me in my own country and rejected by a race of my own colour! The questions about my darkness continued to haunt me until I met this lovely black woman with no name. I cannot remember how

I met her or where except her words that changed my life forever. She looked at me as other observers had done. Bracing myself I listened as she went on to marvel at how beautiful my dark skin was, how lovely my eyes brought out the beauty in the shape of my forehead. As she spoke into my life I could swear that the sun began to shine brighter and brighter and layers of rejection peeled off like soft rose petals. Indeed, how beautiful are the feet of those who bring good news. I know now that I met an angel that day and slowly my voice started to emerge, to form and I began to walk in my own track according to the Book of Life.

24

19 & 39

A mother and daughter remember

Nyarai Majuru and Manyara Matambanadzo

I am 39, not 19.
Birthed from Dzimambwe,
A land of tangerine sunshine, of bronze grass, of
    thundering waterfalls,
A land 19 knows is her home, but without the
    bond like with 39
For 19's blood is of the House of Stone, but has
    been diluted,
For she is 19 and not 39

I am 19, young, free and bold
Early memories of the motherland, reside in my
    childhood,
Everything seen through innocent, and wonder-
    fully naïve lenses
The joy and laughter of going to *kumusha*,
A time when technology had no real place,
Where our imaginations were wild, where play ran
    amok,
Building mudhouses with the red earth,

Filling our bellies with ripe guavas and juicy
   mangoes
Before the age of Twitter, and Facebook
Which consumes so much of my experiences to-
   day,
Where now at 19, this land seems distant to me,
Laughter slightly muzzled, and the vibrancy of the
   sun, that little bit duller.

39 continues to make sure 19 does not forget
Reminiscing with her
When she was once 19 remembering a time of in-
   nocence, of laughter, of joy, of pain,
Of confusion, of uncertainty, of boldness, of fear-
   lessness
Memories of boarding in high school,
Where allegiances were marked by a rainbow of
   blazers; maroon, green cream red, blue, brown
And sporting war cries of '*We are Vale, couldn't be*
   prouder,
If you can't beat us, shout a little louder!'
Where exeat weekend meant Karigamombe
   Centre on Saturdays,
Dairy Den, the Kines, friends, boys and then home
   via Rezende Street
Seems like it was yesterday, a time when I was 19.

At 19 my boarding experiences remain a distant
   memory
When my Gogo would drag me back school on a
   Sunday night.
Instead, I remember being the new black girl,
With a funny, long name, from a strange foreign
   land
'How come you speak like that?', 'How come you
   wear your hair like that?'

And being so aware of how quickly I slipped into
    Shona
But very soon, I was just another kid, not that dif-
    ferent from my peers,
Giggling about boys in the PE changing room,
    singing in the drama studio
Hitching up our skirts when walking to the school
    gates,
Realising that we had more in common that dif-
    ference
Away from our blood home, but adapting to this
    new home,
On these shores of the Queen, our former colonial
    masters

I wish 19 had similar experiences to my childhood
To have had my family closer to me, to not feel so
    alone
But I understand, and accept
That 19 is not only a child of Zimbabwe, but has
    her place in the world,
Blossoming as a woman in independence, in ma-
    turity, in purpose
Charting her own path,
Trusting that it's not simply about where you come
    from
How we have traversed that uncertain road,
Of life away from our spiritual home, but made,
Our Diaspora kaleidoscope of experiences, count.
I am 39 and she is 19.
I am her Mother. And she is my Daughter.

25

Independent

Maryanne Situma

I was sixteen years old. Kenya had just experienced its first coup attempt from a rather disgruntled army. The population was restless after years of what they perceived as an oppressive government. It was the first sign that for many, life was not as rosy as they might have liked to think.

Namibia and South Africa were still fighting colonialism. Zimbabwe was a newly independent republic with a revolutionary president and leadership. The great African leaders at the time included Julius Nyerere, Kenneth Kaunda, Samora Machel, Kwame Nkrumah and Robert Mugabe of the newly minted Zimbabwe. The idea of revolutionaries and of fighting for African freedom was a new and fascinating concept to those of us who were 'born free'.

Fast forward. My father transfers his family to Zimbabwe. Now, you can imagine, I was coming from a country where white people had basically been given the green light to leave soon after Kenya's independence in 1963 (long before I was born). Jomo Kenyatta had already instituted an early version of land reform.

I arrive in Zimbabwe in the early eighties to a country where milk, bread and mail is still being delivered to your doorstep. The streets were very clean and everything was planned and orderly. I am sure there will be readers who can relate to this. Harare was interesting. I couldn't believe that a whole capital city would be devoid of people in the business district by 6 p.m. in the evening.

Coming from the chaos of Nairobi it was a bit of a shock. The idea of street addresses was not a strong feature in the Nairobi I knew, so the whole idea of the postman coming to deliver your mail? in Africa? was astonishing, though I must say I became the biggest spotter of the postman while waiting for the mail from my high school sweetheart. How I wish people still wrote letters... How I looked forward to receiving mail in the mail box, especially during the school holidays.

I remember the first day I went to school. My English teacher was surprised that I could read Shakespeare – and be understood. Yes, be understood. It was also the first time I came across a high school class dedicated to preparing you to become an executive assistant, or more precisely, an executive secretary. If my memory serves me well, this was an avenue to a well-paying job while waiting for the proverbial prince charming to come along.

Having spent all my early school life in a convent school in Nairobi I was extremely pleasantly surprised with the private school to which I was promptly enrolled. I encountered something called M-levels, after which, if you passed, you were eligible for university in South Africa. You did not have to do A-levels unless you were destined for some western country which actually required them or you were going to the only university in the country at the time.

Mark you, looking back, getting those M- and A- levels was a lot of work and getting into the University of Zimbabwe required a minimum of five points. It was rare for anyone to do more than three A-levels, so maximum points were 15 I think. Very hard-won points I may add and all lucky enough to be accepted into the university had this information printed in *The Herald*. I look at the kids today having to achieve more than 12 points in order to get into university.

There is now something called an A star for marks which I understand is genius territory.

So back to this private school, where seniors had their own common room and tea with cake and sandwiches at ten in the morning, tea in the afternoon, as well as lunch. What struck me was how few black students there were. And because I did not understand the local lingo, those in my year had a field day talking about me and getting me to repeat 'bad' words.

This school only had like a metre high Salwire fence on the side where the seniors' hostel was and I was shocked to discover that some of the occupants would have their boyfriends park on the back road, hop over the fence and enjoy a half night sleepover!

Coming from a strict convent school, I could not believe the level of freedom the high school students were given. Naturally, I promptly adjusted to such freedoms. When in Rome... I remember all the farmers' daughters who were boarders were allowed to bring their cars and park them at the school. Actually, even the day scholars could do so. VW Polo, Datsun Pulsar and the ever popular Mazda 323 were some of the cars given by doting parents to their teenage daughters.

Does anyone remember something called a 'desk fee' which parents paid to ensure a place at a school? Or a time when extra lessons were strictly for those who were 'academically challenged'? Back then, you went to class and the teachers taught and exams gave you the justice you deserved. Being made to repeat was not an option. If you did do extra lessons you certainly did not advertise it. Nowadays, it's almost a necessity to ensure kids get through exams.

School kids were not allowed to be seen anywhere except school in their school uniform especially during school time, and any random adult could stop you and interrogate you as to why you were not in school. Some overzealous ones would even phone the school if they recognised the uniform. So, if you were planning to bunk, you had to make sure you had your civvies with you.

Oh, the death of the phone booth. I remember the days of the land line in our house. There was one phone which was in a prominent place where it could be answered by a parent. Who remembers the party line where the whole neighbourhood could listen to your conversations?

I'm sure you all remember in those high school days something called an orange phone which could be used for 20 cents. And people soon figured out how to make those 20 cents last for hours. Parents would actually padlock the phone to stop over-use and a press button phone was the height of sophistication.

There were like five or six clubs in the city. The first time I actually went to one of these I was surprised to see that lights went on promptly at 3 a.m. and the music stopped. Kenya back then had 'day and night' clubs, and while I'm sure they must have had operating hours, I never heard of lights being switched on in the popular Nairobi clubs. Mark you, given my strict parents, going out at night was an exercise in negotiation and planning and it did not always end well.

I remember the First Street Mall when it was the centre for all the best shops: the Barbours restaurant, Greatermans, the Woolworths chocolates in winter. Zimbabwe used to produce the most amazing leather products and beautiful locally made underwear.

I got my first curly perm which cost Z$10 (big curls) and I recall how curl activators would steam in the sun. There was a sticker back then that read, 'I like your perm but not on my window'. Zimbabwe was the first country where I saw locally made hair products for black hair, being produced by titans called Kubi Indi and Sue Peters. These business women opened the doors to a lot of black business women by showing that you can do it too... I digress... The thing about this perm was that if you wanted to set it, you could and then you simply washed your hair to restore the curls. This was not possible with any perm I had come across before and how it stank when being done. I would always save up for that curly perm!

The eighties were the time for colour blocking – purple and yellow, blue and white, red and yellow. It was a time for the big belts, big hair, elastic belts, and I even rocked in Sandak shoes in all their glorious colours. There were those lovely pumps that used to cost Z$30. Who did not have a pair? People rocked in viscose shirts and the chiffon dresses – the London look!

Madonna's hit song 'Holiday' was a club anthem. Remember the singers Luther, Kashif, Evelyn 'Champagne' King? 'Rock me Tonite' by Freddie Jackson was a favourite lover's tune, for the reggae fans. Gregory Isaacs was a big deal. I remember being so excited to meet Tuku (Oliver Mtukudzi) and Lovemore Majaivana. The way I loved live shows, I'm sure I must have been a groupie of some sort in another life. Remember the Frontline concert when Tracy Chapman and Bruce Springsteen came to town? How about Paul Simon and Gracelands?

This Harare was heaven coming from the then disorganisation of Nairobi. Everything was planned: each suburb with a school, a shopping centre, a post office, and so on. Mark you, schools were zoned until the government did away with that arrangement.

Transport was a bit of a strange arrangement for me. There was a bus system which worked efficiently, you could actually arrange to meet your friends on a particular bus and bus route. There were bus timetables that were adhered to and strangest for me was those DAF buses which only had one door. (Kenyan buses had two doors and you had to be a combo of a sprinter, wrestler, high jumper, monkey, etc. to ensure that you *got on* to a Kenyan bus, that you *stayed on* and that you *got off* at the right stop. The *matatu* stories of that time are real! Learning to mount a Zimbabwean bus was an exercise. I am at a bus stop trying to get home. The bus arrives and I ran to the back door to get on. No back door!

So I ran round the bus like one demented until I found the only door, the front door! And I didn't know that you had to pay the driver; I grew up paying conductors.

Can you remember the Harare without kombis? Or those taxis which you had to be careful getting in and out as sharp metal edges could tear your clothes? Do you remember if you missed the last bus home from the city centre after 6 p.m., you would have to take your chances hitchhiking or hope that the good old Peugeot pirate taxis went in your direction. And, if you lived in those leafy suburbs, you'd better make sure to have cab fare back home as a back-up.

The city had cycle tracks and it was the norm for day scholars to cycle, walk to school, or catch the school bus. The posh schools had their own buses and the rest coped nicely with buses laid on by the ZUPCO bus company.

It was an interesting time back in the eighties and nineties. The last colonised African states were free. The University of Zimbabwe back then was an exciting place to be. I know many of our kids today can't imagine that this was so. The place had students from the ANC, PAC, SWAPO,[1] etc. – all sorts of young revolutionaries filled the lecture halls. We met Nelson Mandela soon after he was released. We protested against corruption. We ate cheap meals in the Students' Union and spent many happy hours having discussions and gossiping while seated outside the Great Hall. How I wish google had existed then. I recall how learning to use the library required a lesson on how to master those index cards. Students were taught by some of the finest minds around.

It was the place where I met many people who have gone on to become movers and shakers in their worlds. How proud my parents were when I graduated. I was the first born and first girl in the clan to finish university.

We actually saw Chicken Inn and Nando's grow as a brand. Before them I don't recall a fast-food chain in Zim. I

1 African National Congress, Pan-African Congress, South West Africa Peoples' Organisation.

do remember the chicken from Arizona on Samora Machel and putt putt at East 24. Creamy Inn does not have anything to match the good old Dairy Dens. Has anything ever tasted as good as a polony and cheese sandwich made from hot fresh bread, two-inch-thick slices all squashed together and eaten? Remember bread was not sold wrapped, and the Lobels man would come down the streets with his cart. What about the adverts? The classic *'Ngwerengwere Sadza'* with the Rusike Brothers, Samson the bull, etc. – jingles that still ring in my mind. Do you remember getting excited about getting the next video from the video club?

I could go on forever down this memory lane … it can become a bit like purging yourself.

Everyone has a place and time with which they identify when they became of age. Harare was that place for me and I thank God every day, because it is where I met wonderful men and women who have shaped and influenced my life. I am so grateful God surrounded me with people and circumstances(good and bad) that made me strong and helped me grow up. I have gained sisters that I was not born with, parents with whom I have no biological relationship, advisors that don't take my crap, friends that I still get into trouble with, brothers that have never tired of protecting me, spiritual guides that remind me to put God first, people who love me unconditionally. As to the haters, they know where they can go and what they can do with themselves.

26

From Harari to the BAFTAs

Xoliswa Sithole

It is 2015 August, I am sitting here in San Francisco waiting to go to my oldest friend's fiftieth birthday party where I am to make a speech, and have come all the way from South Africa. It is a surprise birthday party. I went to kindergarten with Munyaradzi Manyika from the age of three, the same year I arrived from South Africa with my mother, Doreen, and sister, Melody. We arrived in Southern Rhodesia as refugees from apartheid South Africa and a year later my mother married Joshua Sithole who raised me; he was the only man I knew as my father. I only met my biological father at the age of 28 in South Africa.

As fate would have it, after kindergarten, Munyaradzi and I continued to the same primary school, Chitsere Primary, where his father was the headmaster. Mr Manyika had been a Fulbright scholar in the 1960s whose research had focused on education. Munyaradzi and I sat in the same classroom until Grade 4, and then my beloved father Joshua died from heart failure.

Not long afterwards, my mother, alone in a foreign country was beset by another tragic loss, Dr Edison Sithole, who had taken the responsibility of being the family caretaker when my dad had died. Dr Sithole was the first doctor of Laws in Southern Africa. He was a human rights lawyer and a political activist who was abducted by Ian Smith in 1975 because of his political activities and was never to be heard of again. These two losses left my mother a heart-broken woman.

Beatrice Cottages

Along with Dr Edison Sithole, my family lived at 14 Rusike Crescent at Beatrice Cottages, Harari (which is now called Mbare), a middle-class area for black people during segregation in Rhodesia. Most of the children in my neighbourhood went to either Martindale, St Martins or the Dominican Convent, 'white' schools that accepted a handful of black children. Having come from South Africa and not being *au fait* with the local language, Shona, logic would have dictated that my parents send me to one of those schools. My father was on the verge of doing so when *Mukoma* Eddie intervened and stated categorically that no Sithole child was to go to any such school until Rhodesia was no more. That's how I ended up going to Chitsere Primary School; my older sister went to Shingirai School. My best friends from the neighbourhood were Bridget Chikosi and Wendy Marumahoko, who both went to black schools. The other kids in the neighbourhood were rather uppity and always showed off with their 'white' English even though our parents were all friends since it was a small neighbourhood. And given the political situation, comradeship was essential.

Monday to Friday I would walk to Chitsere Primary School where I also fought my own wars of being very light-skinned. The kids used to call me *'mukaradhi'* meaning coloured and I did stick out and my Bantu bottom stuck out as well (creating a complex about my beautiful rotund Bantu bottom for most of my life till a decade ago when I grew to love it!), I was teased quite a lot but what may have saved me was that I was quite smart and I always fought for the underdog, which endeared me to a lot of children even though my Shona was quite suspect at that time. The 30-minute walk to school in all kinds of weather stood in stark contrast to the experiences of my peers who went to white schools. They were picked up by bus and this made me rather resentful, looking down through the bus windows the uppity kids were already participating in class warfare – even though they were not aware of what class was about. Nonetheless, as a kid, you just get on with it. Chitsere was a great school, even though I always felt that I was not really understood. My favourite teacher was Mr Mpofu who was the Grade 4 teacher. My mother seemed a rather liberal parent, she was from another country and was learning the ways of the Zimbabwean people. I did not have a very traditional upbringing and was taught to not just accept anything verbatim but to question, *Mukoma* Edison encouraged me to do so, be it with regard to religion, gender and even those aspects of colonialism that a seven-year-old could understand. My teachers, especially Mr Mpofu, were very patient but at times very impatient with me as a result of my need to question. During that time, to question authority was seen as being rude.

My first recollection of Dr Edison is of him being sent to prison, and my mother explaining the situation to me. This was something I never understood because I thought one's parents were the only people who could make any decision on one's life. I could not understand how one could be sent to prison without one's parents being the ones who put you there. I was six years old, or thereabouts, at this point in my life, and really, our parents were our gods. It was traumatic because we were not sure when he would be released. He came home after a week or so. It was then in 1973, when I started to understand or rather to have an inkling about the political situation, when I was told not to talk about *Mukoma* Eddie and that I needed to be secretive about his life and not to air the family linen in public.

Upon the death of my father and *Mukoma* Eddie, it was decided that I had to go to boarding school in Wedza because my mother lost our home. My father's uncle took the property away even though my mother, a qualified nursing sister, had helped pay for it. This left my mother very vulnerable in a foreign land at a time of political turbulence with two daughters to raise. During colonialism, black people were married under customary law and women did not inherit anything, this was of course changed when the country gained independence in 1980.[1] My mother moved to Marandellas (Marondera).

St Mary's Mission Catholic School

Off I went to St Mary's Mission Catholic School. I had no idea what to expect in the middle of the rural area. The new life included pit latrines, sleeping on the floor in the dormitory, eating *mangayi* (boiled semi-dried mealies) and *mbambaira* (sweet potatoes) with tea, and so it was a culture shock. My mother had given me one dollar pocket money which was to last me the whole term and I thought I was very rich. I made friends with Dorothy Choto whose father was a businessman and her grandfather was the chief of the Svosve people in Wedza. For someone like me, who had a sweet tooth, her friendship was manna, as sweets and biscuits were never a problem, since Dorothy could just go to her father's shop ... (The Svosve people were the first people to invade the white farms in Marondera in 1982 and President Robert Mugabe stopped them because he was still trying to negotiate a land resettlement programme with white Rhodesian farmers.)

At this school I grew, I learnt Shona and the ways of the Shona people, one evening a schoolmate of ours called Idonia started having hallucinations, speaking in an old man's voice. I had never seen such and I started asking questions. Dorothy nudged me and told me to shut up, apparently, the girl had a *svikiro*, in other words, she had been possessed by a spirit. A male ancestor was speaking through her, I knew

---

1   The Legal Age of Majority Act was passed in 1982. It gave women the right to choose their sexual partners, inherit property, and engage in economic and political life. It was, however, met with stiff resistance. For a full discussion see *Shemurenga* by Shereen Essof: Weaver, Press, Harare, 2013.

nothing about these things and it freaked me out.

Something else I learned at St Mary's was tilling the land and growing maize, and *kusakura* (weeding). We grew our own mealies for mealie-meal used to make sadza (the staple food) and we also cut sisal to fill the mattresses. My word, I had never ever seen or done any such sisal thing at home. I had a bunk bed from the furniture shop, Pelhams. Life went on however! It was also quite fascinating as we used to go to the bush to collect wild fruits like *hute, zvifokosiyana, matowhe, hacha,* and *matamba,* and that I really enjoyed.

But, one day, I decided that I had had enough of this rural life of pit latrines, unfamiliar food and candles, so I decided to just walk out of the school gate and take the bus to Marondera. And so, I headed home with dreams of lovely food. My mother was livid and I was sent promptly back to school.

During my absence, Dorothy got into trouble and when I got back at assembly on Monday morning I was thrashed by the headmaster in front of everyone. My stubborn nature would not allow me to cry. I honestly did not see anything wrong with what I had done. I had just wanted to go home. I was nine years old.

One evening, sitting in the classroom during study time, a man with an AK 47 jumped through the window and other men followed in quick succession. One of them looked at the history book I was reading and told the class that we were being taught colonial history and he asked me what my name was. I said Sithole, my surname, because my first name XOLISWA, has always been a problem for people to say because of the clicks which do not exist in the Shona language. The man immediately associated Sithole with *Mukoma* Eddie, whom he referred to as a hero. He also spoke about my now late uncle Ndabaningi Sithole, who was one of the founding members of ZANU. I suppose I became a mini-celebrity at the school.

We then went to the sports grounds that evening and that

was my first lesson in the Chimurenga War. From then on, we got used to seeing the comrades at night and singing songs till early hours of the morning and the Rhodesian soldiers coming to school in the morning to arrest student activists. At times, the soldiers would take the older girls and burn cigarettes under their breasts as part of the interrogation process. A friend of ours – let's call her Maidei – also suffered when her father was buried alive by *vakomana*/comrades. He was suspected of being an informer, a *dzakutsaku*. Of course, this was not a conducive environment for a nine-year-old, with the the violence and war looming over our heads. However, it was war – a full-scale war – fought in the rural areas.

By this time my Shona was proficient and when I went home during the holidays, where I would sing those Chimurenga songs... My mother was on the verge of taking me out of the school when there was fighting and an ambush between the freedom fighters and the Rhodesian soldiers and the mission school was closed.

Fast forward one year and I was sent to St Dominic's Catholic School at Chishawasha, an excellent school. Its O-Level results and those of its brother school, St Ignatius, were amongst the best in the country. To gain entry into St Dominic's your Grade 7 results had to be a first-class pass.

The schools that produced the best results were mainly Catholic missionary schools. Julia Sairai was my best friend. I'm not sure what my mother's fascination with Catholicism was because we were not Catholic and I found the system very repressive. Indeed, Catholicism traumatised me so much, I suffered Catholic guilt all my life and afterwards, as an adult, when I was intimate with someone, I always felt my parents were watching me or God was doing so.

I loved dancing and would win disco-dancing competitions during weekends when us girls were bored stiff, and I would win a packet of biscuits each time I won. Olivia Washaya was the organiser of these competitions. The boys from

St Ignatius would come every last Sunday of the month and some had girlfriends. One of my friends, Hazel had a boyfriend Simeon and she told me that Simeon's friend liked me. Let us call him Tendai. This boy started writing me letters and telling me all sorts of 'sweet nothings', at the back of my mind I could hear my mother telling me to keep away from boys, to refuse even their offers of sweets or biscuits: *'Iwawo mabiskit, unowaberekereswa mwana kumsana nawo'* – basically her message was that I would get pregnant.

Somehow, through these letters from Tendai, and subsequently sitting in the park four metres apart, he became my boyfriend. I would sit there not saying a word. Yes, totally mute but he became my boyfriend – this was the courtship phase. But then he broke the spell. He sent me a letter stating that the next time we were to meet he would kiss me and touch my breasts. I had no breasts. Ohhhhh that disturbed me so much and he told me that he would wait for me at the bus stop at the end of the term. So, when the time came I alighted the bus, I ignored him and walked straight past him because I was afraid of being kissed. And that was the end of my first 'love affair'.

By this time Freedom, Zimbabwe (as opposed to Rhodesia), was in the air. It was 1979 and it was magic! There was talk of freedom, political prisoners being released and exiles returning home! The optimism was electric!

I can still see it, feel it and smell it.

Independence in Zimbabwe

In 1980, I was sitting in my French class at a white school, Mabelreign Girls High School having left St Dominics, since the country was going through the negotiation phase, the war had ended and a cease-fire had been declared in 1979. During this period, around April 1980, we were listening to the radio when they announced the triumphant win of ZANU. Most of the white girls cried and talked about how they were going to emigrate to South Africa, while the black girls were jubilant. This was the end of colonial rule. We could now just shoot for the stars: everything, everything was now possible... I remember one of the Chimurenga songs:

ZANULA ZANULA Ishumba Smith inyama
haiwa unengozi... unengozi Smith...
Haiwawa unengozi...

And the Rhodesian army had their own song:

All Rhodesians will fight through thick and thiny
We will keep up
Land the free land, stop the enemy from coming in
We will keep them North of the Zambezi...

From the same time, I remember Thomas Mapfumo the prolific Zimbabwean singer coming onto the scene with his *'Bhutsu Mutandarikwa'*. Then there was my favourite musician and person in the world, Stevie Wonder with 'Master Blaster Jamming' which had the line, 'peace has come to Zimbabwe...' And there was the late comedian Mukadota and Mai Rwizi. What else could we desire?

Of course, I could straddle two worlds. I had gone to school in Wedza and learned colloquial Shona, and I could assume the accent of my 'nose brigade'[2] friends, the ones who had gone to white schools for the majority of their school lives. With them it was Michael Jackson, Shalamar, the Gap Band, house parties and night clubs. Even though I was under-age, I would just go dancing from 9 p.m. till 5 a.m. There was no drugs, no sex, and no alcohol, just good times.

Then came Bob Marley at the Independence Day celebration, when he sang 'Every man has a right to decide his own destiny' in the beautiful song 'Zimbabwe'. I was privileged to watch him perform at Rufaro Stadium at a free concert. Bob Marley was instrumental in stimulating political awareness, especially among the youth. This often created a chasm between our parents' generation and our own. The older folk saw reggae and Rastafari as rebellious

---

2   The colloquial term for people who spoke English through the nose.

music or musicians and, of course, *ganja* and delinquency were associated with them. The brilliance of 'Bob', President Robert Mugabe as a political leader was globally legendary. Listening to him arguing for his scientific socialism was music to the ears of some of us who were not yet politically left but moving towards that view.

By then, my mother, sister and I had moved from Marandellas to Salisbury which later became Harare. I had wanted to be an actress all my life and I performed frequently, but dance was my greatest love. I had even won the inter-schools disco-dancing competition at Prince Edward School in 1981. I used to do fashion shows and be part of the dancing component. Farai Mpisaunga (now Mpofu) was my great *shamwari*. Although we were not at the same school, we hung out a lot.

It was during this time that I had another taste of tragedy. My grandmother, who was visiting from South Africa, was murdered just on the outskirts of Harare, and four months later, I lost my sister Melody to complications due to child-birth. All that was left of the family was my mother, Melody's son Tutu, Nkulu, my other nephew, and myself. That was a very, very difficult time, for my mother especially.

***

We all did our O-Level and A-Level. I used to share a room at boarding school with Nora Chipaumire who is now a prolific dancer in the USA, and my other friend was Yvette Ogiste, someone I had grown up with. Her South African grandmother was related to my biological father. We were very close knit at school. Then we all went to the University of Zimbabwe and Nora was still my roommate. At University, I inevitably discovered dope and sex, Angela Davis, Alice Walker and Sembene Ousmane, and, of course, parties. What a wonderful combination. Even though I do not remember much of my final year, because I think some of my brain cells had found their way into the universe, I remember being rebellious and did not quite understand why. I now think I was bored, creatively, and found my environment too conservative.

After university, I even tried to go study in the US but the pre-requisite was an audition for a film school, which I did and was accepted at Penn State University for the 1989 class. However, this dream was not to be. En-route to my audition, I went to visit Wadzi Garwe who was living in the USA because her father was the Zimbabwean Ambassador to Washington. Farai was there visiting too. I drank Wadzi's father's expensive whisky. Lord! Until now I continue to send gifts to Wadzi's mother to atone for drinking her husband's whisky.

Alfrey Woodard, with whom I acted in the Mandela HBO film with Danny Glover, had organised for my audition at Penn State University. Even though I had been accepted as one of the six out of 450 people, I never went to do my Masters in Fine Arts (MFA), I stayed in Zimbabwe, I met John, followed my heart, lost it and did not carry my brain with me, got stoned for about two years, and don't remember much apart from being socially dysfunctional. With hindsight, I would call it growing up and I chalked it up to experience. Do I regret not going to do my MFA? No, not at all, how my life eventually unfolded was and is still amazing.

I was really going crazy, not being productive at home, literally seeing my dreams go down the gutter and living in my head. One day, Yvette Ogiste advised me to leave the country for a while since she understood how trapped I felt. She noticed my failure at expressing my creative energy. A two-year working visa found me in London. My friend Ruramai Murisi (now Mupfunya) joined me. We worked in old people's homes in London even though it was tough. To while away the time at the old people's homes, I would emerge from behind a curtain with the old gentlemen and old ladies as my audience. For our shows, Ruramai was the MC of the one-woman show: 'Ladies and gentlemen please put your hands together for the amazing Kholiswa Sithole!'.

I would emerge from behind the curtain singing something like, 'It's a long way to Tipperary it's a long way to go.' When the song and act was done Ruramai would ask all of them to clap their hands. The old people would oblige nodding... very very very nice... great actress'.

Most of them had cataracts so their vision was not so great. But nothing happened in those homes apart from television, breakfast, lunch and supper. I was their superstar.

Folks, one has to keep the dream alive!

London was tough, by tough I am referring in particular to the cold, the long working hours combined with just the lack of sun, but what we enjoyed was the 'clubbing'. Fortunately, I had stopped dope by now and that was good for me. Ruramai and I were so broke most of the time, we would have just enough money to go to the Fridge, a nightclub in Brixton; we would smuggle in a quarter whisky, dance and dance and go to the toilet, take a swig in the process, at times we would talk for hours and pontificate on the state of the world whilst sitting in the toilet. Our conversation would go from Malcolm X, Nelson Mandela and gender, it had to be in there somewhere.

There were no boyfriends to speak of.

The male species have never been an important fixture of my life, there was the odd boyfriend here and there, I loved them as friends but I never wanted to marry and still don't. I always felt that boyfriends took up too much space and I always wanted total freedom in my life even though I desired commitment if and when I had a boyfriend, which was not often. Marriage has never been part of my composition. I have had two marriage proposals, one from a friend and the other from a boyfriend. Looking back, I have no regrets, just as well, it is what it is.

My cousin, Agnes Sithole, Edison Sithole's sister was my rock, she was a great support system in London. The city was hard work and yet I think it was the best experience of my life because it humbled me and sobered me up. I lived there during the time of the recession, Margaret Thatcher had decimated the working class by single-handedly destroying the unions, she accelerated privatisation and cut back on public spending. It was tough for a lot of people. It grew me, politically and creatively – I read a lot and had access to a larger creative space which expanded me intellectually, and I travelled within Europe and to other continents because it was cheap and I had the desire to do so.

One day in 1992, I just woke up and decided to visit my biological father in South Africa. I was 28 years old. Ruramai accompanied me. I just knocked on my father's door in the middle of the night as that was the time we arrived. This was the time when South Africa was about to be free. Mandela had just been released. My father asked me to come home and he felt that he had little time left on this earth and he wanted to get to know me. I took up his offer and moved to South Africa in 1994. Having grown up in Zimbabwe, and identifying as Zimbabwean, I had nonetheless never lost my South African roots.

South Africa was a bloody nightmare! The racism was too much for me. Since I had now decided to be a producer as a career move, I started at the bottom, as a receptionist for the BBC on 'The Cecil John Rhodes' series.

I had grown up in a country where we were done with colonialism and black people were in charge in Zimbabwe. South Africa was hard to get used to. But I plugged along. Yes, I plugged along and finally got my bearings right.

My stay in South Africa was made much easier by friends called Gail Smith and Pumla Gqola they taught me a lot about South Africa's journey, history and gender politics. I had family in South Africa and I made other few great friends who made me fall in love with the country and understand where it was coming from. I grasped three hundred and forty-two years of oppression and the pain South Africa has been through.

In all of that I could feel my mother's pain, I could see her face from the time of the displacement of black people in their own land. In every woman I met in South Africa whose face told a thousand stories, I saw my mother, I understood her complexities and I could see her face, her loneliness of being in a foreign country when her beloved Joshua died. I understood. Yet she had kept going, in whichever way she knew how.

On her dying bed, the only way I could salute her was to tell her that if only I had possessed a tenth of her strength, I would have been the first president of the World. She smiled with that faraway smile and I knew she had already begun her journey into the after-life. She smiled the same way my sister had smiled the last day I saw her alive.

In 1997, I fell in love and lived with a lovely Jewish boy of mixed Afrikaner ancestry. He was and is still an active member of the African National Congress. He taught me a lot about the politics of South Africa, as he comes from a family of political activists. His grandfather was one of the founding members of the South African Clothing Workers' Union in 1928, which aimed at addressing the concerns of black workers in the clothing industry and his grandmother was Moses Kotane's secretary. Kotane was the Secretary-General of the South African Communist Party in 1939. I had a lot of respect for his commitment to South Africa and his integrity. It seemed as if politics was going to follow me all my life.

I worked for different companies, gaining experience, including Hollywood films, I did not enjoy working for most of them. I worked for famous people, something I am still ambivalent about. All in all, experience was had.

I lost my mother to HIV AIDS in February 1996, and I lost my biological father Simon Maratuna that same year, September 1996. He and I had managed to build a good relationship and he never stopped thanking my mother and Joshua Sithole for having raised me. There was a time I

216

found South Africa very tough, in terms of its racism, blatant patriarchy and misogyny.

I wanted to leave. I went to visit my father in tears and he sat me down told me of the road they had travelled during apartheid and how they had done their bit and were passing the baton on to us.

These were his words, 'If you ever thought it was going to be easy and that white people would relinquish power, my child you are mistaken. With Mandela's release things have begun to ease up and if you leave and decide to come back a decade later do not complain if white people are still in power. It is up to you to make South Africa and Africa work for you. And it is your responsibility to work at uplifting black people in whatever way you can.'

The rest is history. My film-making career took off. I found my creativity and my drive. It became my life's passion.

I was awarded my first BAFTA[3] in 2005 when I was nominated for an International Emmy award,[4] and my second BAFTA in 2010. I had been nominated for two BAFTAs in 2010. I then received a Peabody award[5] in 2010.

There have been many other great awards as a producer or director of human rights documentaries. I give tribute to Dr Edison Sithole who had a profound human rights influence on my life.

When I was asked to write this essay, I was conflicted, I did not think that I could write a decent piece. As an artist who values honesty and openness, how was I going to write about my wayward wonderful, serendipitous, glorious life and at the same time pay homage to a country that raised me?

How would I write an essay about a country that grew me

3 Awards given annually by the British Academy of Film and Television Arts.

4 An Emmy Award, or simply Emmy, is an American award that recognises excellence in the television industry, and corresponds to the Oscar (for film), the Tony Award (for theatre), and the Grammy Award(for music).

5 This American award, established by George Peabody, and American philanthropist honours the most powerful, enlightening, and invigorating stories in television, radio, and online media.

and most importantly, to a mother who knew that there had to be something better than apartheid even though it was still Rhodesia when we arrived in 1970.

Zimbabwe was home. It is home.

Not once did I ever feel that I did not belong and do not belong in Zimbabwe. Whether I entered politics in Zimbabwe or chose to be anything I wanted to be, politics had to be something. I was even informed by the late Chief Justice of Zimbabwe, Godfrey Chidyausiku, that if I wanted a farm all I would have to do was to apply for a farm. Nobody has offered me a farm in South Africa. I am sure Zimbabwe would give me a chance to be an official of some sort, Comrade Xoliswa Sithole. Then again (maybe not) – *ndakushaina handiti? Pasi ichokwadi.*[6]

Most importantly my life debunks that notion of what family is, the belief that blood is thicker than water. The Sithole family have always made me feel that I do belong. They are my family. I am closer to them than my blood family. The people mentioned in this story are family to me and when I go up on any platform, I always say that I am a ZIMSA. South Africa is home to me, so is Zimbabwe.

I want to say to Wadzi and Farai, thank you for making me do this, I am still your Colie – Fari gave me this name and it stuck, that's what all the 'ma nose' call me, while the SRB's[7] call me 'Koriswa'.

Coming full circle

Back to Munyaradzi's fiftieth birthday speech with which I began this essay. How could I condense into words a speech about someone who has mirrored my life since I was three years old? How do I speak about a friend I kept through primary school, high school, university and beyond?

How do I condense my journey into what I have become?

All I could do when I stood up was to say a few words, then

---

6 I'm showing off – but it's the truth!

7 Jokey acronym or description as it's opposite, MuSalad; an SRB refers to Someone with a Strong Rural Background.

forgot what I had to say and started crying and telling him how proud we all are of him.

Most importantly we salute our parents, for dreaming that it was possible; freedom came in their lifetime – a freedom they fought for, this very freedom which is complicated, but which we are still enjoying. To all my friends' parents who took me in and nurtured me, I salute you too. All the aunts and uncles, and my sister's friends, especially Elsa, who thought I had potential even during my wild times. Most importantly from my early childhood development at nursery school and Chitsere Primary School, I received the confidence to fly.

What did Zimbabwe give me?

Everything. Zimbabwe gave me the Sithole name that I carry with honour, a sense of family, the Shona language that I simply love and a great education. Zimbabwe prepared me for greatness.

What did South Africa give me? It gave me the platform to walk into my greatness. It gave me beauty, passion, *joie de vivre*, gender awareness and Mandela. For without passion I would be nothing.

It has all come full circle.

As for my mother, she taught me to make the sky my blackboard and to claim my space in the sun!

Over the next 50 years, I look forward to raising my daughter, so that she continues to grow me, and to show her that life is about serving humanity. I hope to teach her to live her best life, knowing that God comes first in everything she chooses to do.

I look forward to loving better because that is what one does as they get older. I want to love better whether it will be with one man or a couple of lovers along this journey called life. For a season for a reason for a lifetime to love is a gift in whatever form it comes. Who knows?

Very importantly, I look forward to having better sex with age. I look forward to drinking wine – sitting under the African sky, dancing, writing, getting into academia, nurturing my relationships with friends and family, and, most importantly, moving from glory to glory and not apologizing for this wonderful God-given life I have led so far.

Life is phenomenal, warts and all. We fall we get up and we rise. One must never give up even if they tell you, 'you're crazy' something I've heard all my life and 'who do you think you are?'. Keep at it keep your eyes on the prize. Live your truth, be kind, be generous, have faith and have courage.

27

Lioness Heart Awakening

Chiyedza Nyahuye

As a toddler, the seeds of self-reliance, fighting for my space and place in this evolving country, let alone, global landscape were planted.

Yes, my parents worked hard, developing their businesses to ensure that I got access to the best education in Zimbabwe. This led me to win scholarships to schools in Hong Kong, China and the United States. The pursuit of education has always been popularised as a free ticket from poverty, and as a means to salvation from backward ways to civilisation, sophistication, and knowledge of the workings of this western dominated world. Yet, even after attaining all of this education – two degrees under my belt, I still felt restless. I was programmed, from an early age, that I could only be somebody if I was called Dr Nyahuye or had, at least a PhD., but even that dream was not meant to be – well at least not yet. Instead, life decided to show me that even this narrow way of thinking could not imprison my vibrant yearning soul that demanded so much more from life. This could not have been made clearer to me than when I was completing my master's degree in the US.

In March 2004, in response to my lamentation over a rejection letter from the Harvard School of Public Health PhD Program, my *sekuru, handzvadzi,* dear friend, Ibrahim

(Ibro) Garba of the Kerekere people of Northern Nigeria sent me this prophetic email.

My dear, let things wash for a couple of days ... rain clouds are not an infinite entity. Besides, they are responsible for growth. There is so much ahead of you. You have one precious life to live and I firmly believe that what you have to offer and what others have to offer you in the next phase of your life cannot – and should not – be confined by the narrowness of some New England school, whatever letter of the alphabet it starts with. Chiyedza, your dreams can be as high and ambitious as you like, but please don't let them be that narrow. Life is too precious and the world too rich for us to buy into the lie that we need a certain degree from a certain type of school to maximise our respective potentials. We already know more than we need to give our best to life TODAY, and giving our best to life today is all that the world and its Maker can ask of us.

We have many educated imbeciles running around – some running this country – and many of them have come out of our so-called top-tier schools. There is something in us Africans (who have grown up on the soil of the continent) that we need to come to terms with as we pursue an education in the States, or in Europe for that matter. No one can do this for us and I think that if we don't come to terms with it in time, the schools we attend overseas will rob us of it – or they will give us something else to live for – even though it may appear as if we are acquiring the tools we need to 'help' our people...

If you have already come to terms with this thing, then let Harvard's reply at worst draw only disappointment from you. This is a normal reaction to not getting something we have dreamed about, planned for, invested in. If you have come to terms with it, Harvard is simply one locked door in a hall of many others, even if it is one that you really wanted to go through.

But if you have NOT come to terms with this thing, then Harvard's response is probably the best thing that could happen to you. Your experience there would have deprived the world of what Chiyedza Nyahuye of Zimbabwe, my muzukuru, had to offer it.

*It would be a royal waste of time and, more tragically, a loss for
Africa, of one of her children.*

*Whether or not you have come to terms with this thing inside
you, is a question only you can answer. But if what you are
planning for your future (your goals, your idea of fulfilment) is
derailed or crushed by Harvard's response, then perhaps we need
to go back to the drawing board, or better yet, back to the Chiyedza
whose ancestors' feet danced to the beat of a different drum. The
prism of Harvard cannot bring out all the variety and colour that
my* muzukuru *has to offer the world.*

*Disappointments are difficult, no doubt, especially when they come
in the form of non-acceptance letters from schools we really want
to attend. I don't think what I've said will make this fact any less
real. In fact, I think I might need a talk like this a week from now
as I come to terms with an unpleasant letter from Notre Dame. But
my point is this: you have so much to give and so much to live for.
A time like this may make you doubt this fact, but surrender to no
such thought. Just take it easy for a few days and let yourself be. Let
this be a time to look around at other aspects of your life: family,
relationships, roots, passions, etc. Perhaps too much was being
sacrificed on the altar of Harvard and distant, noble dreams. In
other words, this might be the time to 'keep it real' – as an African.
When you have found your centre, then you can go out and meet
the world on those terms. Harvard and any other school or a job
you apply to thereafter will find their proper place in the grand
scheme of things.*

So my dear muzukuru, *I have succeeded in saying many words,
and where words are many, errors abound. But I believe that the
spirit speaks where the word fails. So read with your heart as well as
your mind.*

Sleep child. And dream.

Sekuru Ibro

I let this profound message marinate for two weeks, gradually
realising how pregnant, how powerfully potent Ibro's words
were on many levels. I was then flooded with questions like:

- What do you mean about not letting my dreams be too narrow?

- So how do we maximise our potentials? For what purpose?

- How do you develop a relationship with this ongoing internal struggle of achieving higher educational ideals knowing that you are being educated to fulfil a European agenda that takes you away from your people?

- What is it that we already know, is that all we need to give of our best of today?

- What is it that we Africans who have grown up on the soil of our continent need to come to terms with as we pursue higher education overseas?

- What is it that these European schools rob us of? What is it that we sacrifice at the altars of European higher education?

- What is the 'something else to live for' that Europeans give us?

- What does 'helping our people' look like to you Ibro?

- What then do you do when you feel so defeated because all the doors keep slamming shut in your face?

- What is the essence that you see that can bring out the variety and colours that we have to offer the world?

- So where is our place at home and the rest of the African continent? What do we bring? What do we compromise? Where do we find acceptance? From whom? Why do we continue to strive for this?

I so wanted to talk to Sekuru Ibro about all of this, face to face, but at the time, I was in Minneapolis, Minnesota while he was in Waco Texas, also completing his master's degree program. I was trying to come to grips with why certain things were happening to me at that time; it was almost driving me crazy and pressing me to come back home. We are yet to have this conversation in person. However, having been home in

Zimbabwe for the past eight years, layers of answers to these questions have revealed themselves in intricate, complex, enlightening ways.

I came home in June 2004 feeling that with at least a master's degree and with some work experience in public health, surely I would gain quick employment, even more so with a UN agency of some sort. Another layer I learned was that nobody knew me, nor did I know many people, so why would they hire me, an over-qualified black woman who has been away from home for so long and who could possibly take their job? Over 600 job applications later, that still hasn't happened. Instead, I have survived, economically, through short-term consultancies that I was introduced to when I met Chipo Chung at a party. She linked me to her mother, Dr Fay King Chung, whom I have worked with over the years in various capacities empowering women through advancing their education, leadership training for teachers and parliamentarians, and more so, in peace building and conflict resolution with Envision Zimbabwe Women's Trust as founding members. I also had opportunities to explore my artistic talents by performing in various plays at the Reps theatre, my favourites being when I played Delores/Sister Mary Clarence in *Sister Act*, where my bum became famous during the halleluiahs. I also played Lady Marmalade, the She-Devil in *Disco Inferno*. I wrote and performed my own play, *Telling HerStory: Warrior Women of Zimbabwe*, and sang in multiple cabarets and I'm constantly involved in the arts sector.

The one full-time job I have had in all these years for just over one year was with the Solidarities International, where I designed business oriented models for horticulture gardens in high density areas of Harare. I felt it was integral to the success of these gardens to link them to viable markets and develop relationships with possible buyers and input suppliers to ensure the sustainability of such efforts. These projects are still thriving, contributing to the green belts initiative in Zimbabwean urban and peri-urban contexts.

Lately, I have become more passionate about finding ways to economically empower the two million or so of the millennial generation, those born between 1980 and 1995 who are sitting on their hands due to the severe lack of opportunities not only in Zimbabwe but globally in the current recession. I have found a very exciting opportunity, through World Ventures, that continues to blow my mind not only with its very lucrative business model, but more so, with its powerful personal development aspects and the stellar training from its leaders who are mostly multi-millionaires.

We need to let go of this miseducation mantra of urging ourselves and future generations that getting good grades, guarantees a good job and a good life. Believe me, I know that is not true. I'm not dismissing education, but our current education system is out of date, not having been revised since 1983. How can we be competitive in this world if our reference points continue to be three decades old?

What I'm learning more so, is the urgent need for us to transform the way we think and do things. The world continues to rapidly change and as Zimbabweans, we need to learn to transform our thinking and practices if we do not want to be left behind. We deserve to live wonderfully abundant, fulfilling, prosperous lives.

All too often, 95% of us choose to be mediocre, choose to stay small, trapped in our cocoons of fear. Poverty is a choice. It is our poor thinking and poor decisions that keep us living such uninspiring lives, focused on survival.

This lioness heart refuses mediocrity. I'm one of the 5%. I believe that God did not make me in *her* image to live like a coward. I am fearfully and wonderfully made. The only way I can bless God and thank *her* is to be who *she* created me to be, dangerously and powerfully with every cell in my body.

I have been able to tap into virtually every sector of Zimbabwe. I have this incessant yearning to become more relevant to my context on the African continent, to find ways to also develop and share my God-given gifts whilst still trying to grapple with how to gain the material and spiritual trappings that supposedly show some level of success and achievement in life.

So yes Ibro, you are right, coming home in 2004 has allowed me to let my lioness heart awaken to her complex layers of existence, yet, I still feel my journey has only just begun.

Ini ndini Chiyedza
Anenge achinditevera
Ndini Chiyedza,
Chiyedza chepasi,
Chiyedza cheupenyu

(I am the light, whoever follows me, I am the light, I am the light of the world, I am the light of life.) My *amai* gave me that song as a gift when I was 22 years old. What an honour and a tall order to have my purpose given to me on a silver platter. Yes, I'm learning to claim my space as a star on this earth and in the universe. My *amai* always taught me that as long as you have breath in your body, you can create whatever world you choose to live in, even if you have to fight every day and night with respite here and there.

28

Family is First and Foremost

Esther G. Madzivire

I was born in 1971, in the throes of the struggle for the freedom of Rhodesia, at the maternity ward known as *kuGomo* – Harare Hospital.

In the late sixties, my father, Betserai Madzivire graduated from Ohio State University as an accountant and returned home to work at Bible House. My mother was the first African physiotherapy university graduate matriculating from St Louis University and returned to Rhodesia in 1969 to work in Bulawayo. They met in the US, got married and moved to Harare. The young couple happily set up in Highfield but then trouble set in. Three months after I was born, my father was arrested for his participation in the liberation struggle and incarcerated for seven years, leaving my mother a newly married single parent. So many wonderful people stepped in to help my mother raise this girl child that I never once felt a lack of love and attention. So many bonds were formed that have framed the person who I am now. While I was fully aware that something about my family was different from those of my friends, I never once felt bereft. From those bonds, I inherited my wonderful extended family of sisters and brothers who, although having no blood links to us, are as close to me as my own siblings.

As a pre-schooler, I spent the school terms with the

Mupawose family. Their son, Taurai, who was born the same year as me, is as close to me as any brother. While his older sister was in boarding school, we played together, shared a bedroom, got up to all sorts of stuff in Chisumbanje. I still have very vivid memories of picking oranges, going to the river-side, and eating together. In their home, my aunt and uncle embraced me, loved me, fed me and taught me. There was never a lack of love or affection, never once did I feel like a visitor – I was one of them.

Then there was Auntie Phillie and Uncle Eddie Garwe and all of their extended Garwe and Mbofana family. My dad and Uncle Eddie had a brotherhood that spanned decades, from their youth. My father would go home with Uncle Eddie when they were at Goromonzi High School in their teens. I sense that he, too, was treated as one of their own, and that bond was passed to their children. I still remember Uncle Eddie coming to the farm *kwa*Gutu to see my grandfather. Any major event in either family was 'in our family'. My big sisters are still my big sisters and my role models today and my baby sisters, fine young women in their own right, are very dear to my heart. Someone once asked of my dad what relation are those girls to him and he replied; 'Those are my children'.

I think many people were touched by the plight of this child, whose father was removed from her before she had a chance to know him, be protected by him, taught by him, shielded by him as any daughter would. I mentioned the Garwes and Mupawoses because I lived with them, but there were many others – too many to mention, who came to my rescue. In addition, I had the strongest mother ever, and what a wonderful role model she was. As such, much as I totally adore my father, my mother and I have an indelible bond, wrought out of necessity and need. She did not have much, but I never felt without. My mother says I was a good child and never really asked for anything, but I think it was because I knew there was not much extra to give. I went to

Gwelo Convent for grades 1 and 2, and I showed up with a second-hand small orange suitcase that functioned as a book case. As embarrassing as that was, I knew my mother had done her best and I said nothing. The other children were so nice no one else mentioned it either. I was never made fun of. I think my mother is still wracked by guilt over the things others had that I did not have, and yet, if anything, I am brimming with gratitude for all the sacrifices she made to make me who I am.

I was old enough to understand the struggle for Zimbabwe and the sacrifices of so many for the freedoms we now have. My mother is a daughter of Jasper Zengeza Savanhu, who was the first African Member of Parliament. He was handsome, tall, graceful and educated, such a gentleman, a man so beyond his time. I have vague memories of living in Beatrice Cottages in Harari (Mbare) at 7 Mlambo Road. There I spent many afternoons playing with neighbourhood friends, cooking in tin cans on the fires outside, playing house. I also watched my Uncle Alex, my dad's youngest brother, meet with his friends, planning and participating in the revolution, as young men are wont to do. I remember thinking that the policemen were my father's friends, until, finally, my Sekuru JZ explained that they were his jailors, not his friends. I learned about our own system of apartheid, and became more acutely attuned to my surroundings and circumstances.

Our lives were all shaped in some way by the history of our country. The absence of my dad and the circumstances of his imprisonment are fairly central to the evolution of who I have become. As dark as some of the details may be, I remember a bright, cheerful, happy and somewhat carefree childhood. It is only now, looking back, that I realise what a treacherous period we lived through as we grew up. The curfews, petrol coupons, bombings, road blocks... They were all there in the periphery of my consciousness, but life carried on. I would accompany my mother to visit my father

at Gwelo Central Prison and from a child's perspective it was
almost like a fun field trip. How brave our parents were to
live in those times.

So, what did I learn?

Hard Work. Nothing in my life has come easy. I have always
had to work and work and work at it. But in the end, success
has been my reward, my blessing.

Love. I have been blessed with such abundance of love in
my life, from my own immediate family to extended family
and friends. When you open yourself to love, and give of
yourself, you are blessed with so much more.

Faith. Be open to the plan that God has for you. My path
has been absolutely amazing. I applied to only one college
in the US while already in medical school at the University
of Zimbabwe. I wanted to travel! I got into that one college,
and not only did they accept me, they gave me a generous
scholarship. While in college I met some of the closest and
most influential women in my life, one of whom is now
my son's godmother, as well as the Mayor of Washington
D.C. I then applied to only one medical school and got
in. There I met whom I consider my baby brother, Pierre
Detiege, who is my daughter's godfather and whose family
bonded so closely to mine that even though he missed my
wedding in Zimbabwe, his mother and sister came all the
way from New Orleans. While in med school I met my big
brother Allen Chiura, who guided me through that process
with his wisdom, encouragement and an all-encompassing
brotherly love. While on a rotation at Harare Hospital
during my residency, I met my husband Vin at Allen and
Nozipo Chiura's wedding. If I had not been in Harare at that
rotation, I may not have been at that wedding, may not have
met Vin, may not have borne the greatest blessings of my life,
my two babies. My son, the first born, was a micro preemie at
1 pound 7 ounces. He endured much, but survived to be a
healthy wonderful beautiful boy. I happened to be in Boston

at the time and he was born at the Brigham, one of the top Neonatal Intensive-Care Units in the country, which has a lot to do with his survival and outcome. What are the odds?

Along the way, I tried different things, applied for different things, but God would not open those doors. Those avenues that were paved for me, despite my resistance, ended up gracing my life with more than I could ever ask for. My mother bought me a beautiful painted tile for my dresser that says 'Be Still and Know...' How true that is. When times are rough, when things don't seem to be going your way, just stop, be still and know...

Family is first and foremost. I would be nothing without the generations that came before me. I witnessed their struggles. I remember, because I was old enough to see and understand when my father was released in 1978. My parents then had to live in exile in Cameroon until Independence in 1980, leaving me in the very loving care of the Garwes. After their return, they had to start from nothing. I remember that first car, the Renault 12 that would frequently break down on the way to or from school and my dad would have to get out and push it out of the way of the traffic. I remember when I lost a library book and had to pay $2 and my dad took forever to get it to me (remember pocket money back then was 25c per day so $2 was a LOT of money). I vividly remember his palpable relief when the book was found and I didn't have to pay the fine. I also remember his pride in me that I'd been honest enough to tell him that he could keep the money.

Now, I look at the struggles of the generations before us who were able to withstand the test of time through perseverance, prioritisation, unity, faith, and they are an inspiration to me. They never compromised their principles or took the easy road; they were fuelled by love not by material desires. I treasure my parents, uncles, aunts, grandparents – all of the wisdom and support they have showered upon us. They all instilled the belief in my sister and me (both girls!) that we can to *anything* we set our minds to.

As a woman, you must strive for independence. The one thing no one can take from you is your education. Have your own career, income, mind, and respect yourself, if you expect people to then respect you. Do not compromise your integrity for any one or any thing. Believe in yourself.

I do not profess to have any wisdom at all. I just share my experience in this life in the hope that one day it may inspire even just one person.

Thank you for this privilege.

29

My Guiding Truths

Geraldine Chengetai Matchaba

When I was invited to be a part of this lovely project, I wondered what 'words of wisdom' I could possibly share with the younger generation. Times have changed from when I was in my teens; the younger ones now have so much at their disposal, so much to choose from, and much faster access to information. I am, however, not sure that this abundance in choice is necessarily a good thing. If anything, it can lead to confusion.

What I wish to share is not a blueprint for success, believe me, even in my late forties, I am still looking for answers and ways to get certain things right and be 'successful'. However, what I do know is that there are some universal truths, which will never change, and this is what I wish to share.

Hard work

It really is true about hard work being the only way to the top. I lost my parents recently, both to cancer within 18 months of each other, and now, almost every day, I remember their advice about life and specifically hard work. I will be forever grateful for that teaching, and I am sure my siblings will agree. I give my son the same advice and when I talk to him about the importance of working hard, I can hear my parents talking through me.

Such guidance might sound very old fashioned. You might hate your parents and teachers for repeating it and roll your eyes and sigh. You might think you can get by on half the effort because you managed to pass your last test without much reading. Perhaps you will tell your parents about the rich and famous people who dropped out of high school. You will probably also think that luck will get you places, and if not, you will work hard later. Or someone will give you a 'through pass'. If you're a beautiful girl, you may even think you will become the next supermodel, maybe like Iman or Kim Karsdashian or whoever your idol is. Social media today has given us the impression that one can become a celebrity overnight; but if you do your research, you will discover that only a few are making money out of it per se. Every career requires hard work, patience and some strategising about the right content to keep your audience engaged.

You may also think that your parents will always look after you. Maybe they drive the latest cars and are quite wealthy. Maybe they've even bought you an apartment or a house! Lucky you! But the reality is that they probably owe money on that house and those cars and they will certainly not be able to look after you forever. That car they have left for you will require service and insurance; the house will require maintenance and you will need to put food on the table – every single day. Please understand, there is a time to play, but remember that you will always have to work hard. And most times, hard work does pay.

Respect

When you are a teenager or ten going on 16, you will surely think that your parents and the older generation are clueless as far as you're concerned. You will think you know better and that they are old fashioned. True, they may be. They may not know how snap chat works or what new fashion is trending, but when all is said and done, they will still know way more than you do about life and survival. They have something you don't have, and it's called experience. They were also once teenagers, they also probably thought they were smarter than their parents, but they have probably had their fingers burnt, so they know better. If there is one thing I always admire about our African culture, it is the respect that we are taught to give to all our elders, and not just our parents. Giving respect does not mean not speaking your mind. But there is a way to speak to adults and there is a way to manage conflict even with your parents. Talking back or sulking for days on end is certainly not the way to behave. If you are lucky, your parents will whip your butt to teach you a lesson or they may use other methods, like withdrawing your pocket money. I am not talking about abuse but discipline. If you are disciplined you are lucky, at least your parents are paying attention to you. Please understand this, even the Bible talks about the need to respect your parents. It's not something that is negotiable. You will be blessed in your life. Also remember that one day you will be a parent. Karma sucks, do the right thing.

Peer pressure

Much as you think you are unique and there is no one like you in this world, and indeed there is only one you; the challenges that you will face are nothing new. Other young people are going through the same and those before you also went through similar challenges. But there is one nasty thing, and it's called 'peer pressure'. Be careful, the chances are that at one point in your adolescent life you will give in to it. Some of it will be for a good cause but most of it will not. They say experience is the best teacher, so it may not be a bad thing to get yourself into trouble because then you will learn. But some trouble is too deep and too dangerous. Please be careful about what you do just in order to belong to be 'cool'. No one is a saint. we all did unsavoury things when we were young but know where and when to draw the line. Remind yourself that you are indeed unique. If you always follow the crowd, one day you will realise you're lost, at the edge of a cliff with one foot off the ground and you may fall. In such a case, maybe only a miracle can save you otherwise you may be lost forever. Being young is fun. The sky is the limit. But be sensible. Save some fun for later in life. Have your own set of values, preferably the ones taught to you by your parents. Read the Bible, it has guiding lessons which if we all followed, we would not experience half the trouble in life.

Many ways to success

I wish I could give you a formula for success or even define what success is. Everyone defines it differently and at different stages of your life, your definition of success will also change. Success might mean having material things, a job, marriage, money, etc. The level of success differs from person to person and through the different stages of your life. I know, for example, that a job that may have seemed very attractive to me four years ago is not necessarily what I want today. I also know that whilst an office would have been important to me 20 years ago, all I need today is a desk and a chair, I will be happy sitting anywhere in the office including next to the water cooler!

I have been told that I have had a successful career and whilst I am grateful for what I have achieved, I don't define it as absolute success and am still hungry for more but not necessarily in the sense of wanting to earn more money or hold a bigger title. I have been fortunate to work in four very different markets. Currently I am based in Johannesburg. Previously, I was in Hong Kong and before that in Mumbai and, of course, my home country Zimbabwe. When I was in Hong Kong, I had many people telling me how lucky I was to be living and working there. The same people also asked how I survived in India. I still get asked that question today and I ask what they mean. Most reply, they could never live in India and I usually respond – 'Oh, just as many say they could never live in Africa'.

These are the people who want an opportunity in London, New York, Dubai, Singapore, Hong Kong, Sydney or some other first world city. I made lifelong friendships in India., friends who would invite me into their houses today if I went back to visit. What I learnt there has shaped me into the person I am today and I wouldn't give that back for any experience anywhere in the world. I am sad I never had the time to visit places like Rajasthan, Kerala, and Kashmir. But never before have I come across a people with such a rich culture, not to mention the food! The tandoori chicken, the *gosht rogan josh*, the *palak paneer*, I could go on. The moral of the story is that there are many paths to success – focus on yours and be open to what life has to teach you. I also loved Hong Kong but in India, I learnt more about life than what I learnt in first world Hong Kong.

Be open to opportunities, don't just go where everyone wants to go. Thinking like that will not get you very far in your career or in life. You can live in London, I am sure, but you may not have a decent job; in fact you may not have a regular job at all. Others are lucky and have thriving careers in those cities but not everyone. The people there work very hard. Nothing comes easy in life. So when it comes to your career, keep an open mind. I need you to understand that some opportunities don't appear glamorous at first sight, but are actually pure gold.

Finally, you are young; the world is your oyster. Learn from your older siblings, learn from your parents, learn from your good friends and learn from your mistakes. Don't ever give up; there are many paths to success. Have fun but be responsible. We all have just this one life.

30

Freedoms Imagined and Real

Runyararo Bertha Faranisi

I have no struggle credentials. I have had a privileged life by any standards. Born unaware of the oppression around, relocated to foreign climes, only to return home to Zimbabwe in 1982, and to freedom. What could I possibly teach anyone? Me, who returned unable to speak my mother tongue but the language of the oppressors, not by choice but somehow that part of my formative years was overlooked. Perhaps a calculated plan by parents wanting to have confidential conversations in front of their then only child? The result – having to start again from scratch and to be constantly ridiculed for my intonation and poor Shona vocabulary, and still be on a quest to master Shona. But should I be defined by my ability to speak *The* language? Is it not who I am rather than how I speak that should matter? Over the years, I have transitioned from label to label from being a member of the 'nose brigade' to being a 'musalad', and on to the next trendy derogatory term, but though these appellations have changed, my character has remained consistent. I love to communicate with people based on their personality, not their linguistic ability. I will speak to anyone who cares to speak to me with care and concern, and the respect that we all deserve. What matters is that we understand each other and feel the offer of love that is being extended and we give each other time. There is no shame in being me. Flawed I am, but I know my strengths far outweigh my weaknesses. We all have different paths to follow. These may not fit the ideal or may not appear to make sense now – we are what we are.

As I sit here, in my forties, middle-class mother, auntie, wife, sister, daughter, relative, friend and stranger, I am not where I was projected to be or where I saw myself. Friends despaired and discarded me when I found a mate whom I eventually married. Marriage did not form a part of their plans for me. My long-suffering, surviving parent despaired when I chose love over employment and independence; relocating to build a new life without a job offer in sight. Imagine a parent's disappointment when I failed to find employment, while many around me were able to penetrate a market that seemed to be doing everything possible to box me out. I therefore became a reluctant housewife, and when my daughter was born, I acquired the fancier title of 'stay-at-home mom'.

All those years of a private school and a tertiary education down the drain… Really? Am I at peace? Seven years down the line I am … almost. The shame and insecurity I feel by not being a career woman is compounded by those who judge me, but choose not to know my story or believe my journey. For many, nothing is more important than being an income-earner. But am I less of a woman because I earn nothing but love, hugs and kisses? Do I deserve any better? Maybe: but now I count my blessings every day. I am loved and appreciated by those that I stay at home for – my priorities - my husband and my daughter, friends and family, all of whom can call me whenever they need to talk, consult or make a request. I am privileged to know my child, to enjoy mutual fearless communication with her, and to always have time for her. I am not high flying or schmoozing, just forever available. The countless hours in doctors' waiting rooms may feel a curveball some days, but at least I can be there. I am my own parent's joy and sadness, pride and disappointment.

Freedoms Imagined and Real by Runyararo Bertha Faranisi

A product of private school because a struggle was fought and won, one which allowed us to have the education our parents only dreamt about. A product of our parents' yearning for their children to have more opportunities in the future. I am eternally grateful for my freedom but oppressed by the disdain of my fellow middle-class aunties, my peers. Sometimes our plans do not work out as we wish, but we cannot stop planning or moving forward. Love who you are and what you can be to those in your sphere of influence. Embrace your idiosyncrasies and enjoy your journey, only you have a deep understanding of where you are now and where you want to be. Let us enjoy our freedom be it imagined or real.

31

Love in Great Abundance

Sophie Chamboko

I was born Sophia Shingai Chamboko at five minutes to midnight on 16 April 1971. My mother has never let me forget the five minutes to midnight as she insists on staying up every year so that she can call me at this exact time in order to wish me a happy birthday.

Today I live in Johannesburg, South Africa. I am one of many Zimbabweans living in the diaspora. I have a pretty decent lifestyle and am blessed with a pretty great job. Yet when I reflect on this, my life is due to the amazing foresight and perseverance of my parents.

My parents are Jeremiah Chamboko and Joyce Chamboko (née Patsanza, born and raised in Chivi, Masvingo and Hwedza respectively). Coming from such humble beginnings, both of my parents had to overcome many challenges in life, no doubt much like many of your parents. When I think of where they came from, I marvel at how they came to achieve so much, how they even came to dream the dream that led them to life in Harare and Bulawayo and to the University of Lesotho.

Both of them were employed as civil servants for many years and yet somehow managed to send four children to private school on their very modest earnings. Money was always short, but love always in great abundance.

The life lessons learnt were many:

From my dad: love of family and all people, to show and speak openly of affection, to worship God and pray often, to exercise regularly (both mind and body), appreciation of good food and whisky and to reward oneself every now and then.

From my mum: fiscal discipline, to keep going in the face of adversity, an iron will and steely determination and how to keep a sense of humour through all of life's challenges.

From both of them: to worship God and pray often, honesty, to treat people with respect, a fierce loyalty to family, the beauty of hard work, to run my own race and not be preoccupied with the lives of others, to take action and not indulge in self-pity.

These are just a few of the many, many lessons that my parents have taught me and my siblings. Because of these lessons my siblings and I, their spouses and their kids are each other's best friends. We are very close and love spending time with each other. We care and look out for each other. We laugh together and play together and, most of all, we pray together.

I have deliberately not mentioned education, job titles and work experience. All of these are important yes, but for me, they are a means to an end. What really gives me purpose, happiness and comfort in life is my faith in God and my relationship with my family. That is how this township girl was raised.

Glossary

The Shona words and spelling in this glossary use the standard orthography.

Agogo	An old fashioned dance styling where dancer poses
amai or *mai*	mother
amainini	younger mother (mother's younger sister)
amaiguru	mother's elder sister
ambuya	grandmother or with a slightly different pronunciation, mother-in-law. Also used colloquially to respectfully address a woman.
ara uru	catch – the children's game
baba	father
babamukuru	(older father) uncle or elder sister's husband
babamunini	(younger father) uncle or young sister's husband
bhabharasi	a hangover
bhudhi	brother
chaya	hit
chimambaira	landmine (colloquial)
chihwandehwande	hide-and-seek – the children's game
chirimo	autumn – the harvesting period before winter
chikomo/chikomba	rural area
chingwa	bread
chisveru	children's game similar to tag
chitorobo	cattle whip plaited from bark skin
chomolia	a leafy vegetable
dhoro	traditional seven day's beer
dombo	stone
dura	granary
Dunhu	children's ball game

dzepfunde	Of the reed (A response in storytelling, encouraging the teller to continue)
gavi	bark
gudo	baboon
handei	let's go
hanzvadzi	a sibling of the opposite sex
horda	mobile bakery
hosho	traditional rattles made out of dried gourd
ipwa	type of sugar cane
*kamu ye simb*i	metal comb
kukwesha	scrubbed
kumunda	farming fields
kumusha	rural area
kwa and *ku*	(preceding a noun) means 'at' i.e *kwa*Tsambe means at Tsambe or *ku*10 Miles means at 10 Miles
kupunungura magwere	shelling maize husks
mafeso	upside down/weed like growth
mabhunu	Boers/white people
magandanga	rebels, a term also used to refer to the freedom fighters
maiguru	(older mother) maternal aunt or wife's older sister or elder brother's wife
mainini	younger mother) maternal aunt, or wife's younger sister, or young brother's wife
majita	(colloquial) guys
makadä	greeting: 'how are you?'
Manyika	people or dialect of eastern Zimbabwe
matohwe	[plural] chewy wild fruits
mbuya	grandmother
mbira	traditional musical instrument
mhamhatsi	red ants that bite
mudhumeni	agricultural extension officers
mukoma	brother or can be used to refer to a gardener/helper
mugwazo	a portion to complete/a section/working shift

muriwo	green vegetable
mutswairo	traditional grass broom for sweeping
mutsvairo	broom
muzukuru	niece, or nephew, or grandchild
musalad	member of the 'nose brigade' or snobbish person
na	with (conjunction)
nhodo	child's game
pada	hop-scotch
Paivapo	Once upon a time/ There was…
putugadzike	tea
Raka-raka	child's game
Rezende	A bus station in Harare city centre
rugare	joy
ruva	flower
rwaenga	roasting pan used on an open fire
sekuru	grandfather (or mother's brother)/maternal uncle or refer to an old man
shamwari	friend
sisi	sister
shamu	small thin twig, used to whip
svikiro	spirit medium
taitamba ma-records	we danced to (music) records
tete	aunt (father's sister, advisor to all and keeper of traditions)
tsoro	children's game
tsime	well
tsubvu	wild, black fruit
tsuro na gudo	hare and baboon
tsuro	hare
va or *vekwa*	[preceding a noun] denotes belonging or 'from' i.e vekwa Chari means from Chari
vakomana	boys
vakomana	[plural] boys used also to refer to freedom fighters (the boys)
varukwa nemawoko	had hair done by hand

vahosi	elder wife in polygamous marriage
vakuru	elder
vanavangu	my children
vaprofita	prophets
vetkoek	(Afrikaans) deep fried yeast buns that can be served as a snack, for breakfast or lunch
zhizha	summer (rainy season in Southern Africa)
Zezuru	people or dialect in central Zimbabwe

Printed in the United States
By Bookmasters